Integration of Technology into the Classroom: Case Studies

Integration of Technology into the Classroom: Case Studies has been co-published simultaneously as *Computers in the Schools*, Volume 16, Number 2 and Volume 16, Numbers 3/4 2000.

The *Computers in the Schools* Monographic "Separates"

Below is a list of "separates," which in serials librarianship means a special issue simultaneously published as a special journal issue or double-issue *and* as a "separate" hardbound monograph. (This is a format which we also call a "DocuSerial.")

"Separates" are published because specialized libraries or professionals may wish to purchase a specific thematic issue by itself in a format which can be separately cataloged and shelved, as opposed to purchasing the journal on an on-going basis. Faculty members may also more easily consider a "separate" for classroom adoption.

"Separates" are carefully classified separately with the major book jobbers so that the journal tie-in can be noted on new book order slips to avoid duplicate purchasing.

You may wish to visit Haworth's website at . . .

http://www.HaworthPress.com

. . . to search our online catalog for complete tables of contents of these separates and related publications.

You may also call 1-800-HAWORTH (outside US/Canada: 607-722-5857), or Fax 1-800-895-0582 (outside US/Canada: 607-771-0012), or e-mail at:

getinfo@haworthpressinc.com

Integration of Technology into the Classroom: Case Studies, edited by D. LaMont Johnson, PhD, Cleborne D. Maddux, PhD, and Leping Liu, PhD (Vol. 16, No. 2/3/4, 2000). *Use these fascinating case studies to understand why bringing information technology into your classroom can make you a more effective teacher, and how to go about it!*

Information Technology in Educational Research and Statistics, edited by Leping Liu, PhD, D. LaMont Johnson, PhD, and Cleborne D. Maddux, PhD (Vol. 15, No. 3/4, and Vol. 16, No. 1, 1999). *This important book focuses on creating new ideas for using educational technologies such as the Internet, the World Wide Web and various software packages to further research and statistics. You will explore on-going debates relating to the theory of research, research methodology, and successful practices. Information Technology in Educational Research and Statistics also covers the debate on what statistical procedures are appropriate for what kinds of research designs.*

Educational Computing in the Schools: Technology, Communication, and Literacy, edited by Jay Blanchard, PhD (Vol. 15, No. 1, 1999). *Examines critical issues of technology, teaching and learning in three areas: access, communication, and literacy. You will discover new ideas and practices for gaining access to and using technology in education from preschool through higher education.*

Logo: A Retrospective, edited by Cleborne D. Maddux, PhD, and D. Lamont Johnson, PhD (Vol. 14, No. 1/2, 1997). *"This book–honest and optimistic–is a must for those interested in any aspect of Logo: its history, the effects of its use, or its general role in education." (Dorothy M. Fitch, Logo consultant, writer, and editor, Derry, New Hampshire)*

Using Technology in the Classroom, edited by D. LaMont Johnson, PhD, Cleborne D. Maddux, PhD, and Leping Liu, MS (Vol. 13, No. 1/2, 1997). *"A guide to teaching with technology that emphasizes the advantages of transiting from teacher-directed learning to learner-centered learning–a shift that that can draw in even 'at-risk' kids." (Book News, Inc.)*

Multimedia and Megachange: New Roles for Educational Computing, edited by W. Michael Reed, PhD, John K. Burton, PhD, and Min Liu, EdD (Vol. 10, No. 1/2/3/4, 1995). *"Describes and analyzes issues and trends that might set research and development agenda for educators in the near future." (Sci Tech Book News)*

Language Minority Students and Computers, edited by Christian J. Faltis, PhD, and Robert A. DeVillar, PhD (Vol. 7, No. 1/2, 1990). *"Professionals in the field of language minority education, including ESL and bilingual education, will cheer this collection of articles written by highly respected, research-writers, along with computer technologists, and classroom practitioners." (Journal of Computing in Teacher Education)*

Logo: Methods and Curriculum for Teachers, by Cleborne D. Maddux, PhD, and D. LaMont Johnson, PhD (Supp #3, 1989). *"An excellent introduction to this programming language for children." (Rena B. Lewis, Professor, College of Education, San Diego State University)*

Assessing the Impact of Computer-Based Instruction: A Review of Recent Research, by M. D. Roblyer, PhD, W. H. Castine, PhD, and F. J. King, PhD (Vol. 5, No. 3/4, 1988). *"A comprehensive and up-to-date review of the effects of computer applications on student achievement and attitudes." (Measurements & Control)*

Educational Computing and Problem Solving, edited by W. Michael Reed, PhD, and John K. Burton, PhD (Vol. 4, No. 3/4, 1988). *Here is everything that educators will need to know to use computers to improve higher level skills such as problem solving and critical thinking.*

The Computer in Reading and Language Arts, edited by Jay S. Blanchard, PhD, and George E. Mason, PhD (Vol. 4, No. 1, 1987). *"All of the [chapters] in this collection are useful, guiding the teacher unfamiliar with classroom computer use through a large number of available software options and classroom strategies." (Educational Technology)*

Computers in the Special Education Classroom, edited by D. LaMont Johnson, PhD, Cleborne D. Maddux, PhD, and Ann Candler, PhD (Vol. 3, No. 3/4, 1987). *"A good introduction to the use of computers in special education. . . . Excellent for those who need to become familiar with computer usage with special population students because they are contemplating it or because they have actually just begun to do it." (Science Books and Films)*

You Can Do It/Together, by Kathleen A. Smith, PhD, Cleborne D. Maddux, PhD, and D. LaMont Johnson, PhD (Supp #2, 1986). *A self-instructional textbook with an emphasis on the partnership system of learning that introduces the reader to four critical areas of computer technology.*

Computers and Teacher Training: A Practical Guide, by Dennis M. Adams, PhD (Supp #1, 1986). *"A very fine . . . introduction to computer applications in education." (International Reading Association)*

The Computer as an Educational Tool, edited by Henry F. Olds, Jr. (Vol. 3, No. 1, 1986). *"The category of tool uses for computers holds the greatest promise for learning, and this . . . book, compiled from the experiences of a good mix of practitioners and theorists, explains how and why." (Jack Turner, Technology Coordinator, Eugene School District 4-J, Oregon)*

Logo in the Schools, edited by Cleborne D. Maddux, PhD (Vol. 2, No. 2/3, 1985). *"An excellent blend of enthusiasm for the language of Logo mixed with empirical analysis of the language's effectiveness as a means of promoting educational goals. A much-needed book!" (Rena Lewis, PhD, Professor, College of Education, San Diego State University)*

Humanistic Perspectives on Computers in the Schools, edited by Steven Harlow, PhD (Vol. 1, No. 4, 1985). *"A wide spectrum of information." (Infochange)*

Integration of Technology into the Classroom: Case Studies has been co-published simultaneously as *Computers in the Schools*, Volume 16, Number 2 and Volume 16, Numbers 3/4 2000.

The development, preparation, and publication of this work has been undertaken with great care. However, the publisher, employees, editors, and agents of The Haworth Press and all imprints of The Haworth Press, Inc., including The Haworth Medical Press® and Pharmaceutical Products Press®, are not responsible for any errors contained herein or for consequences that may ensue from use of materials or information contained in this work. Opinions expressed by the author(s) are not necessarily those of The Haworth Press, Inc.

Cover design by Thomas J. Mayshock Jr.

The Haworth Press, Inc., 10 Alice Street, Binghamton, NY 13904-1580 USA

Library of Congress Cataloging-in-Publication Data

Integration of technology into the classroom: case studies/D. LaMont Johnson, Cleborne D. Maddux, Leping Liu, editors
    p. cm.
    Co-published simultaneously as Computers in the schools, v. 16, no. 2 and 3/4, 2000.
    Includes bibliographical references and index.
    ISBN 0-7890-1047-X (alk. paper)–ISBN 0-7890-1048-8 (alk. paper)
    1. Educational technology–Case studies. 2. Computer assisted instruction–Case studies. 3. Internet in education–Case studies. I. Johnson, D. LaMont (Dee LaMont), 1939- II. Maddux, Cleborne D., 1942- III. Liu, Leping.

LB1028.3 .I5654 2000
371.33′4–dc21

00-059809

Integration of Technology into the Classroom: Case Studies

D. LaMont Johnson
Cleborne D. Maddux
Leping Liu
Editors

Integration of Technology into the Classroom: Case Studies has been co-published simultaneously as *Computers in the Schools*, Volume 16, Number 2 and Volume 16, Numbers 3/4 2000.

The Haworth Press, Inc.
New York • London • Oxford

Indexing, Abstracting & Website/Internet Coverage

This section provides you with a list of major indexing & abstracting services. That is to say, each service began covering this periodical during the year noted in the right column. Most Websites which are listed below have indicated that they will either post, disseminate, compile, archive, cite or alert their own Website users with research-based content from this work. (This list is as current as the copyright date of this publication.)

(continued)

*Special Bibliographic Notes related to special journal issues
(separates) and indexing/abstracting:*

- indexing/abstracting services in this list will also cover material in any "separate" that is co-published simultaneously with Haworth's special thematic journal issue or DocuSerial. Indexing/abstracting usually covers material at the article/chapter level.
- monographic co-editions are intended for either non-subscribers or libraries which intend to purchase a second copy for their circulating collections.
- monographic co-editions are reported to all jobbers/wholesalers/approval plans. The source journal is listed as the "series" to assist the prevention of duplicate purchasing in the same manner utilized for books-in-series.
- to facilitate user/access services all indexing/abstracting services are encouraged to utilize the co-indexing entry note indicated at the bottom of the first page of each article/chapter/contribution.
- this is intended to assist a library user of any reference tool (whether print, electronic, online, or CD-ROM) to locate the monographic version if the library has purchased this version but not a subscription to the source journal.
- individual articles/chapters in any Haworth publication are also available through the Haworth Document Delivery Service (HDDS).

Integration of Technology into the Classroom: Case Studies

Contents

ABOUT THE EDITORS

D. LaMont Johnson, PhD, is Professor of Education in the Department of Counseling and Educational Psychology at the University of Nevada, Reno. He is also Program Coordinator of the Information Technology in Education program. He teaches courses on the application of technology in education and trains teachers across the state of Nevada in using the Internet in their classrooms. The co-author of the textbook *Educational Computing: Learning with Tomorrow's Technologies*, now in its second edition, Professor Johnson has written or co-written numerous books and articles on educational computing and information technology in education.

Cleborne D. Maddux, PhD, is Professor of Education in the Department of Counseling and Educational Psychology at the University of Nevada, Reno, where he teaches courses on statistics and on integrating technology into education. He trains elementary and high school teachers in the state of Nevada on how to make the Internet a regular feature of their classroom agendas. Senior author of *Educational Computing: Learning with Tomorrow's Technologies*, a textbook now in its second edition, Professor Maddux has authored or co-authored numerous professional articles and books on informational technology in education and educational technology.

Leping Liu, PhD, is Assistant Professor of Education in the Department of Reading, Special Education and Instructional Technology at Towson University. She received her PhD in Information Technology in Education and Statistics from the University of Nevada, Reno. She teaches courses on the application of technology in education. Her research interests focus on integration of technology in classroom teaching/learning, technology and mathematical thinking, multimedia learning environment and cognitive development, and computer achievement modeling. She has authored or co-authored several professional articles and co-edited two books.

INTRODUCTION

D. LaMont Johnson
Cleborne D. Maddux
Leping Liu

Integration of Technology into the Classroom: Case Studies

Through our involvement in teacher training programs, we have come to recognize that an important part of bringing pre-service and in-service teachers to a point where they can effectively integrate information technology into the classroom is to provide them with a variety of good examples. In this spirit, we have collected case studies on successful integration projects for publication in this volume. The case studies being published were selected from a broad sample of case study reports that were submitted after we sent out a call for papers. In that call, we requested reports of successful experiences where teachers had harnessed the power of technology to enrich and enhance teaching and learning experiences in their classrooms.

We asked interested parties to prepare case study reports that would communicate two things to our readers: (a) the rationale and justifica-

[Haworth co-indexing entry note]: "Integration of Technology into the Classroom: Case Studies." Johnson, D. LaMont, Cleborne D. Maddux, and Leping Liu. Co-published simultaneously in *Computers in the Schools* (The Haworth Press, Inc.) Vol. 16, No. 2, 2000, pp. 1-2; and: *Integration of Technology into the Classroom: Case Studies* (ed: D LaMont Johnson, Cleborne D. Maddux, and Leping Liu) The Haworth Press, Inc., 2000, pp. 1-2. Single or multiple copies of this article are available for a fee from The Haworth Document Delivery Service [1-800-342-9678, 9:00 a.m. - 5:00 p.m. (EST). E-mail address: getinfo@haworthpressinc.com].

1

tion for integrating technology into a particular teaching and learning situation, and (b) the techniques and procedures involved in carrying out such an integration project. Our goal was to publish case studies that would help teachers discover why the integration of technology would enhance a teaching and learning situation and would help them understand theoretical and/or philosophical principles that form the underpinnings of the case study. Further, we wanted to publish case studies that would enable teachers to see how they could apply the techniques and procedures described in the case studies to their own situations–assuming similar interests and resources.

Our instructions to case study authors were to answer two questions in their reports:

1. How and why did you think the integration of technology into this teaching and learning situation would cause students to learn more efficiently, more thoroughly, and more deeply?
2. What evidence can you offer to show that you were correct in your assumptions?

We were pleased with the response to our call for papers. We received case study reports from educators working in a wide variety of situations, and the reports ranged across the entire gambit of grade levels and curricular interests.

It is our hope that these cases will further the integration of information technology into school curricula and that they will inspire other teachers to document their integration efforts and prepare well-written reports for publication. We believe that providing teachers with a rich source of ideas relating to this important endeavor is one important step in fully capturing the potential of information technology in teaching and learning.

RESEARCH

D. LaMont Johnson
Leping Liu

First Steps Toward a Statistically Generated Information Technology Integration Model

SUMMARY. One hundred and two case studies relating to integrating information technology into the classroom were analyzed using logistic regression. The purpose of this procedure was to generate a statistical model that would reflect the significant components present in successful case studies. In order to accomplish this, we identified instructional components that were common to all case studies. Through this process, we identified six instructional components that we labeled: Use of Software, Use of Web-Based Instruction, Use of Web Information Resources, Use of Problem-Based Learning, Instructional Design Choice, and Tailoring Multimedia Courseware. These six instructional compo-

D. LAMONT JOHNSON is Professor, Counseling and Educational Psychology Department, College of Education, University of Nevada, Reno, NV 89557. E-mail: ljohnson@unr.edu
LEPING LIU is Assistant Professor, Department of Reading, Special Education and Instructional Technology, College of Education, Towson University, Towson, MD 21252. E-mail: lliu@saber.towson.edu

[Haworth co-indexing entry note]: "First Steps Toward a Statistically Generated Information Technology Integration Model." Johnson, D. LaMont, and Leping Liu. Co-published simultaneously in *Computers in the Schools* (The Haworth Press, Inc.) Vol. 16, No. 2, 2000, pp. 3-12; and: *Integration of Technology into the Classroom: Case Studies* (ed: D. LaMont Johnson, Cleborne D. Maddux, and Leping Liu) The Haworth Press, Inc., 2000, pp. 3-12. Single or multiple copies of this article are available for a fee from The Haworth Document Delivery Service [1-800-342-9678, 9:00 a.m. - 5:00 p.m. (EST). E-mail address: getinfo@haworthpressinc.com].

3

nents were considered variables in the statistical analysis. Three of the six variables were statistically significant and were incorporated in the model (i.e., Use of Software, Use of Problem-Based Learning, and Instructional Design Choice). We recommend this model in teacher training in order for teachers to be prepared to successfully integrate information technology into the classroom. Suggestions are offered for further investigation and refinement of this model. [Article copies available for a fee from The Haworth Document Delivery Service: 1-800-342-9678. E-mail address: <getinfo@haworthpressinc.com> Website: <http://www.HaworthPress.com>]

KEYWORDS. *Statistical model, constructivism, instructivism, integration, information technology*

Expressions of the need to integrate information technology into the school curriculum have become passé. It should be obvious to every person with even a casual interest in the movement to supply schools with new information technology that we are at a point where we must show that these new educational resources can be used for more efficient teaching and learning. Spending millions of dollars to purchase computers, software, peripherals, and connectivity only to add one additional small dimension to the already bloated curriculum cannot be justified. We refer here, of course, to the proposition of using information technology simply to teach students about technology for the sake of having them leave school knowing something about technology. The promise that has been made to the American taxpayer, explicitly or implicitly, is that students will emerge from our public schools with a better education when we spend the money to equip schools with the latest technological advances.

It seems that we are at a point in time where everybody is talking about technology integration, but few practicing teachers profess to know exactly how to proceed. The fact is that real integration requires change. Such change may impact classroom organization, instructional delivery, teacher/student relationships, lesson design, and evaluation. There are many ideas relating to such change floating around, and there are some great success stories. However, what seems to be lacking is a model that teachers can use to guide them through the necessary changes they will need to make to be successful in integrating new technology into their classrooms.

As far as we know, no one has put forth a statistical model for successful integration of information technology in teaching and learning. What have been referred to as integration models are usually anecdotal success stories, which are not to be disparaged, but which are often difficult to generalize from. What we are attempting to accomplish in this article is to lay down some basic building blocks for an elegant integration model– one that will be simple, precise, and generalizable. We recognize the limitations of this initial step, but take it in the spirit of a pioneering endeavor. Our hope is that the model we set forth here will foster contemplation, discussion, and constructive criticism. We further hope that the model will be expanded and refined to a point that it can be used as a referent point in pre-service and in-service teacher training.

WHAT WE DID

In developing our model, we reviewed 102 case studies relating to the integration of information technology into teaching and learning situations. Of these cases, 67 described integration projects that took place in K-12 classrooms, 24 described integration projects that took place in higher education teacher training settings, and 11 described integration projects that took place in in-service training settings. The projects covered all curricular areas and included grade levels ranging from preschool to graduate school.

Each of the case studies was rated in terms of outcome success. Two or more independent evaluators rated each case to determine overall success. The overarching question related to whether the integration project described in the case achieved its stated goals and objectives. Our strategy in developing the model was to try to determine which instructional components contribute to successful learning outcomes. Our strategy was further based on the assumption that, once we could identify instructional components, we could determine which components were the most powerful predictors of successful learning outcomes. Our first step, then, was to examine all 102 case studies to identify common instructional components. This process resulted in the identification of six common instructional components that we labeled as follows:

1. Use of Software
2. Use of Web-Based Instruction
3. Use of Web Information Resources
4. Use of Problem-Based Learning

5. Instructional Design Choice
6. Tailoring Multimedia Courseware

In order for the reader to relate to these instructional components, we provide the following explanations:

Use of Software

Here, we are not speaking of whether or not software was used or not used in an integration project; rather, we are referring to the nature of the software use. Using a distinction made by Maddux, Johnson, and Willis (1997), we categorized software use as Type I or Type II. In this distinction, *Type I software* tends to turn the computer into a teaching machine. It is usually drill and practice, or tutorial in nature. It tends to render the learner passive and the computer active. It is designed to help teach specific skills, processes, or concepts. Integrated Learning Systems (ILS) software generally fits this distinction. *Type II software* tends to turn the computer into a tool to enhance learning by allowing the learner to create, manipulate, and produce. Application software such as word processing, database management, spreadsheet, and graphics programs fall into this category. This type of software tends to render the learner active and the computer passive. Any type of software where the user is the creator and the computer provides the creative medium (e.g., Adobe Photoshop) tends to fit this designation.

Use of Web-Based Instruction

The Web-based instructional component refers to the use of the Web to deliver online lessons. For example, when a teacher develops a tutorial using authoring software and subsequently delivers the tutorial over the Web, we consider it Web-based instruction. Another example would be where a teacher develops a PowerPoint presentation and a set of assignments to be completed, and this entire instructional package is delivered via the Web.

Use of Web Information Resources

In this instructional component, we refer to the Web as a general information resource. Whether the teacher searched the Web for information relating to a learning situation or the students searched the Web for information, we categorized the case study as having used the Web as an information resource.

Use of Problem-Based Learning

The problem-based instructional component is characterized by the teacher setting up a problem to be solved and allowing the students to pursue activities that lead to solving the problem. Such a process leads students toward experiencing what a thing or idea is and how it works. The presence of this component might be viewed as the opposite of what is sometimes referred to as rote learning. There are strong discovery and experiential learning elements present in the case studies that are categorized as possessing this instructional component.

Instructional Design Choice

To simplify the instructional design component, case studies were categorized as either using a constructivist approach or an instructivist approach. Realizing that these categories are broad, we differentiated between them by looking at the degree to which the learner had an opportunity to explore and create his/her own learning outcomes. Constructivist cases tended to provide more open-ended assignments with ample opportunity for students to select their own learning materials and to be creative in their approach. Instructive cases tended to focus the learning outcome more narrowly and be more structured in terms of what the learning outcome would be and the procedures required for reaching the learning outcome.

Tailoring Multimedia Courseware

The tailoring multimedia courseware component refers to the presence of any attempt in the case study to create tailored multimedia learning materials. Such learning materials range from short lesson segments to entire tutorials created with authoring software such as HyperCard, ToolBook, or Director. Cases were also listed as possessing this component if they used tailored multimedia materials created for the Web.

Generating the Statistical Model

Each of the 102 cases was evaluated to determine whether it had been successful in terms of having met the goals and objectives established for the learning project upon which it was based. Each case was then evaluated to determine into which category it best fit with respect to each of the six instructional components. In other words, we evaluated each case to determine if software was used for Type I or Type II computer applications, whether Web-based instruction had been used, whether Web information resources had been used, whether problem-based learning had been used, whether the instructional design was constructive or instructive, and whether tailored multimedia courseware had been used. Categorizing the cases in this way resulted in a data table (see Table 1). Table 1 illustrates how the cases were dissected and how the results were organized preparatory to running a logistic regression–the statistical procedure we used to generate our model.

Logistic regression is a form of statistical modeling that is often appropriate for categorical outcome variables. It describes the relationship between a categorical response variable and a set of explanatory variables. In our analysis, the response variable was the outcome of the learning project described in each case and was categorized as successful or unsuccessful. The explanatory variables in our analysis were the six instructional components previously defined. The purpose of the logistic regression analysis is to try to identify a set of variables (i.e., instructional components) that can best predict the out-

TABLE 1
Variables in the Logistic Regression

Response Variable	Explanatory Variables		
(Y) Outcomes		Successful	Unsuccessful
	(X1) Use of Software	Type I	Type II
	(X2) Use of Web-Based Instruction	Yes	No
	(X3) Use of Web Information Resources	Yes	No
	(X4) Use of Problem-Based Learning	Yes	No
	(X5) Instructional Design Choice	Constructivism	Instructivism
	(X6) Tailoring Multimedia Courseware	Yes	No

come of a technology integration case study (i.e., whether it was successful or unsuccessful). The logic of conducting such an analysis is that, if we can determine which variables predicted success in our sample, we should then be able to recommend those same variables to predict success in other technology integration projects.

WHAT WE FOUND

After running the logistic regression analysis, it was determined that the best model (i.e., the best set of variables) for predicting the success of a technology integration case study was a model that included variables X1, X3, and X5 (Use of Software, Use of Problem-Based Learning, and Instructional Design Choice) as can be seen in Table 2.

Table 2 shows that three of the original six variables (see Table 1) are significant in predicting the success of a case study (Use of Software, Use of Problem-Based Learning, and Instructional Design Choice). In other words, we are confident that these three variables will consistently contribute to success in integrating information technology in the classroom. It is important to point out the direction of these significant variables. Based on our analysis, we can say with confidence that the chances for successful integration are enhanced when:

1. Type II software is used.
2. Problem-based assignments are given.
3. Constructivist learning environments are established.

It is interesting to think about the three nonsignificant variables (Use of Web-Based Instruction, Use of Web Information Resources,

TABLE 2
Logistic Regression Analysis Results

Variable	DF	Parameter Estimate	Wald Chi-square	P > Chi-square	Odds Ratio
Intercept	1	− 5.2783	14.1148	0.0002	
Software	1	2.9049	12.3779	0.0004	18.264
Problem-Based Learning	1	3.9173	9.3159	0.0023	50.266
Instructional Design Choice	1	3.2694	6.5084	0.0107	26.299

and Tailoring Multimedia Courseware). We speculate that the reason the "Use of Web Information Resources" did not achieve significance lies in the fact that there was almost no variance in this instructional component. Almost all of the cases used this resource and therefore it added nothing to the prediction of success. This variable then, is probably best viewed as a ubiquitous integration resource. Use of the Web-based Instruction and Tailoring Multimedia Courseware, as we have defined them, are quite similar. Both imply some degree of programmed instruction the designs of which can be based on instructivist or constructivist approaches. Cases using Web-based instruction or tailoring multimedia courseware with constructivist design principles tend to have expected learning outcomes and to be successful cases. Evidently, what really made a difference was the approach to instructional design. This is why the use of these two instructional components cannot be used to predict successful cases (they are not significant to the model).

Using the three significant variables, a visual representation of the model (Figure 1) generated by the logistic regression analysis follows.

WHAT THE MODEL MEANS

The model that was statistically generated from analyzing 102 cases where information technology was integrated into the classroom curri-

FIGURE 1
The Integration Model

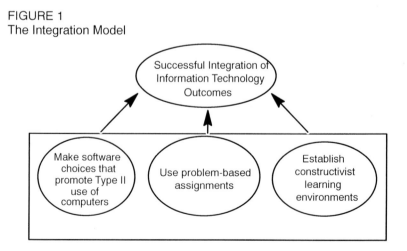

culum verifies much of what we already knew. The three instructional components (i.e., Use of Software, Use of Problem-Based Learning, and Instructional Design Choice) that were significant in predicting successful integration projects represent mainstream thought relating to technology integration. From the beginning of the microcomputer age, those interested in harnessing the power of the new technology in the classroom believed that the computer should be used as a tool, that students should use this new tool in problem-based learning situations, and that the constructivist philosophy of education provided the most effective grounding for designing such instruction.

With the statistical verification provided here, we believe we have created a visual icon that can be used to form the underpinnings for instructional design training in both pre-service and in-service settings. The model represents an elegant reference for both training in technology integration and evaluating proposed integration projects. Instructors can take the stance that the best predictor of a successful integration project depends heavily on the extent to which these three elements have been given thoughtful consideration. Using this model in teacher training suggests that, in order for teachers to be prepared to successfully integrate information technology into the classroom, they need to be competent in a variety of Type II computer applications, they need to be able to design interesting and challenging problem-based learning situations, and they need to understand and become comfortable in designing constructivist learning environments.

NEXT STEPS

At the beginning of this article, we were careful not to claim too much. We view this effort as an initial step and recognize the limitations of the statistically generated model we have created. We propose that others use this first step to conduct other studies and suggest the following as possible research directions:

Refinement of the instructional components–We chose and labeled the six instructional components that constituted the variables in the statistical analysis. These instructional components need refinement. They need to be more elegant in terms of representing simply stated powerful concepts.

Expansion of the instructional components–It is fine to say that our model can serve as an icon for technology integration design, but the real meat of the model lies in the expansion and fleshing out of the three instructional components. The model needs to be expanded to include efficient ways of teaching concepts and techniques relating to each component (e.g., What are some effective ways to create problem-based learning situations?).

Replication of the study–It would be interesting to apply our model to other collections of cases to determine whether the three significant instructional components of the model hold up as the chief predictors of success.

Controlled experimentation with the model–At some point, studies with tighter experimental controls will be necessary to add validity to our model. It would be interesting to conduct a research project involving different groups being trained in technology integration where integration modeling serves as the experimental variable. Such studies are difficult to design and conduct, of course, but would do much to either validate or dismiss our integration model.

REFERENCE

Maddux, C.D., Johnson, D.L. & Willis, J. W. (1997). *Educational computing: Learning with tomorrow's technologies*. Needham Heights, MA: Allyn & Bacon.

Cleborne D. Maddux

Case Studies:
Are We Rejecting Rigor
or Rediscovering Richness?

SUMMARY. *Case studies are receiving renewed interest as an alternative to traditional research methods and reports. This interest is part of a more general trend involving the rejection of modern science and scientific methods in the social sciences and helping professions, and what is often a strident and ill-informed advocacy of qualitative research methods. Qualitative research in general and case studies in particular have a number of disadvantages and should not be substituted for quantitative research methods. Nevertheless, case studies probably can make a worthwhile contribution to the search for knowledge in education by helping to communicate the richness of human interactions, and by providing examples of how theories and philosophies can actually be applied in real situations. [Article copies available for a fee from The Haworth Document Delivery Service: 1-800-342-9678. E-mail address: <getinfo@haworthpressinc.com> Website: <http://www.HaworthPress.com>]*

KEYWORDS. *Case studies, qualitative research, constructivism*

CLEBORNE D. MADDUX is Associate Editor for Research, *Computers in the Schools*, and Professor of Education, Counseling and Educational Psychology Department, College of Education, University of Nevada, Reno, NV 89557. E-mail: maddux@unr.edu

[Haworth co-indexing entry note]: "Case Studies: Are We Rejecting Rigor or Rediscovering Richness?" Maddux, Cleborne D. Co-published simultaneously in *Computers in the Schools* (The Haworth Press, Inc.) Vol. 16, No. 2, 2000, pp. 13-16; and: *Integration of Technology into the Classroom: Case Studies* (ed: D. Lamont Johnson, Cleborne D. Maddux, and Leping Liu) The Haworth Press, Inc., 2000, pp. 13-16. Single or multiple copies of this article are available for a fee from The Haworth Document Delivery Service [1-800-342-9678, 9:00 a.m. - 5:00 p.m. (EST). E-mail address: getinfo@haworthpressinc.com].

13

One of the interesting educational developments of the last decade has been a resurgence of interest in case studies as research tools. This interest is part of a more general trend involving the rejection of modern science and scientific methods in education.

That trend has produced a number of movements other than a return to case studies. For example, modern anti-science thinking has resulted in many calls for *qualitative research strategies* in education, of which case studies are a case in point. Some of the advocates of qualitative research strategies suggest only that such strategies should be more widely used and more widely published than they currently are; while other, more extreme proponents maintain that we should totally abandon quantitative research and the entire scientific method.

It is difficult not to be cynical after reading the arguments of many of these extreme would-be reformers, who attribute their positions to a mixed bag of popular and formal culture and philosophy. Indeed, it would be difficult to take any movement seriously whose advocates pay lip service to such diverse ideas as *postmodernism, relativism, naturalism, feminism, neo-Marxism, progressivism, deconstructivism,* and *constructivism* (Maddux & Cummings, 1999).

However, no matter how amusing it may be, an over-reliance on words ending with the same suffix is not sufficient grounds for rejecting an educational trend. Nor is it relevant that many of the conclusions of the more extreme advocates of qualitative research seem impractical, to say the least. For example, at a recent conference of educators interested in information technology, some of the more unusual suggestions made by presenters included the contention that (a) science has never provided a true answer to any research question; (b) educational research is whatever the researcher says it is, and can thus be a poem, a statue, a play, a short story, etc.; and (c) any project or activity that advances the cause of an oppressed group should be considered a legitimate doctoral dissertation in information technology in education.

I must confess that I find much that is shallow in the anti-science movement of the last decade or so. Although there are exceptions, it seems to me that few of the most extreme critics of the scientific method have bothered to master the theoretical and philosophical tenets upon which they say they base their own positions. Many allude to the "-isms" listed above, but seem to have little, if any, real understanding of the ideas the terms represent. An obvious example can be found in even a cursory reading of the recent literature advocating "constructivism" in education. It is painfully obvious that many of the authors of this literature have never read translations of the work of theorists such as Piaget and Vygotsky, and what little many know about the ideas of these seminal thinkers has come from the often erroneous interpretations of their ideas found in secondary sources. Another example is the educational literature suggesting that "chaos theory" should be used to reform elementary and secondary education, counseling, special education, and just about every other facet of professional educational practice. A small percentage of this literature is coherent and logical, but much of it seems based on a depth of understanding of chaos theory gleaned solely from a casual viewing of the film *Jurassic Park*.

Quite simply, much of the current popularity of modern anti-science in general and many of the "-isms," such as "constructivism," seems based on little more than fad and fashion. Why education is so prone to vagary is a matter for conjecture, but few would argue that the phenomenon exists. We have all witnessed the meteoric rise and rapid demise of a long list of educational fads, of which anti-science and constructivism may be the most recent examples.

Nevertheless, while we may reject some or all of the suggestions of ill-informed extremists, the real question is whether or not case studies have anything to offer us as researchers and practitioners. If they do, there is no reason why they cannot be used in addition to, rather than as substitutes for, more traditional quantitative research methods.

I believe that case studies *can* make a worthwhile contribution to educational research. Their strength is their potential to communicate the richness of human interactions, and to provide examples of how theories and philosophies can actually be applied in real situations. (Of course, their ability to do this is highly dependent on the skill of the writer, which may be even more important when preparing case studies than when writing more traditional research reports.)

The disadvantages of case studies must also be kept in mind. One critical disadvantage is the difficulty in generalizing findings from the specific environment described in the case study to environments encountered by others in the field. It was primarily this disadvantage that was the most pressing reason for abandoning case studies several decades ago, and it is this disadvantage that mitigates for case studies merely augmenting, rather than replacing, quantitative strategies.

There is no great danger, and indeed, there is almost certainly much to be gained, in expanding our list of research tools to include well-written case studies. This journal welcomes the submission of case studies, and good ones will appear alongside well-written research reports of studies employing both quantitative and qualitative methods.

Case studies can be as productive as our other, more widely accepted research methodologies, but their recent increased popularity may be a symptom of something dangerous. The strident and ill-informed advocacy of some of the current devotees of "constructivism" who dismiss all quantitative research as irrelevant and useless is the first real example of the educational *true believer* in our new field of information technology in education. Does this signal that our new field will be as dominated by fad, fashion, and the consequent infamous educational pendulum effect as have elementary and secondary education? I hope not, because I believe that elementary and secondary education have not been well served by these phenomena.

The title of this article asks whether the increasing popularity of case studies means we are rejecting rigor or rediscovering richness. I believe the answer is both. Some seem to endorse case studies and other qualitative methods because they fear numbers, dislike careful advance planning, and never mastered quantitative theory and method. Others see the benefit of case studies in illustrating clinical judgment and providing a bridge between theory and method. I believe that if we can adopt the latter stance, and refrain from "choosing up sides" in an emotional and bitter debate between advocates of the two approaches, we can avoid some of the educational mistakes of the past and further the search for better methods in information technology in education.

REFERENCE

Maddux, C.D., & Cummings, R. (1999). Constructivism: Has the term outlived its usefulness? *Computers in the Schools, 15*(3/4), 5-20.

Nancy Yost

Electronic Expressions: Using E-Mail to Support Emergent Writers

SUMMARY. *This article discusses the use of e-mail in a kindergarten classroom. The article presents information on how e-mail can be used to support emergent writers. Information is given as to how one kindergarten teacher set up an e-mail program that encourages autonomy. The article includes suggestions about how the writing done by the children can be documented and examined for emergent writing development. [Article copies available for a fee from The Haworth Document Delivery Service: 1-800-342-9678. E-mail address: <getinfo@haworthpressinc. com> Website: <http://www.HaworthPress.com>]*

KEYWORDS. *Kindergarten, writing, emergent writers, technology, computers, early childhood, e-mail, elementary school*

The creative urge of the child to write down his own ideas was considered by teachers to be the important thing to be fostered in written language.

–Marie M. Clay (1975)

When was the last time you had children asking if it was their turn to write? Or children going home upset because they had not gotten to

---

NANCY YOST is Assistant Professor, University School, Indiana University of Pennsylvania, 570 S. Eleventh Street, Indiana, PA 15705-1087. E-mail: njyost@grove.iup.edu

[Haworth co-indexing entry note]: "Electronic Expressions: Using E-Mail to Support Emergent Writers." Yost, Nancy. Co-published simultaneously in *Computers in the Schools* (The Haworth Press, Inc.) Vol. 16, No. 2, 2000, pp. 17-28; and: *Integration of Technology into the Classroom: Case Studies* (ed: D. LaMont Johnson, Cleborne D. Maddux, and Leping Liu) The Haworth Press, Inc., 2000, pp. 17-28. Single or multiple copies of this article are available for a fee from The Haworth Document Delivery Service [1-800-342-9678, 9:00 a.m. - 5:00 p.m. (EST). E-mail address: getinfo@haworthpressinc.com].

17

write today? Or a child crying to write one more piece, after having chosen to write for an hour of choice time? I have experienced all of these situations in my kindergarten program. These are not isolated incidents, but fairly regular occurrences. Most of the children in my programs look forward to writing. How did I accomplish this? Through the sending of electronic expressions, or e-mail messages, between the kindergartners and their families and friends.

I have struggled as an early childhood teacher looking for ways to encourage young children to write in truly meaningful and authentic ways. Even though creative writing has been a part of many early childhood classrooms, including mine, these creative writing activities have felt contrived and teacher driven at times. A child's creative urges need outlets beyond story writing. The National Association for the Education of Young Children (NAEYC, 1998) stated that print rich environments by themselves "do not make most children readers. Rather, they expose children to a variety of print experiences and the processes of reading for real purposes" (p. 34). Likewise, having children write in a limited number of genres does not create writers. Children need to write through a variety of experiences and processes. Engaging children with e-mail allows them to begin to see that writing as a dynamic communication tool.

Traditionally kindergarten children use a variety of writing implements. They write using pencils, crayons, markers, pens, or paints. Computers simply add another tool to this "pencil box" of writing implements. Just as their individual choices for writing implements change, so do their developmental needs. A typical kindergarten class might have children with literacy levels anywhere from a three-year-old to that of a typical eight-year-old (NAEYC, 1998). It is important to provide emergent writers with scaffolds that support their individual development. Holdaway (1979) presented multiple ways to scaffold the individual emergent writer. The children are presented with choices of how to carry out their writing. Using traditional writing tools, a child might:

1. Write using sound spellings independently.
2. Request sound spelling assistance from the teacher or a peer.
3. Request assistance with the writing from the teacher when the child is tired of writing.
4. Ask the teacher to write the words so the child can copy the writing.
5. Ask the teacher to act as scribe while the child dictates a story.

When writing e-mail messages, the same scaffolding practices continue. Following Holdaway's suggestions, I issue invitations to the children when writing e-mail. I begin by asking if the child wishes to do his own typing. Frequently, this is the only invitation I need to offer. If the child says no, then I ask if he/she wants me to help. My assistance might range from the child typing some words independently, to support with sound spelling, to writing words down for the child to type from, or our taking turns typing. If none of these options meets the needs of the child, I ask if he/she wants to dictate the e-mail message for me to type. The needs of children vary from day to day. Sometimes the most capable writer might want to dictate the message instead of typing it independently.

Initially, I did not set out to establish the sending of e-mail messages as a major part of my kindergarten writing program. It has evolved into this over several years. Teaching at a university laboratory school allows me the opportunity to explore new curriculum and teaching methods. The first year I used e-mail with the children was simply to send messages to parents with needed classroom information. The early messages from the kindergartners might say, "Please help me remember my library book" or "I need a new drink bottle in the classroom."

Only a couple of families used e-mail that first year. Some of the families were related to the university and had begun to have access to e-mail in their offices. As the number of families with e-mail access increased, so did my e-mail usage with the children. Four years ago, I discovered that, with one exception, all kindergartners had one family member with e-mail access. At this point, I decided to incorporate e-mail more systematically into my kindergarten curriculum.

I feel strongly that children this age write only to family and friends. I prefer to have the children interact with known persons. The abstract nature of communication through computers is sometimes difficult for children to understand. By writing to people they know, and will see face to face on a regular basis, the children can also engage in verbal discussions about the messages they send through the computer. This begins to allow the children to construct an understanding that the messages are going to an "actual" person, not just a machine.

However, there is a little more to this activity than just sending e-mail. In the following section, I will explain what goes into the background project. I will not only explain what I do, but also make some suggestions on how you will be able to implement this project in your own classroom.

PULLING IT ALL TOGETHER

Early in the school term I send a letter to the parents discussing the e-mail project as a part of the writing program. I request that the parents send in information on any family members or friends who would enjoy communicating with their child. I ask the parents to check with the people before submitting their names and e-mail addresses. It is important that the people to whom the children write *want* to interact with the young writers. The responses sent back encourage the kindergartners to write. Also the family and friends must understand and not be disappointed or discouraged when the child does not always write back. Some adults become overly enthusiastic and send multiple messages in one day. The children become overwhelmed with so many messages and often stop writing for a brief period.

My initial letter contains a one-paragraph explanation of the e-mail project followed by space for the parents to write the names of the contact people, their relationship to the child, and the complete e-mail address. I ask for the relationship information to assist with my conversations while the children write.

The address information is used to compile a set of classroom e-mail directory pages. I use Netscape Composer to create the pages, but that is a personal choice. Any editor or word processor that creates hypertext pages will work. The first page I create is a list of the students in the class (see Figure 1).

This list can be organized to suit the needs of your students. For kindergartners at the beginning of the year, I use only the first names in alphabetical order. If you have non-readers, you might want to use a picture clue before the name. I might add the children's last names as we begin to work on learning to recognize and write them later in the year. Use a font that is large enough for the children to click on comfortably. If you have a large class, you might want to use columns so that all the names will appear on the screen at one time. If you teach two different groups of children, I suggest that you create a page for each class. The child's name is linked to an individual e-mail directory page.

The individual e-mail directory page contains a list of the e-mail names for that specific child. For example, clicking on Alex's name in the class directory page brings up a page similar to Figure 2.

When Alex wants to write to a person on his list, he clicks on the person's name. This click produces an e-mail composition window be-

FIGURE 1
E-Mail Directory

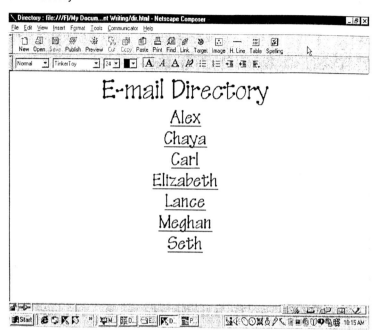

cause of the html code in the background. The e-mail composition window
is addressed, ready to have a subject line and the message added (see
Figure 3).

These pages create some type of autonomy in the children's writing
program that I strive for in the other areas of my kindergarten program.
The pages are easy to create with a brief five- or ten-minute lesson on
how to use one of the basic editors. All pages are stored on the hard
drive in one folder. Changing the browser preferences establishes the
class list directory page as the home page. Now the computers are ready
for my children to send e-mail anytime the browser is open.

I have found that most children can learn to use these pages and the
mail program with a minimum of instruction. The next section looks at
what the children actually do when they send e-mail in my kindergarten
class.

FIGURE 2
Individual Student's Directory

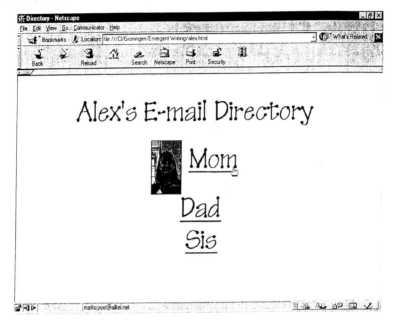

Mail Call

What had begun as a home/school communication tool turned out to be a writing bonanza. We usually look for ways to integrate technology into subject areas, or themes with special projects and activities. For me integrating technology through e-mail became a core of my writing program, a daily occurrence no matter what the topic of discussion in the room is. Just as Chang and Osguthorpe (1990) found that older children write longer passages and in greater depth, so do the kindergartners. With traditional writing tools like pencils and markers, the children seem to spend much of their effort with the manipulation of the pencil forming the letters. The children must focus so much of their attention to recall sound/symbol relationships, the shapes of the letters, where on the paper to begin writing, and the directionality of the letters, that there is little energy for them to consider the content and writing conventions. Children writing e-mail are able to focus on the sound/symbol relationship, writing conventions, and content. These

FIGURE 3
Sending Messages

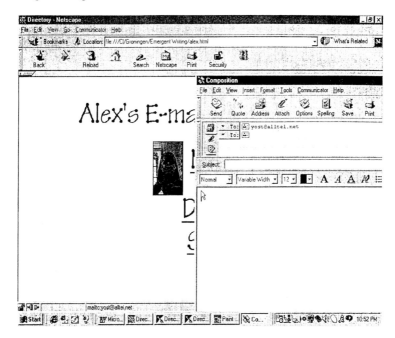

young writers also learn quickly to take advantage of editing features such as deleting, copying, inserting, and moving text. This allows them the same ability to rewrite and revise that older writers have demonstrated ability in using when doing computer compositions (Borgh & Dickson, 1992; Jones, 1994; Schrader, 1990; Seawel, Smaldino, Steele, & Lewis, 1994).

Usually the children in my program write e-mail during two blocks of time, before school and during center time. Either my student teacher or I assist with the e-mail. Children choose when they want to write e-mail. While we do ask each child to read, or have read, their individual messages, responding is left up to the individual. The children write by choice. We do discuss the social obligation of responding, but ultimately the choice is the children's. As we observe the children writing, the student teacher and I document the writing behaviors.

The first thing that all the children *must* do is to type their name in the subject line frame. This means that all children do type *something* and for some, their name is sufficient. Then the children generally write messages in one of three styles.

Some children simply type away on the keys. These children are beginning to understand that text has meaning and that letters create words. However, they have not broken the code of letter/symbol relationship. But they do know that this is a way to communicate with another person. While the text in Figure 4 appears to carry little meaning, observing and documenting the child during the process created a different interpretation. Usually the child will be talking about his writing as he types. When this happens, we actually treat the conversation as dictation and write the information in the notes for the child.

After the child has sent the message, I will send a second note to the same person. This time the subject line will read "translation of (child's name)." I type the "dictated" message into the message box so that the recipient can read what the child had "written." This translation does not undermine the child's belief in being a writer but allows the receiver to respond appropriately to the message the child sent.

Another child might exhibit a rudimentary understanding of the sound/symbol relationship. Figure 5 provides an example of this child's message.

In isolation, Meg's message might not convey much meaning. However, when documenting this child during her writing, she actually had sounded out the words to write:

FIGURE 4
Random Typing

```
flkdjqoeruc p j gikkfv ;pofqa;vf;v;afamv.m ;kvpvfk
alfjaopfjqamf pok   pg;vp   kasg'pka'[p   0P4TI 0
ga';"JF OURT GI
  OGTI
]IHYJ[ULSK'IY[PBLVC[ET[PEA GAK'PRQ.  PGP'G
AFVGP[AQ1ajf[of p oqfu t q[09qir] 0ir  53]   -vgfvb'p]   VBGJ
lvjapoc ['fu8  gtu'
   iai]--qK'V.NLNP-Q[AM pp-q   [ ;g[yhqpba'  'g'aq '0ghlngbn'
gq'ag ;gafggu  OAF;;qu ;ogbvl
```

Hi Mom. I love you. Can we go buy me a new beanie baby?
Love, Meg

Children who are writing at this stage are demonstrating that they are beginning to understand the sound/symbol relationship. However, they are missing the understanding of space between words as well as the full command of letters and sounds. After a few translations of this type of writing, adult readers generally do not need to have translations sent.

Children functioning on the high end of literacy development usually type in complete sentences. Some have even actually broken the codes of punctuation and capitalization. A typical message for these children might look like Figure 6.

You can see that this child has a well-developed use of traditional spelling. She understands the use of spacing between words and the use of a period. However, only observation and discussion with this child can answer the question of capitalization. She might understand the concept, but has chosen not to use it. Another child might choose to write in all capital letters. Perhaps the teacher could select a mini-lesson on when capital letters are conventionally used or on how to use

FIGURE 5
Moving Toward Traditional Writing

himomilvucnwegobymeanwbenebabe

luv

meg

FIGURE 6
Traditional Writing

dear grandma how are you. i cant wait until we go to 7 seasons.
how is chula.
love stacy

the shift key on the keyboard to produce capital letters. We can answer these questions by observing and discussing the writing process. Stacy also seems to have a well-developed sense of how to construct an informal letter.

Last year I developed a form to assist us with documenting the children's work. This form has helped the student teacher and me to be consistent with our observations and documentation. The form contains the following information:

1. Child's name?
2. Date?
3. Teacher's name?
4. Who was the message from or to?
5. What was the attitude of the child sending e-mail, eager, willing, so-so, reluctant?
6. Who read the e-mail?
7. Who wrote the e-mail?
8. What did the child type?
9. What observations were made concerning the child's reading.
10. What observations were made concerning the child's writing.
11. What observations were made concerning the child's spelling.

A copy of the appropriate e-mail message is attached to this sheet and is filed in the child's portfolio. We are now able to look at a child's writing development over the course of the school term.

Messages for the Future

As the start of a new school year approached, I began to reflect on the program's effectiveness. I realized that I was pleased with all components, but another discovery resulted from the previous year's implementation. I had accepted undergraduate volunteers to assist the children with the e-mail and I realized that I had too many volunteers. While this is not a problem for most teachers, it resulted in a concern worth noting. During the spring semester, two different undergraduate students assisted the children with e-mail for 30 minutes each day. This became overwhelming for the children. Sending e-mail appeared to be no longer a choice, but to be mandatory. The children rebelled; they grumbled when invited to send messages. Some actually stopped typing. The children became less productive and more dependent. For instance, kindergartners began asking the undergraduates to type very brief messages for them instead of typing for themselves. I began considering the role that choice plays in encouraging young children to write, and this choice is an essential component in the success of this writing program. While the assistance was both helpful and appreciated, in this situation less was better.

As I look at the goals for this project–to encourage and nurture emergent writers–I believe that the use of e-mail has been my most exciting find. Using e-mail as a portion of my writing program has gone beyond encouraging and nurturing these writers. This program also:

1. Promotes independence and autonomy in the writing process.
2. Establishes a positive and safe environment for these young writers.
3. Validates the children as writers, by my trusting that the children can and will write to their families.
4. Fosters positive relationships between the school and the families of the children.
5. Establishes authentic and meaningful writing situations for the children.

These are outstanding rewards for a minimal effort.

The program has been relatively easy to establish. The most difficult problem was that of settling on a "time" that the writing could take place. In my program, that is the first half-hour as the children gather and then during the center-time, free-choice hour. The computer becomes a choice for the children during center-time. I open the mail in the morning and invite the children to read any new messages they have received. After that those children who choose to may write messages. Some days more children write messages than on others, just as some days more children paint than on others. For the teacher, it does sometimes become difficult to be at the computer to provide support and write documentation. There are so many places that a teacher needs to be during center time anyway, and this becomes one more. Having a student teacher has helped my situation, but parent volunteers or older student "e-mail" helpers would work. However, the teacher must remember that the intent is not for all children to write everyday, but only an option for those children who choose to write. As in any situation where we are encouraging autonomy, perhaps the hardest thing a teacher must do is to let go and trust the children. I have no magic formulas for this, but only encouragement for them to try and watch what happens.

I hope that through this article teachers may learn how easy it can be to incorporate computers as a writing tool in a preschool or primary classroom. I have provided information and illustrations to smooth the transition toward using e-mail in a writing program by sharing my own experiences and recommendations. I have pointed to ways that writing e-mail assists toward reaching writing outcomes, perhaps even allowing children to do things at a more advanced level than the teacher might see with pencils or markers. As the children begin to explore and see writing as a dynamic communication tool, their electronic expressions become rich, rewarding experiences for all in-volved–the children, their family and friends, and me.

REFERENCES

Borgh, K. & Dickson, W.P. (1992). The effects on children's writing of adding speech synthesis to a word processor. *Journal of Research on Computing in Education*, *24*, 533-544.

Chang, L.L., & Osguthorpe, R.T. (1990). The effects of computerized picture-word processing on kindergartners' language development. *Journal of Research in Childhood Education*, *5*(1), 73-84.

Clay, M. (1975). *What did I write?* Portsmouth, NH: Heinemann.

Holdaway, D. (1979). *The foundations of literacy*. Portsmouth, NH: Heinemann.

Jones, I. (1994). The effect of a word processor on the written composition of second-grade pupils. *Computers in the Schools*, *11*(2), 43-54.

National Association for the Education of Young Children. (1998). Learning to read and write: Developmentally appropriate practices for young children. *Young Children*, *53*(4), 30-46.

Schrader, C.T. (1990). *The word processor as a tool for developing young writers* (Report). (ERIC Document Reproduction Service No. ED 212 431).

Seawel, L., Smaldino, S.E., Steele, S.L., & Lewis, J.Y. (1994). A descriptive study comparing computer-based word processing and handwriting on attitudes and perfor-mance of third and fourth grade students involved in a program based on a process approach to writing. *Journal of Research in Childhood Education*, *4*(1), 43-59.

Barbara Weiserbs

Social and Academic Integration Using E-Mail Between Children With and Without Hearing Impairments

SUMMARY. Children with and without hearing impairments participated in an e-mail project where each student had a year-long opportunity to exchange messages with a peer to learn about that person's experiences and interests, working in a low-stakes (risk-free) environment. Students were asked to function as teacher/resource by describing information they had learned in their social studies curriculum or other areas and as learners by further questioning their partners about their topic. In this model, knowledge would be deepened through rethinking and recording ideas, and by replying to questions that were sent to e-mail partners. E-mail is used as a collaborative tool and is applied in a purposeful and highly motivating context, one that does not fit the traditional classroom use of writing. Differences in teaching methods and values resulted in differences in e-mail accessibility for students. [Article copies available for a fee from The Haworth Document Delivery Service: 1-800-342-9678. E-mail address: <getinfo@haworthpressinc.com> Website: <http://www.HaworthPress.com>]

KEYWORDS. *E-mail, curriculum, hearing impairments*

BARBARA WEISERBS is Associate Professor, Department of Behavioral Science, Kingsborough Community College, 2001 Oriental Blvd., Brooklyn, NY 11235. E-mail: weiserbs@sci.brooklyn.cuny.edu

[Haworth co-indexing entry note]: "Social and Academic Integration Using E-Mail Between Children With and Without Hearing Impairments." Weiserbs, Barbara. Co-published simultaneously in *Computers in the Schools* (The Haworth Press, Inc.) Vol. 16, No. 2, 2000, pp. 29-44; and: *Integration of Technology into the Classroom: Case Studies* (ed: D. LaMont Johnson, Cleborne D. Maddux, and Leping Liu) The Haworth Press, Inc., 2000, pp. 29-44. Single or multiple copies of this article are available for a fee from The Haworth Document Delivery Service [1-800-342-9678, 9:00 a.m. - 5:00 p.m. (EST). E-mail address: getinfo@haworthpressinc.com].

29

E-mail offers a connection between populations of students that have not had opportunities to communicate with one another. In this project, we used e-mail to bring students and teachers in special and general education into communication and cooperation with the goal of enhancing their academic programs and improving their social awareness of one another.

BACKGROUND

Until recently, education of students in special and general education has been mostly separate and, although the separation has decreased, some populations of students and teachers remain isolated in separate schools. This has two consequences.

First, attitudes that children develop about other groups of children often rely on stereotyped images that can contribute to distorted information (Gottlieb & Gottlieb, 1977). Additionally, negative attitudes equating "us/they" with "in/outgroups" impede successful integration attempts.

Second, a similar insulation occurs for teachers at the special school because these teachers primarily speak with colleagues at their own school and miss the diverse approaches that are continually being refined and replaced in general schools. Thus, teachers in special schools develop their own culture, which reinforces its own values and approaches, and primarily supports their expertise in the area of the child's disability. The assumption underlying this notion is that the disability is the main educational target rather than the general needs of the child. E-mail serves to bridge this school culture gap by acquainting teachers with other models. E-mail provides collaborating teachers a window with which to observe and gain insights to alternative teaching methods and perspectives by sharing ideas and materials and by meeting in one another's classrooms and viewing first hand the method that their counterparts use.

OBJECTIVES

These considerations led us to consider e-mail as an interesting environment where educational opportunities, both academic and social, could be combined to bridge the gaps between these populations through a cooperative learning approach. In our project, e-mail functioned as a tool through which children could exchange knowledge that had been acquired in their social studies curriculum or about any other topic of interest. In this way, children assumed a teaching role and simultaneously were resources for one another. For students, learning takes on greater meaning when ideas are reviewed, reorganized, and rethought in an effort to actively explain them in writing.

E-mail provides a motivation for writing: communication in an open-ended fashion to learn about another person's experiences and interests.

Besides academic benefits, e-mail helps students recognize similarities and differences between each other, but, more importantly, it helps students understand one another more realistically through first-hand interactions by opening an avenue for communication.

METHODS

We selected children with and without hearing impairments to participate in this study. Fifth-grade children from a hearing impaired class were paired with fourth-grade children from a general education class to help compensate for language differences that existed between the groups. Age was considered a more fundamental basis, and we aimed for matches between children that were not greater than one year.

The children in the general education classroom attended a New York City public school where creative problem solving through student interaction, and constructive discussions between peers were emphasized. Individual and group projects were used as the primary learning tool. The class was a mixed aged group of third and fourth graders. There were equal numbers of boys and girls, and children were racially and ethnically diverse. The children in this class were also heterogeneously grouped with regard to intellectual abilities. All spoke English and had no disabling conditions. Only the fourth graders participated in the collaboration. In this class e-mail was easily integrated into the daily activities. The computer was available for students during any part of the school day with the exception of whole-class meeting times.

The second group consisted of an equally diverse group of children whose common defining characteristic was some degree of hearing dysfunction ranging from severe to profound loss. These children were fifth graders in a school for the deaf in New York City. They shared many of the same ethnic, racial, socioeconomic, and intellectual descriptions as their general education counterparts. The most outstanding difference was their use of American and English Sign Language as their primary means of communication. These children wrote in English, yet they exhibited a slower rate of progress in writing skills because of the disadvantage caused by their hearing loss. Despite the heterogeneity of children's abilities, a whole-class approach was the primary teaching method. Class and e-mail schedules were rigidly followed, although whenever needed, e-mail was preempted by other requirements.

INTEGRATION PROJECT DEVELOPMENT

Rationale and Justification for Integrating E-Mail into the Social Studies and Writing Curriculum

While e-mail is useful to all children, it lends itself well to children with serious hearing limitations for several reasons.

First, it is a visual and tactile means of communication and children with hearing impairments compensate for their loss by relying on these other sensory channels.

Second, children may spend whatever time they need to compose their written messages and e-mail counterparts are unaware of the amount of time needed. Communication disparities between children become diminished because completed messages do not reveal the time or effort spent.

Third, e-mail offers a means of communication between hearing and nonhearing groups of children, which is virtually impossible without this technology because of physical distances between schools. E-mail conventions include abbreviations and idiosyncratic shortcuts. Punctuation and spelling errors are ignored; the interest is in the content of the message.

Perhaps the most important reason for integrating this program between a class of children with hearing difficulties and another class of children without these difficulties is to overcome the isolation that exists between these groups of children. With this in mind, we developed a structured model for e-mail-based communication that fosters both academic and social opportunities in the context of cooperative learning. Playing the role of learner–using the other child as resource/teacher–

breaks down traditional stereotypes, as each child is valued for his/her complementary knowledge.

Theoretical and/or Philosophical Principles
That Form the Underpinnings of the Case Study

There are several perspectives that converge to form the underlying bases for this study. One is that e-mail is part of the whole-language approach to literacy. E-mail encourages reading and writing. Its function is to transmit information and ideas through written language. This project's use of e-mail is compelling because of its personal and, at the same time, social approach. The project is largely based on a cooperative learning model as students informally share information and make requests for help from one another. It encourages systematic use of partners as sources of information. It couples classroom teacher collaboration with paired student cooperation, and integrates a student-driven review of the social studies curriculum with written communication and organization of ideas. It reinforces concepts by using a new avenue for their expression. It extends naturally over the course of the school year, unlike other e-mail projects (Baugh & Baugh, 1997) that are short-lived. Furthermore, this project is completely tied to each student's class curriculum and thus can be expanded into any curriculum area. This can be based on the interests of e-mail partners and collaborating teachers, and with the encouragement of each child's teacher.

Integrating E-Mail Enhances a Teaching and Learning
Situation, Helping Students Learn More Efficiently,
More Thoroughly, and More Deeply

Integrating e-mail into the classroom functions to reinforce and synthesize (Jonassen, 1996) activities that the student has learned through reconstructing them in e-mail messages. This requires the student to select a topic, to develop some thoughts about the topic, and to review and reorganize what he or she learned in order to transmit the idea in a meaningful way.

First, the student must review previous work in a selected area. Second, the student must decide from many pieces of information what aspect to send to his or her e-mail partner. Third, the student must get help either with writing or factual information from peers, charts, previous work, dictionaries, teachers, or other resources. Children take on the roles of both teacher and learner. When playing the role of teacher, learning takes on greater meaning as the child reviews and reorganizes ideas in order to actively explain them in writing to another person. Consequently, his/her own knowledge is deepened through rethinking and recording ideas, and by replying to further questions that the information sent elicits. Assuming this role helps increase self-esteem for all students (Kelly, 1999). With this approach, e-mail serves as a strong motivator for reexamining class work. When playing the role of learner, children learn to ask questions and use peers as resources, ultimately becoming aware that they can learn from one another.

Difficulties Encountered

One troublesome aspect of integrating e-mail into the classroom for new teachers or those using a traditional teaching model may be the lack of direct assessment. There is little concrete assessment or formal feedback from teachers to students using e-mail. Traditionally, grading has been one of the central roles for teachers and the means for measuring students' work. Without a grading system, teachers may feel that e-mail is unimportant. Teachers experience no immediate rewards other than the approval of having "computers in the classroom" from parents and administration.

Teachers Need to Adapt to New Roles

E-mail should be viewed two ways: (a) as a tool with which to reinforce and review previously learned ideas, and (b) as an opportunity to write about what has been learned.

If teachers need information about the value of e-mail for themselves, they should monitor the lengths and frequency of messages over the course of the school year.

In our model, the role of the teacher is not to evaluate e-mail, but rather to encourage and facilitate its use. E-mail support comes in many forms. The teacher solves frustrating technical problems. The teacher can integrate e-mail into the fabric of each activity and curriculum area by developing follow-up activities using the computer. The teacher can show how she values work done on the computer by displaying computer-generated work and by sending individual e-mail messages to students. The teacher can be most supportive by creating an environment where students feel free to access the computer. In an open classroom, this is most easily done. It would be more difficult in a classroom where the predominant teaching method is directed to the whole class or to large segments at one time. In these types of classes, the teacher can control the type of writing by announcing the writing choices and including e-mail among the choices.

Problems for Teachers

While Teacher 1 used e-mail effectively, Teacher 2 was unable to have her children equally benefit from it. For her, three main problems arose, all stemming from management issues: perception of the teacher's role, accessibility of computer use, and integration into the curriculum.

Teacher's Role. Teacher 2, the teacher of the children with hearing impairments, used an approach that was not time-effective and interfered with the peer-to-peer intent of the project. In an effort to help her students transmit understandable messages that would not diminish the students' image, this teacher would correct the students' spelling, grammatical structure, and punctuation. In doing so, she felt diverted from her other responsibilities. As a result, she eventually made e-mail a low priority in her class. This problem is discussed more fully in the Results of E-mail Tabulation section.

Accessibility. Having set aside only one or two times per week for each student's access to the computer, opportunities for use and for timely responses quickly disappeared at School 2. Special school functions such as trips, visitors, and changes in class schedule because of administrative needs further reduced computer time for students. The lack of timely responses caused the most frustration for students. Others have observed this same issue (Allen & Thompson, 1994).

One classroom teacher's behavior supported student independence while the other classroom teacher's behavior supported student dependence. Computer accessibility was easily accomplished in the independent setting but hinged totally on teacher direction in the dependent setting.

Lack of Integration. E-mail is meaningful when it is integrated into the curriculum, and not used as a reward for other work or viewed as a novelty in the class. At School 2 teachers failed to recognize its potential value as a writing tool and as a means of social and academic learning for students and teachers alike. The problematic assumption Teacher 2 made was that "outsiders" who were not trained for the specific disability could not know how to work with the particular group of children. Therefore, she remained closed to its benefits.

Consequences. The limitations in e-mail correspondence at School 2 inevitably had ramifications at School 1. Children became frustrated with lack of and/or delayed responses. They began to question their teacher for reasons that could account for the lack of e-mail. Lack of e-mail reciprocity appeared to have the greatest effect on changing attitudes toward e-mail partners.

Along with her children, Teacher 1 experienced the lack of e-mail reciprocity and wondered how to help her children with this dilemma. She wrote and suggested that Teacher 2 encourage her students to respond. She also encouraged her students to continue to write to their e-mail partners even though they were receiving little or no responses. More teacher meetings were arranged. But as Levine (1995) noted, this does not necessarily effect a change in attitude or in curriculum.

THE INTEGRATION PROJECT

Others may certainly apply the techniques and procedures in this model to their own situation. Technically, two computers with modems and dedicated phone lines connected to an Internet service provider are required. Two teachers at different sites must meet on a regular and ongoing basis to develop the collaboration.

Teachers need to pair children by gender, behavior style, shared or complementary interests, and as closely as possible by writing level in order to promote the social and educational goals of the experiment, ultimately creating the potential for friendships to form.

Participating teachers can integrate this activity into their existing social studies curriculum or into any area of the curriculum they wish. They only need to agree to teach complementary topics. Teachers and students benefit from the strengths of their counterparts' curriculum.

RECOMMENDED TECHNIQUES AND PROCEDURES

In order to get started, a summary of essential points for project viability is useful:

1. The teachers of the paired classrooms must agree to meet monthly.
2. They must agree to provide daily access to the computer for the children. (This does not apply, of course, to trip days and other exceptional circumstances.)
3. Teachers must help children receive and send mail until children are self-sufficient in e-mail protocol.
4. Each teacher should exhibit a list of student questions about the topic that is being taught in the collaborating class and generate new lists of questions as new topics are studied. Children may select questions from this list or ask other relevant questions.
5. Teachers must ensure that their students will be in a position to provide information to their e-mail partner by charting key concepts, ideas, and issues that have been studied in their social studies units.

Some guidelines for organizing students' newly acquired concepts are suggested below:

1. Review the most interesting aspects of the topic the class has just completed. Then display charts recording this information.
2. Have charts, books, and other materials available as resources.
3. Allow children to work individually or in groups when they need assistance.
4. Focus on the content of the message and not on a grammatically correct message. (We are intent on giving positive feedback for on-task efforts rather than creating a daunting task.)

Teachers could introduce message exchanges by using some variation of the following model.

Children in class x have been studying _____ for a few weeks now. Instead of me teaching this to you, I'd like you to find out as much as you can about this topic from your e-mail partner. Let's write up a chart of questions we want to find answers to. Then each of you can print out what you've learned. We can put this information together into a book by the students in class x and y or we can make a chart that answers our questions.

The following is a list of suggestions that specifically encourage writing in the project:

1. Discuss and display topics for writing.
2. Encourage students to help one another and use one another's knowledge as a resource.
3. Share successful work, either one's creative works or information learned in class.
4. Generate questions that could be asked of e-mail partners, such as (a) Could you mail me an example of your class work on _____? (b) If you were going to add to your work, what else would you write?
5. As a culminating experience, compile a class book of all messages pertaining to the specific topic or make a collection of each child's messages.

EVALUATION:
EVIDENCE SUPPORTING OUR ASSUMPTIONS

Several assumptions underlie this project. The first assumption is that e-mail is a highly interesting and strongly motivating platform that encourages written language expression. It offers a different source for reinforcement of writing. Feedback comes directly from peers in the form of e-mail response and not from teachers in the traditional positive/negative teacher feedback or grading scheme.

Evidence that supported these assumptions came from two sources. The first was our direct observation. We witnessed an outpouring of excitement that was unparalleled with any other classroom observation. As an indicator of their enthusiasm for the new medium, one after another, children spontaneously stood up, introduced themselves to us. A typical comment was:

Hi, I'm A___ or I'm J___. I'm the one who wrote to you about X.

The second source of evidence was the content in the e-mail itself. Early communications reflected the same initial excitement.

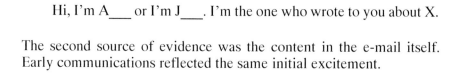

hi it is me ____I am so glad you wrote to me. my favorite tv show is the same one is yours. I will like to see you one day in person. i hope you will like to see me to.

Dear_____,

Isn't the Net cool?! I mean, I can't see you but I can read what your thinking from miles away (or just 10 minutes away). Okay we have alot of catching up to do. My favorite color is blue . . .

The second and equally important assumption is that teacher collaboration and support are essential for the success of this project. When teachers met to evaluate how effective the e-mail collaboration was functioning in their classes, they discovered that they themselves were pivotal in assuring success of the project. The more interested and invested teachers were in the project, the more support, time, and encouragement they gave to students. After collaborating teachers met, students' messages were longer and more frequently sent. After the fourth meeting, the two collaborating teachers decided to encourage their students to send examples of poetry on which children had worked.

Examples:

Dear (teacher's name),
Can you ask (e-mail partner) to write to me because she has not bene writeing me
thinks
(name)

Teacher responds,

Hi (student),
I will make sure (e-mail partner) writes to you on Monday or Tuesday. I'm sorry you have not received mail from her recently. She has a hard time writing sometimes. But I will make sure she writes to you this week.
Bye, (teacher's name)

Dear (e-mail partner),
Yes have poem. Like it lot. Peom very, very very good.Here my animal poem
+ Frogs
+ Ribbit, ribbit
+ On water

+ get food
Love, (e-mail partner)

dear, (e-mail partner)
want t'here a poem I wrote:
I AM A KID
I am akid who's a kid

who's a kid
who's still a kid
who knows some kids
who's freinds with kids
who has fun with kids
by (e-mail partner)

The third assumption is that open access to the computer was essential. For teachers to welcome this approach, teachers needed to integrate e-mail into the curriculum and not to view it as a reward for finishing scheduled assignments or as a separate entity.

RESULTS OF E-MAIL TABULATION

Tabulation of e-mail traffic revealed a sharp disparity in the number of e-mail messages sent between the two classes, consistent with the imbalance of class time that was set aside for e-mail use. Greater than twice the amount of messages were sent from children in one class than were received by them. The total number of messages that were sent between dyads in any kind of ongoing, reciprocal correspondence indicated that by more than a factor of 2, far more messages were sent from children without hearing impairments ($n = 179$) than from children who were hearing impaired ($n = 81$).

School 1. E-mail was available throughout the day. Children maintained high use throughout most of the year. However, responses were infrequent. Many messages illustrated frustration with not receiving mail. One child wrote, "write to me, write anything!" With continued limited response from their partners, by June the children were not enthusiastic but rather were dissatisfied and reluctant to participate. One youngster, speaking to his teacher, said, "Do I have to?"

School 2. Teacher 2 spent a considerable amount of time helping each child compose a literate message. She was very motivated by a need to shelter her students from any negative feedback about their written English (of which none was reported). In doing so, she allocated more time than she could afford and because of this expenditure, she devoted less and less time to the project and became less invested in it. Each child had designated time each week for checking, responding to, and sending new mail. However, these times were often preempted by other work. The end result was exactly what Teacher 2 did not want to happen, although her actions were largely responsible for the outcome: Children used e-mail when the teacher told them to do so, the task becoming an assignment that lost the joy and natural curiosity it was expected to promote. External constraints placed upon them interfered with the timeliness, the ability to freely communicate, and the development of interest in the child with whom they were paired.

CONCLUSIONS

There were several successes in the project. For teachers, e-mail served to bridge the separation that existed between the general and special education teachers. It served as the foundation for the relationship that developed between teachers. The most interesting insights occurred through visiting one another's school and recognizing differences that existed in their teaching styles and in their interactions with their students.

For children, the brightest and most academically mature were able to reorganize and express factual information into coherent paragraphs. Others could transmit examples of creative writing that they had generated. Students functioning at a more basic level were successful at written repetition of simple factual information. All children were comfortable with describing personal experiences and self-information.

A Bonus Function of E-Mail:
Low-Stakes Writing

Some students are reluctant writers for a variety of reasons. Some are unwilling to share personal emotions and feel vulnerable to expose their inner feelings. Others find writing an unsatisfying experience because the assigned work is inevitably done for teachers to read and evaluate. Consider peers, family members, and oneself as alternative readers with whom communication is not typically done. Children need the opportunities to experience writing in a variety of forms and for a variety of purposes (Dyson, 1993): for expression of opinion, emotion, description, information, questions, and directions, to name a few. They need both high- and low-stakes experiences. Typically, writing in class is a high-stakes activity because the teacher evaluates it. Low-stakes writing is almost risk free and does not involve teacher scrutiny. To be successful, writers need to feel satisfied with the process and product of their work. Teachers can encourage active participation in writing by offering low-stake writing opportunities.

E-mail is a low-stakes writing opportunity. Writing is directed to a peer instead of an adult. Writing errors are overlooked. As long as there is computer access and response from one's e-mail partner, students will continue to be active writers. Using e-mail as a writing tool functions to enhance learning and gives the student a platform for self-expression. The more the student writes, the more effective will his/her writing become and a greater fluency will be achieved.

Finally, students need time to compose written work. Teachers must recognize that each child will need different amounts of time to generate thoughts. Writing offers the slower or more reflective child a chance at self-expression. Speed of response is removed as a factor with e-mail writing, especially if the teacher does not put artificial time limits on the student.

E-Mail as a Follow-Up Tool

Follow-up activities are developed to review, reinforce, and enhance previous activities. In the present model, e-mail can be integrated into the curriculum if it is conceptualized as follow-up to current lessons. Not only are topics within the particular curriculum reviewed and reorganized, but writing becomes a fundamental part of the follow-up activity. For teachers who are trained in a teacher-centered approach, e-mail can be structured into lessons with this framework. It is easily integrated into a child-centered classroom, given its highly self-motivating character.

Changes for Future Use

This year-long collaboration supported several interesting insights for e-mail use. The most basic change is the necessity for both collaborating teachers to accept e-mail as an integral part of the curriculum, and to recognize its value as a writing tool that reinforces and extends classroom activities. Projects of shorter duration tend to overlook these fundamental features.

If teachers emphasized interpretation of facts, more personal opinions could be expressed. Comments from peers are a valuable feedback from which children can benefit, especially if constructive criticism were developed in the curriculum at both schools as part of the writing process. Such a change would produce richer e-mail transmissions.

To remedy the skewed message exchange that occurred in the current project and the disparity between management styles that ultimately led to differences in e-mail use, mutual integration of e-mail into the curriculum and ongoing regularly scheduled meetings between teachers are essential. Frequent discussions and identification of problems are the first steps toward resolving problems that arise (Norum, Grabinger, & Duffield, 1999).

Although we tried to find sites that were matched by similar teaching approaches, it would be more productive to use this endeavor as an opportunity for teachers to gain methodological insights from the collaboration and to take advantage of the curriculum strengths of the collaborating teacher. The main requirement for success is a willingness to share ideas and to agree to consistent meetings to discuss curriculum and problems (technical and other issues as they arise) over the course of the school year.

REFERENCES

Allen, G., & Thompson, A. (1994). Analysis of the effect of networking on computer-assisted collaborative writing in a fifth-grade classroom. Paper presented at the *Annual Meeting of the American Educational Research Association*, New Orleans.

Baugh, I., & Baugh, J. (1997). Global classroom: E-mail learning communities. *Learning and Leading with Technology, 25*(3), 38-41.

Dyson, A. (1993). *Social worlds of children: Learning to write in an urban primary school*. NY: Teachers College Press.

Gottlieb, J., & Gottlieb, B. (1997). Stereotypic attitudes and behavioral intentions toward handicapped children. *American Journal of Mental Deficiency, 82*, 65-71.

Jonassen, D. (1996). *Computers in the classroom: Mindtools for critical thinking*. Englewood Cliffs, NJ: Prentice-Hall.

Kelley, R. (1999). Getting everybody involved: Cooperative PowerPoint creations benefit inclusion students. *Learning and Leading with Technology, 27*(1), 10-14.

Levine, S. (1995). Teachers using technology: Barriers and breakthroughs. *International Journal of Educational Telecommunications, 1*(1), 53-70.

Norum, K., Grabinger, R., & Duffield, J. (1999). Healing the universe is an inside job: Teachers' views on integrating technology. *Journal of Technology and Teacher Education, 7*(3), 187-203.

Marianne K. Dove
Susan C. Fisher
Dwight L. Smith

Internet Learning Connections Between Second-Graders and University Teacher Education Electronic Mentors

SUMMARY. The dynamic nature of technology integration requires making many more connections than simply an electronic connection. This case study documents other necessary links in establishing Internet learning connections between second-graders and university teacher education students. Connections also include: collaborating with

MARIANNE K. DOVE is Assistant Professor, Department of Teacher Education, Beeghly College of Education, Youngstown State University, Youngstown, OH 44555-0001. E-mail: mdove20122@aol.com

SUSAN C. FISHER is Assistant Professor, Department of Teacher Education, Beeghly College of Education, Youngstown State University, Youngstown, OH 44555-0001. E-mail: sfisher433@aol.com

DWIGHT L. SMITH is Second-Grade Teacher, Louisville Elementary School, 1025 Washington Avenue, Louisville, OH 44641. E-mail: lsmith@alliancelink.com

The authors wish to thank the following whose belief and dedication made Project CONNECT possible: The Martha Holden Jennings Foundation; second-grade students, Louisville Elementary School, Louisville, Ohio; and, secondary teacher education students, Youngstown State University, Youngstown, Ohio.

[Haworth co-indexing entry note]: "Internet Learning Connections Between Second-Graders and University Teacher Education Mentors." Dove, Marianne K., Susan C. Fisher, and Dwight L. Smith. Co-published simultaneously in *Computers in the Schools* (The Haworth Press, Inc.) Vol. 16, No. 2, 2000, pp. 45-58; and: *Integration of Technology into the Classroom: Case Studies* (ed: D LaMont Johnson, Cleborne D. Maddux, and Leping Liu) The Haworth Press, Inc., 2000, pp. 45-58. Single or multiple copies of this article are available for a fee from The Haworth Document Delivery Service [1-800-342-9678, 9:00 a.m. - 5:00 p.m. (EST). E-mail address: getinfo@haworthpressinc.com].

university and public school colleagues, seeking funding to implement innovative online projects, integrating content learning and literacy development with technology skills, and utilizing non-traditional teaching strategies such as electronic mentoring and e-mail exchanges to encourage young children to make the reading/writing connection. Project CONNECT represents the first attempt for primary grade online learning in the Louisville City School System, Louisville, Ohio, and the first venture for cyberfield placement for teacher education students at Youngstown State University, Youngstown, Ohio. [Article copies available for a fee from The Haworth Document Delivery Service: 1-800-342-9678. E-mail address: <getinfo@haworthpressinc.com> Website: <http://www.HaworthPress.com>]

KEYWORDS. *Electronic mentors, e-mail exchange, collaboration between university and public school, curriculum and technology integration, cyberfield placement*

In the summer of 1997, three educators (a second-grade teacher, a secondary teacher education professor, and an educational technology professor) met to brainstorm ways they could integrate technology into the curriculum. At that time, the State of Ohio Department of Education had issued its strategic technology plan, and Ohio universities and public schools were trying to make inroads for Internet technologies. Our respective institutions, Youngstown State University and Louisville Elementary School, had recently been wired for the Internet and e-mail and both of our educational environments were now capable of engaging in the first stages of online learning. This first phase of technology readiness has been coined the "WWWW" stage by Judith Boettcher, a researcher at the Corporation for Research and Educational Networking. This acronym refers to "Waiting, Watching, Wondering, and Wishing" (Boettcher, 1998). Boettcher explains during this first stage that "people are waiting for a better time; watching to see what others are doing; wondering what fits for them; and wishing they knew what to do" (Boettcher, 1998, p. 22).

This case study reflects our efforts to move beyond the "Waiting, Watching, Wondering, and Wishing" first stage for online learning and documents our initial collaborative efforts as "early adopters" of e-mail technology to establish learning connections between second-grade students and university teacher education electronic mentors.

MOVING BEYOND THE "WWWW" STAGE

As teachers, the three of us considered ourselves to be revisionist educators and very open to the possibilities and promise of integrating educational technologies in the curriculum. Therefore, we were not entrapped by traditional teaching methods nor caught in the web of waiting or watching to see what others would do.

Prior to our online literacy project, the second-graders were confined to learning activities conducted within the traditional walls of the classroom, and university teacher education students were also confined to classroom learning activities and field placements limited to area public schools. The second-graders' reading and writing time was limited to individual classroom teacher instruction that consisted of whole group or small group arrangements and centered on paper and pencil lessons. The teacher education students had little prior understanding of the developmental process of learning to read and write other than information gleaned from synoptic textbook accounts. Thus, the teacher education students had theoretical understanding of the reading process but no experience with real students to create the reading and writing connection. Additionally, the curricular integration of educational technology was cursory at best, and consisted of traditional media such as overhead projectors, VHS tapes, and educational television programs.

Clearly, we wanted to take advantage of online teaching opportunities and provide our students with new tools to acquire technology skills needed in today's world. We believed that strengthening connections between the university and public schools was imperative to facilitate such change. Therefore, our initial discussions centered on "wondering" what we could do collaboratively. What connection could be of greatest benefit for both subgroups of students–second-graders and secondary teacher education students? Which technology should we try to implement first? What did the research literature reveal about successfully integrating and using technology?

The technology literature indicated that e-mail's simplicity and usefulness made it the most far-reaching, widely used Internet tool (*Classroom Connect*, December 1997/January 1998). E-mail was also lauded as one of the greatest communication tools currently available, and telecomputing technology was praised for its potential to facilitate collaborative learning (Newman, 1994; Naugh, Levin, & Smith, 1994). We reasoned that e-mail was the necessary, rudimentary tool for our initial attempts to integrate technology in the classroom. Thus, if we were going to use technology in our classrooms and model technology applications on a regular basis, we must first establish e-mail as an online communication tool for our students.

Focusing on e-mail as our technology connection, we then decided that we should integrate e-mail exchanges with the curriculum and agreed to target literacy development. The public school's curriculum identified literacy development as a primary learning goal. The second-grade teacher, in turn, was committed to providing opportunities to promote his students' love of reading and writing, and the university professors were eager to help secondary majors become more aware of how young children learn to read and write. We made a decision to read the print version of *Time for Kids*, a news magazine that provides information about current events and features interesting topics, as a means of establishing a communication connection between the second-graders and the education students.

Time for Kids is published 26 times during the school year (September-May) by Time, Inc. (customer service, 1-800-777-8600) for $3.95 per student subscription. Thus, subscription fees for Project CONNECT were approximately two hundred dollars. As electronic mentors, the university students would be asked to generate questions related to the *Time for Kids* articles as well as interpersonal exchanges and transmit their e-mail once a week during the academic year to their second-grade cyberpals. The second-grade students would then respond to the content-related questions and also include their personal thoughts.

In order to make our "wishing" come true, we submitted a grant proposal to the Martha Holden Jennings Foundation, Cleveland, Ohio. We believed our grant would be of interest to the foundation because its purpose is to foster the development of young people and to explore new frontiers in secular primary and secondary schools in Ohio as well as to promote more effective teaching in those schools. We were grateful to be awarded the necessary funds for our online literacy project entitled Project CONNECT. This project represented the first attempt for primary grade online learning in the Louisville City School System, Louisville, Ohio, and the first venture for cyberfield placement for teacher education students at Youngstown State University, Youngstown, Ohio.

GOALS FOR PROJECT CONNECT

Goals for our online integration project targeted integrating literacy strategies with technology because second-graders' reading and writing achievement was a primary performance goal of the elementary school curriculum. We reasoned that providing meaningful reading/writing experiences by means of electronic mentor e-mail exchanges would promote second-graders' practice in making the reading and writing connection. Teacher education students would gain greater understanding about children's literacy development and the power of using technology to stimulate active learning. The development of technology skills was inherent to the project and required all participants to use e-mail as the means for communication, thus, developing a community for learning. Collaboration between the university and the public school would also be enhanced through the year-long interaction of the cyberfield placements.

Based on this rationale, the goals for Project CONNECT included the following: (a) to provide students with technology skills and the opportunity to engage in online learning; (b) to integrate literacy strategies with technology; (c) to develop student awareness regarding the uses of e-mail; (d) to promote second-graders' literacy development by means of technology tools and electronic mentors; (e) to expand secondary education students' understanding of the reading and writing process and its development with young children; (f) to strengthen connections between the university and public schools to promote more effective teaching and learning opportunities; (g) to integrate technology in the curriculum to personalize learning; (h) to extend the public school's and university's classroom walls electronically; (i) to provide secondary education students with an alternative teaching placement (cyberfield placement); (j) to work collaboratively to facilitate technology integration efforts between the public school and the university; and (k) to learn and experiment together as a community of learners.

PROJECT CONNECT INTEGRATION ACTIVITIES

At the beginning of the project, the second-grade teacher engaged the class in whole class instruction (23 students) in order to demonstrate the correct use of the e-mail software and also to teach the children the proper format for composing e-mail in a friendly letter format. The teacher then identified four students that had shown mastery of these skills and asked them to serve as peer tutors for their 19 classmates. These four peer tutors worked one on one with their fellow classmates for approximately three computer sessions per week for a three-week duration. After these peer-training sessions were completed, only three students continued to experience difficulty and required extra assistance. Thus, the teacher individually assigned a peer tutor to help these three youngsters with their communications and also had the peer tutors provide continuing support when small glitches arose in the e-mail communication process with fellow class members.

It is important to explain, in addition, the writing process in which the children engaged to complete and send their e-mail. On a weekly basis, the teacher constructed a writing web with the whole class that reflected the topics of the *Time for Kids* magazine plus other timely events, concerns, or experiences that were of importance to the children. The class was also instructed to reread the e-mail message from their electronic mentor and answer the mentor's questions about the magazine's articles. This procedure enabled the youngsters to focus and organize their thoughts in order to compose a handwritten rough draft for their individual e-mail exchange with their university electronic mentor. The teacher required the proofreading of handwritten, rough drafts not only by the individual child, but by a student partner as well. Only then were the children able to type their e-mail messages (please note this final handwritten, edited draft also fulfilled a requirement for the children to receive a handwriting grade). Once the e-mail messages were typed, the children were instructed to save them and close the file. Typically, the teacher read the children's e-mail messages after school dismissal. This was a conducive time to screen all e-mail for spelling and grammatical errors, proper format, and paragraph construction before sending these messages as a group mailing to the university account.

To initiate the project at the university level, the college professors completed the necessary paperwork for establishing university e-mail accounts for the secondary education students enrolled in the methods course and scheduled weekly computer lab times for the students to send their e-mail messages. All education students participated in a training session on how to use e-mail. Education students who were familiar with e-mail (approximately one-third of the class) also helped with this instruction. The project directors arranged to send the education students' exchanges to the second-grade teacher's account in order to facilitate management of the electronic communication at the elementary school.

Prior to the initial communication, the second-grade teacher visited the methods class and gave the education students background information regarding each individual child's interests, skills, and personality. The elementary teacher also explained the reading and writing abilities of second-graders, and suggested developmentally appropriate strategies useful in facilitating communication with the youngsters. The college professors also visited the second-grade classroom, interacted with the children, and surveyed the available technology (five computers, of which three were networked and grouped in a pod, and two portable Alpha Smart Boards). These on-site visits helped to launch the project as we embarked upon the cybercommunication adventure.

The first exchange involved education students e-mailing written physical descriptions of themselves to their second-grade key pals so that the youngsters could draw a picture of their university cyberpals.

Sample:

University electronic mentor's first e-mail to second-grader.

Hi Madisson!
My name is Mike. I am 6' tall and I weigh 225 pounds. I have short brown hair and brown eyes. My favorite sport is football. I am a member of the Youngstown State University Penguins football team. My jersey number is 36. I like school and lifting weights.
I have a few questions for you. Open up your *Time for Kids*. What is your favorite dinosaur? I like the Tyrannosaurus rex. How big was the Tyrannosaurus rex and where did he live? Have you ever seen a fossil? What is your favorite food for lunch? Pizza is my favorite. I hope to hear from you soon.
Your friend,
Mike

Sample:

Second-grader's initial response to university electronic mentor.

Dear Mike,
I have brown hair. I also have brown eyes. My favorite color is

purple. My favorite food is chicken. My favorite thing to do is play with my best friend. I am 4 foot 1. The T rex was 20 feet tall. *Tyrannosaur* rex was my favorite *dinosaur.* North America is where the T rex lived.
Your friend,
Madisson

The project directors also took digital pictures of the students during visits to the university and school classrooms and shared these with the student participants. It was helpful to match cyberpals' names to faces by viewing the children's artwork and by looking at digital photographs. Although e-mail is a good medium for expressing ideas, communication, especially with young children, may be more difficult because youngsters cannot "see" their electronic mentor. This is an issue to consider because much of the "content of personal communication is best expressed through tone, inflection, and body language–all of which are missing with e-mail" (Creed, 1999, p. 8).

Throughout the course of this year-long project, students exchanged weekly e-mail related to the *Time for Kids* magazine articles. University students served as electronic mentors and helped second-graders explore such topics as the planets and distant stars, the disarming of land mines, the wolf packs in Yellowstone National Park, the secrets of ancient Nubia, rain forest fires, the World Series, spiders, changes in minting U.S. currency, and dinosaurs. The e-mail dialogues regarding these readings served to open the youngsters' eyes to the world around them and the education students' eyes to the literacy abilities and interests of second-graders.

ADVANTAGES OF THE PROJECT

The outcomes of integrating the e-mail project with literacy skills and curriculum content were numerous. The second-graders developed many skills including basic typing skills and keyboard awareness, greater ability to write original sentences and paragraphs, the ability to read with purpose, the ability to compose answers to university students' questions about the magazine's topics, dictionary skills, peer editing skills, and oral reading abilities (they loved to share the e-mail they received from the university students with their classmates).

The secondary education students had an opportunity to engage in a "cyberfield placement" which none of them had experienced previously. They quickly realized the power that technology holds as a communication tool. They honored the opportunity to nurture a one-on-one relationship with a child. It was interesting to note that by the fifth week of the e-mail exchange, the second-graders were sharing some poignant questions and concerns with their university cyberpals. Examples include: "Do you have a dad?" "Yes I did read about the world heating up and that's not right burning our world up." "My dog died and I am sad." "Would you like to go fishing with me?" "I am sad because this class is over and this is my last letter. I liked all of your letters." University students became much more aware of the importance of serving as counselors and trusted advisors for the children. The education students gained valuable insights about the literacy development of young children (e.g., invented spellings like "I like fruits *exspeshuly* apples." "Your *freiand* Johnathan."), and often struggled to carefully construct sentences that were not too lengthy or did not contain vocabulary that was too difficult for second-grade readers. The education students also witnessed the positive effects generated by this technology experience (e.g., improved writing, reading, and computer literacy skills), and they became more confident regarding their ability to integrate technology in classroom practice.

The most rewarding benefit for the project directors was the opportunity to collaboratively team in order to integrate technology and curriculum for our students. Teaming was possible because we knew each other well (the second-grade teacher was a former student of the methods professor, and the methods professor and technology professor were colleagues at the same university) and we had previously shared positive experiences working together. Just as trust is important to the classroom environment, trust and respect for one another's professional perspectives are critical to successfully teaming for an educational project. Project CONNECT would not have been implemented without first considering ourselves to be friends and our individual capacities for collaboration. There were many times throughout the experience that it would have been easy to disband the project given the frustrations and obstacles we jointly faced.

OBSTACLES OF THE PROJECT

An analysis of the obstacles encountered involved concerns that can be loosely grouped into the following three categories: technology

operations, project management strategies, and ergonomic considerations. Scheduling the weekly use of the computer technology for
e-mail exchanges proved to be a daunting experience at both the
elementary school and college level. Although the elementary school
network had a direct connection to the Internet, connectivity at the
college was limited to three dial-up connections to the campus electronic network. Therefore, access to the university's Unix server became problematic because the number of university students attempting to access the network via the modem connections exceeded the
capacity of the university modem pool. On many days, it was simply
impossible for the education students to quickly and efficiently log-on
to the network. Additionally, throughout the project, the university
system continuously and randomly severed the phone connections.
The resulting frustration served to dampen the education students'
enthusiasm regarding the ease of implementing technology in the
classroom.

At the elementary school setting, the second-grade teacher and his
students also experienced similar frustrations because the electronic
lines of their system were down several times during the project. The
lack of technical support to reestablish electronic communication capabilities was particularly vexing to both the classroom teacher and
university professors. A number of long-distance phone calls were
placed between project sites to explain the respective situations and to
assure one another that we would try to send again as soon as possible.

The classroom teacher faced an additional problem because his
classroom was limited to the use of three networked computers and
two Alpha Smart Boards. Given that second-grade students' typing
skills are not very advanced, it became very time consuming for 23
children to compose and send e-mail to their university cyberpals. By
its very nature, student computer work does not lend itself well to
whole-group instruction (DeVoogd, 1995). The classroom teacher had
to constantly shift from whole-group activities to small-group work
and also provide individual help to the children working at the computer pod.

The need for well-developed management strategies and organizational support became evident during the initial phase of the project.
Although a grant award was obtained in order to finance the project,
conditions of the award restricted expenditures toward the purchase of
supplies and materials for the public school; thus, no supplies could be

purchased for the university students. Teachers often spend their own money to purchase necessary supplies for their classrooms. However, technology undertakings are not inexpensive and it should be noted that approximately nine hundred dollars was expended for this project to purchase technology supplies, paper, subscriptions to *Time for Kids*, and funding to print a booklet of the students' e-mail exchanges and art work. The project directors did not foresee funding problems at the college level because the university students were required to pay a lab fee that covered unlimited use of computer supplies in the college computing laboratory. Since the education students were going to create and retrieve their e-mail exchanges in this lab, we erroneously thought that there was no need for additional supply funds.

On paper this project was well-designed, reasonable, and workable. However, during the first week of the project, circumstances changed drastically. Enter Murphy's Law of technology use! Access to the university system via the college laboratory's computers became unavailable during the methods class scheduled lab time due to scheduling conflicts. Unfortunately, this sole computing laboratory had to accommodate the needs of both undergraduate and graduate education students, as well as educational technology classes. Additionally, the university computing services department took more than three weeks time to provide education students with personal Unix accounts. The project directors quickly had to develop a contingency plan that involved sending the university students' e-mail message from the professors' office computers and their home computers, as well as receiving the second-graders e-mail by means of this same connection. This created a weekly log jam on the professors' personal computer systems. Unfortunately, no funds were available for the purchase of essential supplies such as diskettes, printer ink cartridges, and paper for these locations.

Management problems also occurred in the elementary school classroom as the second-grade teacher attempted to track which students had responded to their university cyberpal and which students had not yet replied. The teacher valiantly tried to maintain an accurate account of who had mailed their responses; however, this task was a difficult undertaking when compounded by the tasks of dealing with network problems, teaching the regular curriculum, and attending to the needs of all students. Absenteeism among the second-grade students and university students was also difficult to manage for prompt e-mail exchanges.

The three networked computers in the second-grade classroom were arranged on trapezoidal tables in a three sided semi-circular pod. This arrangement enabled the teacher to create a computer learning center in one section of the classroom. The pod arrangement allowed the teacher to decrease the chance of student injury by placing electric cords, computer cables, and printer cables in the center of the pod well out of the reach of the second-grade students. However, this safety advantage created a problem that involved the lack of adequate table space for students to use for their materials. The table surface proved entirely too small to accommodate a computer system, student papers, and necessary reference materials. The need for adjustable computer tables and chairs in the elementary classroom was also apparent. Not only were the tables too high for the second-grade students to correctly position their hands and wrists for typing, but the seats of the chairs were too high and many students' feet could not touch the floor. This situation highlights the need for the purchase of suitable equipment for technology integration at the elementary level. Telecomputing efforts must address all of these glitches, and educators must be forewarned about how easily these activities can be thwarted by the unreliability and lack of equipment, the difficulties of technology operations, the vexations regarding technical problems, the challenges of imperfect classroom environments, and the inadequate ergonomic conditions experienced by students.

EVALUATION OF PROJECT CONNECT

The recent literature on evaluation regarding technology implementation indicates that "effectiveness is not a function of the technology but rather of the learning environment and the capability to do things one could not do otherwise" (Jones, Valdez, Nowakowski, & Rasmussen, 1999) Indeed we were able to extend the walls of the public school's and university's classrooms and provide learning opportunities that had previously been impossible. It was a "first" in many respects: the first time second-graders had ever communicated by e-mail; the first time education students had participated in a cyberfield placement; the first time primary students in the public school had engaged in online learning; the first time secondary education students corresponded with primary students; the first time reading and writing opportunities between children and pre-service teachers were grounded in real-life contexts; and, the first time both university professors and the second-grade teacher had worked collaboratively for an entire academic year. According to these "firsts" we judged Project CONNECT to be a highly successful undertaking. Project CONNECT has also served as the prototype for other teachers in the district to apply for grants and engage their students in e-mail exchanges.

Evidence of effective teaching and learning that occurred during Project CONNECT was also compared to criteria specified by Barbara Means of SRI International. She has identified seven variables that, when present in the classroom, indicate engaged and effective learning. These variables are: (a) children are engaged in authentic and multidisciplinary tasks; (b) assessments are based on students performance of real tasks; (c) students participate in interactive modes of instruction; (d) students work collaboratively; (e) students are grouped heterogeneously; (f) the teacher is a facilitator in learning; and (g) students learn through exploration (Jones, Valdez, Nowakowski, & Rasmussen, 1999). Project CONNECT participants and directors were involved with collaborative online learning opportunities that concerned real-life tasks that valued learners' personal interests and supported multidisciplinary learning. The students' art work and e-mail communications were published in booklet form so that parents and the educational community could read about the meaningful learning activities of Project CONNECT.

CONCLUSION

Integrating technology into the curriculum is no simple task, and our experience with Project CONNECT has revealed that educators should expect glitches and disruptions throughout such a process. Despite the obstacles encountered, we recognize that technology integration efforts work much better when educators make connections that address the systematic changes required for successful technology applications in public school and university classrooms. These connections include collaborative efforts between university and public school educators, funding for innovative educational projects provided by foundations, integrating interdisciplinary versus single subject learning with technology, and the willingness to be "early adopters" and engage in experimental approaches to teaching such as electronic mentors.

Although we faced difficulties, which at times short-circuited our connections, the electronic exchanges served to motivate and improve second-graders' writing, reading, and computer literacy skills. It also provided the opportunity for pre-service teachers to practice effective technology applications and experience how to integrate technology to promote student learning. The success of the project indicated that second-graders are capable of undertaking electronic exchanges and that a methods course is a natural point in the sequence of a teacher education program at which to establish the connection for technology integration. Lastly, some of the most valuable benefits of Project CONNECT were the momentum generated for learning by all individuals connected to this endeavor and the realization that the dynamic nature of technology integration requires making many more connections than simply an electronic one.

REFERENCES

Boettcher, J. V. (1998). Taking off with distance learning: Are we there yet? *Syllabus*, *12*(4), 22-26, 53.

Creed, T. (1999). Make e-mail work for you. *Advocate*, *1*(6), 5-8.

DeVoogd, G. (1996). Cultural congruence in the technology literate classroom. In B. Robin, J. Price, J. Willis, & D. A. Willis (Eds.), *Technology and Teacher Education Annual, 1996* (pp. 14-18). Charlottesville, VA: Association for the Advancement of Computing in Education.

Jones, B. F., Valdez, G., Nowakowski, J., & Rasmussen, C. (1999). New times demand new ways of learning. *Plugging In: Choosing and Using Educational Technology.* [Online]. Available: *http://www.ncrel.org/sdrs/edtalk/toc.htm* (1999, June 10).

Naugh, M. L., Levin, J. A., & Smith, K. (1994). Organizing electronic network-based instructional interactions, Part 2: Interpersonal strategies. *The Computing Teacher*, *21*(6), 48-50.

Newman, D. (1994). Computer networks: Opportunities or obstacles? In B. Means (Ed.) Technology and educational reform: The reality behind the promise (pp. 57-80). San Francisco: Jossey Bass Publishers.

Using e-mail to teach writing. (1997, December/1998, January). *Classroom Connect*, *4*(4), 4-5.

Richard Knee
Ralph Cafolla
Kristine Haller

Integrating Standards-Based Education in a Telecommunications Project: A Case Study

SUMMARY. *This case study describes a project that used computer-mediated communication (CMC) to facilitate the new types of learning made possible by modern technology. This paper reports the results of a project designed to use modern telecommunications technology to establish an e-pal or keypal project between second-grade students in south Florida, an English-as-a-second-language class in Finland, and a class of second graders learning English in Slovenia. Rather than just providing a media for cultural exchange, this project integrated specific curriculum standards in geography and language arts. Because the goal of education for students K-12 is to develop content-based knowledge and to incorporate higher level thinking skills to interpret, analyze, and synthesize the data, technology-based projects allow for this development through a constructivist approach to learning. [Article copies available for a fee from*

RICHARD KNEE is Assistant Professor, College of Education, Florida Atlantic University, Educational Technology and Research, Davie, FL 33309-1616. E-mail: knee@fau.edu
RALPH CAFOLLA is Associate Professor, College of Education, Florida Atlantic University, Educational Technology and Research, Boca Raton, FL 33341-0991. E-mail: Cafolla@fau.edu
KRISTINE HALLER is Teacher, Broward County School Board, Broward County, FL 33301. E-mail: haller_k@popmail.firn.edu

[Haworth co-indexing entry note]: "Integrating Standards-Based Education in a Telecommunications Project: A Case Study." Knee, Richard, Ralph Cafolla, and Kristine Haller. Co-published simultaneously in *Computers in the Schools* (The Haworth Press, Inc.) Vol. 16, No. 2, 2000, pp. 59-72; and: *Integration of Technology into the Classroom: Case Studies* (ed: D. LaMont Johnson, Cleborne D. Maddux, and Leping Liu) The Haworth Press, Inc., 2000, pp. 59-72. Single or multiple copies of this article are available for a fee from The Haworth Document Delivery Service [1-800-342-9678, 9:00 a.m. - 5:00 p.m. (EST). E-mail address: getinfo@haworthpressinc.com].

59

The Haworth Document Delivery Service: 1-800-342-9678. E-mail address: <getinfo@haworthpressinc.com> Website: <http://www.HaworthPress.com>]

KEYWORDS. *Telecommunications, e-pal, instructional communications, Research, Analysis, Communication model (RAC), tellecollaborate*

Many educators assume that the only way for learning to take place is for a fixed number of students to spend a fixed amount of time in a fixed place in face-to-face communication with a teacher. Modern computer technology, including the Internet, has forced us to consider a new set of assumptions. For example, computer-mediated communication (CMC) relies on computer technologies that enable individuals to share information while working and learning together. Students from all around the globe are able to learn cooperatively using both synchronous and asynchronous telecommunications (Jonassen, 1996).

This paper describes a project that used CMC to facilitate the new types of learning made possible by modern technology. The project was based on the well-known, traditional "pen-pal" projects that teachers have used for years. In this type of project, teachers attempt to broaden the cultural perspective of their students by establishing a one-to-one connection between their students and students from other cultures and countries. These projects have traditionally been limited by several factors. First, the use of regular mail caused long delays between communications. It would seem that students, particularly younger ones, could benefit from more immediate feedback. Teachers that are familiar with more modern forms of communications address this issue by setting up electronic connections with teachers and students internationally.

While modern forms of communications like e-mail successfully addressed the delays and costs of traditional mail, these traditional pen-pal type projects were also limited in that they were often undertaken without addressing specific curriculum issues. While a cultural exchange might be a worthy goal in and of itself, such a project offers the opportunity to integrate the curriculum into the pen-pal experience. Cultural exchanges provide knowledge acquisition at a first-hand and personal level. Students learn what life is like for children their own age in different parts of the world. By giving thought to how the standards and goals of the curriculum can be developed through international and intercultural projects, teachers can enrich and enhance goals for student achievement. The goal of education for K-12 students is to develop content-based knowledge and to incorporate higher level thinking skills to interpret, analyze, and synthesize data.

This paper is a case study of a project designed to use modern telecommunications technology to establish an e-pal or keypal project between second-grade students in South Florida, an English as a second language class in Finland, and a class of second-graders learning English in Slovenia. Rather than just providing a media for cultural exchange, this project integrated specific curriculum standards in geography and language arts. This technology-based project incorporated a constructivist approach to facilitate this learning.

PROJECT GOAL

The goal of this project was to integrate two content areas of the curriculum, geography and language arts, in a telecommunications exchange between students from various cultures. Florida, like most other states, has adopted standards and benchmarks in various curriculum areas. The curriculum standards and benchmarks used in this project come from the Florida Sunshine State Standards in geography and language arts (*http://sun3.firn.edu/doe/curric/prek12/frame2.htm*). Additional goals and objectives from the school's improvement plan were also used. The American school used the Broward County School District *Standards Driven Instructional Model* (see Figure 1) as a model to develop the instructional standards. This model was developed to encourage teachers to think about standards as a focus for instruction, and then design learning activities that specifically teach the standard. This is then followed by assessment to measure student understanding and to help teachers modify, change, or improve instruction.

The general theme of social studies for the second-grade curriculum is "Cultures Near and Far." The Florida Sunshine State Standards core concepts of continuous progress indicators (CPIs) define expectations for progressive student achievement. Three CPIs for geography for second grade include the ability to differentiate between urban and rural places, the ability to compare natural resources in terms of relative surplus or scarcity, and demonstrate the ability to describe how the sun-earth relationship impacts how people live in different global locations. Students were also expected to understand that a region's

FIGURE 1
The Standard Driven Instructional Model of Broward County School District

Stages	Activity		
Planning	**What should be taught?**		
	Standards, Outcomes, Competencies		
Implementation			
	How should it be taught?		
	Integration, Technology, Constructivism		
Decision Making			
	Design and delivery.		
Assessment			
	How should it be assessed?		
	Authentic, Traditional, Writing, Presenting		

climate is based on its location on the earth and its relationship to the sun. To illustrate this characteristic of climate, the class from Finland used a graphics program to demonstrate how they understood their location and relationship to the sun in the physical world. They were then able to attach this graphic file to an e-mail and send it to their American counterparts.

BACKGROUND

Computer technology, like the older technology of writing, maximizes its potential for enriching intellectual performance when the individual is consciously engaged in the mind-technology partnership. Some changes in performance occur only in interaction with the tool; other change is more generalized and longer lasting (Salomon, Perkins, & Globerson, 1991). Salomon (1981) also focuses on the reciprocal nature of instructional communications, the instructional setting, and the learner. Salomon argues that schema play a major role in determining how messages are perceived–in terms of creating an anticipatory bias that influences what information is selected and how it is interpreted. Furthermore, various media create new schema which affect subsequent cognitive processing. The *symbol systems theory* developed by Salomon is intended to explain the effects of media on learning. Salomon's work is very close to Gardner's theory of multiple intelligence (Salomon, 1981).

One of the critical concepts of Salomon's theory is that the effectiveness of a media depends upon its match with the learner, the context, and the task. Salomon (1977, p. 112) explains: "Learning can be facilitated to the extent that the activated skills are relevant to the demands of the learning task." Salomon's theory is supported primarily by research conducted with film and television (especially *Sesame Street*). More recent work has extended the framework to computers (Salomon, Perkins, & Globerson, 1991).

In this project, the theoretical framework espoused by Solomon was used to integrate the use of technology with the critical skills required for the learning task–language and geography. The classroom teacher used the Research, Analysis, Communication model (RAC) as the practical pedagogical model to integrate two content areas of the curriculum in a telecommunications exchange between students from various cultures.

THE RAC MODEL

The Center for Educational Progress of the Caroline County Public Schools in Maryland (*http://www.cep.cl.k12.md.us/RAC/RACSite/RACRoots.html*) developed a framework for planning instruction that:

1. Makes effective use of computer technology.
2. Can be easily incorporated into a performance-based classroom.
3. Focuses on teacher planning in addressing state/local standards.

The model, Research, Analysis, Communication (RAC), is an instructional planning framework that integrates technology with research, analysis, and communication skills to teach students and assess their understanding of the required curriculum. Representatives of Apple Computer, Inc., quickly recognized the effectiveness of the RAC model. In 1996, Apple partnered with Caroline County Public Schools to produce a CD-ROM entitled "Apple Performance Activities" (*http://www.cep.cl.k12.md.us/RAC/RACSite/RACRoots.html*).

Benefits of using the RAC model in a performance-based classroom include:

1. Students apply content, skills, and processes as required by state and local standards.

2. A meaningful context for the application of skills is easily integrated into the RAC model.
3. Application of thinking is embedded through the analysis component of the RAC model.
4. A RAC lesson sets the stage for assessment and the identification of performance criteria.

PROJECT OVERVIEW

This project took place over a one and one-half-year period beginning in February 1997 and continuing through June 1998. Three groups participated in the project: (a) twenty-eight second-graders from Broward County, Florida; (b) twenty-six fourth-and fifth-graders from Finland studying English as a second language; and (c) twenty-five second-graders from Slovenia, also studying English. The American students changed as the school year ended and a new group of second-graders continued the project through the next school year. The same group of students from Europe participated throughout the project.

The majority of the American students involved in this project were from upper middle-class families. Reflecting the diversity of south Florida, one-third speaks more than one language, with English as the second language. Many students have Internet access at home, and their parents place a high value on education and student achievement. Most have had varied and enriching travel experiences.

As noted above, this project is based on a traditional pen-pal, snail-mail model. In the traditional model, teachers identify potential pen pals in professional education magazines or through colleagues. The teacher then has to personally contact a teacher abroad to plan the experience. While some of these projects attempt to integrate within the curriculum, most often the goal is communication through letter writing. The ability for deeper development in understanding of people and places is limited in the traditional pen-pal correspondence. Although the classes exchange letters and pictures, the knowledge is limited to the participating classes.

While this project began as an e-mail project, the participants embraced all the resources of the Internet, using it as a resource not available to teachers using traditional mail for key pal projects. Because of the Internet's multimedia capabilities and interactive properties, the World Wide Web makes vast resources available in a variety of mediums to relate to various learning styles of children in a class. The Internet provides teachers with ready access to global projects as well as numerous multimedia (streaming audio and video), multi-sensory information sources.

In a traditional pen-pal project, the news and information about a region are often limited to that area or take days and sometimes weeks to gather and disseminate. Global communication has changed that significantly. For example, when Hurricane Georges approached south Florida last fall, the e-pals not only were able to e-mail their support to their friends, but also tracked the storm and learned about hurricanes. Obviously, this type of immediate learning had an impact on the participants. They learned that a hurricane was not just a storm, but also a profound event that had impact on people they knew in a place they had learned about.

PROJECT DESCRIPTION

The American project began as a means to integrate curriculum standards and goals as part of an Internet telecommunications project developed by NickNacks' *Telecollaborate* (*http://home.talkcity.com/ academydr/nicknacks/NNabout.html*). NickNacks' global education project, *Tellecollaborate–Signs of Autumn-Signs of Spring*, invites students from classrooms around the world to collect and record data about changes happening in their region as the season of spring or autumn evolved. Data are e-mailed and posted on the NickNacks Web site once a week for a period of six weeks. The first year 26 schools from around the world participated, including the schools from south Florida, Finland, and Slovenia.

NickNack's founder and director, Nancy Schubert, developed this project in conjunction with classroom teachers. Ms. Schubert also works directly on each project in a classroom setting to ensure the applicability and feasibility of all activities. NickNacks' *Telecollaborate* can help teachers explore exciting virtual horizons of learning via the Internet. Its primary goal is to encourage telecollaboration among educators and students around the world.

In the American classroom, students spent about two to three hours each week on this project, usually during the social studies and language arts periods. The students were divided into groups of five or six and each week observed, measured, and wrote about the seasonal changes occurring in south Florida. Each group was assigned a leader for the week who was responsible for recording and logging the group's observations about the temperature, plants, animals, and the clothing that people were wearing. The groups stayed the same each week, but the leader changed as did the specific areas they were observing. After gathering the data, the whole group created a final paragraph and a student typed in and saved the observation onto a computer disk. Because the classroom had no Internet access, the teacher took the disk home to send the data to the NickNack Web site. Interpersonal skills were developed as students learned to share and accept input for their section each week. The geography standards were embraced through student-centered/created bulletin boards.

Following the *Signs of Autumn-Signs of Spring* project, both the students and the teacher wanted to be involved in another telecommunications project. The teacher from the American school contacted a few of the teachers from the schools on the *Signs* project, asking if they would like to participate in e-pal letter correspondence. The e-mail letters of request were sent to different schools in Finland and Slovenia who agreed to participate.

At the beginning of the second school year, the teacher from the American school was able to expand all aspects of the project. Starting in September, the American class created individual "Our Wonderful World" notebooks to store their data. The notebooks contained a map of the world that they labeled with common geographical terms (continents, hemispheres, oceans, equator, etc.). They also plotted the locations of the other schools and kept copies of their e-mail correspondence.

To integrate the language arts standards for writing, students used the software program Kid's Works Deluxe™ to create the illustrations and write observations for their notebooks. They also used the software to create illustrations used to express their understanding of the changes around them. Kid's Desk Deluxe™ is an excellent resource because it has voice capabilities that enable students to add voice in both Spanish and English.

This project was designed to be integrated into the curriculum over the long run. Therefore, the project attempted to maintain student interest for the full academic year by adding new and different dimensions as the year progressed. In the beginning of the year, students studied the geographical aspects of our world and participated in the *Signs of Autumn* project. By December, they had incorporated the

Holidays Around the World and brought in parents and other guests to share their culture. One student asked to have a family friend from Finland come in and share items, books, and pictures about the culture and people they had been communicating with. Students tallied the origins of their own families into continents as well as the various languages spoken in class. They also counted the number of schools in the *Signs* projects and plotted the results into the hemispheres and continents they were located in using *The Graph Club.*™ The software enabled students to prepare a spreadsheet for data collection and turn this information into bar, line, pie, and picture graphs. This particular program, designed for K-4 grades, gives students the opportunity to develop cognitive skills for constructing interpreting, and analyzing their data.

PROJECT EVALUATION

The effects of this project, on meeting specific geography and language arts standards was measured using a teacher-generated, schoolwide test. The test, given across the entire grade, indicated that less than five percent of incoming second-graders in September could fill in a blank map and label the continents and oceans. By May, 93% of the same students scored above the 90th percentile. All standards, benchmarks, indicators, and related principles from the Sunshine State Standards were demonstrated and evaluated by works and materials developed for and by students. These artifacts were kept in portfolio notebooks or on student-created bulletin boards. Work was part of the students' grades and results were part of each student's progress report sent home quarterly.

The RAC model that the American teacher used provided a framework for the link between curriculum, technology, and the world of work. Research, the first component of the model, engaged the American students in gathering data for their research. The data included plotting geographic locations of the participating schools in the *Signs* project. Secondary data actually constituted new lesson objectives for measuring student achievement (i.e., defining geographical terms, worldwide temperature, longitude and latitudinal positions in relation to the location of the continent, and so forth).

The second step of the RAC model, data analysis, requires students to use higher order thinking skills to examine and sort data gathered from their research. Students had to determine what data were valuable and how the data fit into various categories. They then had to determine how to graph, write about, or illustrate the results. The primary curriculum goals in each part of the RAC framework encouraged the development of new skills. Technology was not used in every component of skill development; rather it was used only where it was effective and appropriate. Because so much computer technology is available to aid in research, analysis, and communication, these types of technology can be easily and effectively used with a RAC lesson. With this approach, the teaching of curriculum standards remains the focus of the lesson, and technology becomes an effective means for teaching the curriculum (George, 1999).

The third component of the RAC model, communication, was used for accessing student knowledge and understanding of the data gathered. It was through cooperative exchanges that the students' projects demonstrated the knowledge they had gained. The direct link between cooperative learning and successful construction of models to demonstrate knowledge should also be noted. Cooperative learning requires interdependence to be effective. Students' strengths and weaknesses were evidenced in the grouping of the American students. Various ability levels in writing and reading became apparent. It was necessary for students to work out their role and contribution within the group. The process of learning cooperatively actually improves the acquisition and retention of content and skills throughout the curriculum (Dockterman, 1997).

In addition to the direct curriculum benefits noted above, the project had several ancillary benefits. For example, during the exploration of *Seasons of the Year*, one of the students went to Peru to visit her family. While the south Florida climate was heading into spring, Peru, with winter approaching, was quite cold. When the student returned, she excitedly shared her experience of the northern and southern hemisphere weather.

Math, science, and reading curriculum standards and benchmarks of expected student achievement were informally incorporated and achieved throughout the lessons. The standards and goals used by each of the three teachers in this project were different and individually based on the needs of their classes. The classes from Slovenia and Finland never communicated with each other but were an intricate part of the communication necessary to develop the objectives for the American class.

CHALLENGES

Implementing this project presented a few challenges for the class-room teacher. The greatest obstacle was time management. There was limited classroom computer access at the American school. Extra planning on the part of the teacher was necessary to think through the various ways to group students and what the other students would be doing while small groups worked on parts of the project. What was going on in regard to the regular classroom duties and responsibilities was a constant concern. Extra time was also necessary for the teacher to learn the computer software programs used with the students. Naturally, having seven- and eight-year-olds work independently on computers also presented a challenge. To accommodate the developmental level of the students, all letter writing was first done on paper, edited and revised, and then "published" on the computer. Parent volunteers were an invaluable resource to aid students when it came time to publish.

The obstacles were far outweighed by the positive results gained in student knowledge, skill development, and ability to work cooperatively. For example, the teacher from Slovenia was initially concerned about the ability of her second-graders to correspond with American students in English. As the project proceeded, she found that the motivational level of her students more than made up for their lack of language skills.

Although the American students had limited access to computers and no classroom access to the Internet at school, the student enthusiasm was high and very motivating. With no Internet access in the school classroom the teacher e-mailed student work from home after school. The classroom teacher was able to recruit parents willing to assist in this project. This gave the teacher the free time needed to work in other areas. Flexibility on the part of the teacher was necessary to recognize that some days not all students would be able to participate in the lesson or activity in which the rest of the group was engaged in. For example, on publishing day, the parent volunteer would work individually with the appropriate students. Obviously, these students would not be able to participate in the lesson or activity in which the rest of the group was engaged. Teachers wishing to use technology to enhance curriculum goals should keep a few things in mind. Everything did not work smoothly the first time. Start small and work into one project at a time. The global projects for international communication with preset time frames and already established goals provided an excellent starting point. NickNacks' *Tellecollaborate* provided sheets for recording data within a pre-established time frame. With the e-pals, when time lapses occurred, one teacher or the other would write to make adjustments in the schedule.

CONCLUSION

After the project progressed through the year and the adjustments noted were implemented, the project was deemed successful. A letter from one of the teachers in Slovenia demonstrated this success: "I really enjoy working with teachers abroad. I always get some new ideas to improve my teaching and my students are much more motivated if they use the language they are learning for communication. Now they are eager to learn as much English as possible." Clearly the connection with the people in the other countries provided the class with a new acceptance of other students, languages, and traditions.

Telecommunications is a part of today's instructional program. It is now possible for teachers and students to extend the reach for knowledge, to interact and learn through many disciplines. The project demonstrated that through established curriculum standards and goals, while conducting research involving other schools across the state or across the world, learning did take place. It takes planning, but teachers and students can turn data into information and information into knowledge via online projects (Maurer & Davidson, 1998).

REFERENCES

Dockterman, D. A., (1997). Great teaching in a one-computer classroom. Watertown, MA: Tom Snyder Production.
George, D. (1999). FETC connections. Tallahassee, FL: Florida Educational Technology Corporation, Inc.
Jonassen, H. D. (1996). Computers in the classroom: Mindtools for critical thinking. Englewood Cliffs, NJ: Prentice Hall.
Maurer, M. M. & Davidson, S. G. (1998). Leadership in instructional technology. Saddle River, NJ: Merrill.

Salomon, G. (1977). Reexamining the methodology of research on media in technology in education, *Review of Educational Research, 47*(1), 99-120.

Salomon, G. (1981). Communication and education. Beverly Hills, CA: Sage.

Salomon, G., Perkins, D., & Globerson, T. (1991). Partners in cognition: Extending human intelligence with intelligent technologies. *Educational Researcher, 20*(4), 2-9.

APPENDIX

E-Pal Listings:

A Global Classroom Exchange (1999). [Online]. 103 countries, site listed in English, Spanish, French. Available: *http://www.epals.com/*

Intercultural E-Mail Classroom (1999). [Online]. A free service to help teachers link with partner classrooms in other countries. Available: *http://www.stolaf.edu/network/iecc/*

Web Sites for Global Projects:

NickNacks Tellecollaborate (1999). [Online]. A wide variety of global projects with predetermined goals and time frames for K-12 projects. Available: *http:// home.talkcity.com/academydr/nicknacks/NNindex.html*

Globalearn Expeditions (1999). [Online]. Contains international explorations with chats available with explorers, a fee is required. Available: *http://www.globalearn.org/*

The Global Schoolhouse (1999). [Online]. E-pals, lesson plans, global projects, educational resources. Available: *http://www.globalschoolhouse.com/*

The Jason Project (1999). [Online]. A year-round scientific expedition designed to excite and engage students in science and technology and to motivate and provide professional development for teachers. Available: *http://www.jasonproject.org/*

Florida Everglades (1999). [Online]. A one of a kind ecosystem environment, plant life, history, photographs. Available: *http://www.gorp.com/gorp/resource/US_National_ Park/fl_everg.htm*

Software Programs

The Graph Club–Tom Synder Productions. Available: *http://www.tomsynder.com*
- One computer, $79.95; site licenses available
- Win95 or Mac 6.07
- Award winner of Technology Leading and Learning Award of Excellence and the Developmental Software Award
- Prints the graphs you create in regular, big book, or poster size

Kid Works™ Deluxe Knowledge Adventure–Davidson
- Builds writing, reading, and creativity skills
- Combines word-processor and paint programs
- Computer reads words and stories back to students
- English and Spanish
- Single copy $67.95

Elizabeth (Betsy) Baker

Integrating Literacy and Tool-Based Technologies: Examining the Successes and Challenges

SUMMARY. *Elementary teachers have a significant responsibility to foster children's abilities to read and write. At the same time, elementary teachers are encouraged to use tool-based technologies such as the World Wide Web, multimedia encyclopedias, and word processors. However, tool-based technologies do not inherently develop children's literacy abilities. The author conducted an ethnographic study in a fourth-grade classroom in order to examine how literacy and tool-based technologies can be integrated. In this report, the author describes the setting that includes an explanation of the instructional approaches and theoretical underpinnings used by the teacher. While many findings emerged, in this paper the author focuses on the successes and challenges the teacher had while integrating literacy and tool-based technologies. The findings empower teachers to consider*

ELIZABETH (BETSY) BAKER is Assistant Professor, Literacy Education, University of Missouri-Columbia, 478 McReynolds Hall, Columbia, MO 65211. E-mail: bakere@missouri.edu

The author would like to thank the teacher and students who graciously invited her into their daily explorations with technology. She would also like to thank the following persons who helped with data collection and analysis, debriefing, and/or manuscript development: Charles K. Kinzer, Deborah W. Rowe, Robert Sherwood, Susan Bunch, and Joy Whitenack.

[Haworth co-indexing entry note]: "Integrating Literacy and Tool-Based Technologies: Examining the Successes and Challenges." Baker, Elizabeth (Betsy). Co-published simultaneously in *Computers in the Schools* (The Haworth Press, Inc.) Vol. 16, No. 2, 2000, pp. 73-89; and: *Integration of Technology into the Classroom: Case Studies* (ed: D. LaMont Johnson, Cleborne D. Maddux, and Leping Liu) The Haworth Press, Inc., 2000, pp. 73-89. Single or multiple copies of this article are available for a fee from The Haworth Document Delivery Service [1-800-342-9678, 9:00 a.m. - 5:00 p.m. (EST). E-mail address: getinfo@haworthpressinc.com].

73

potential successes and challenges they may have and to decide how they might replicate the successes while addressing or circumventing the challenges. [Article copies available for a fee from The Haworth Document Delivery Service: 1-800-342-9678. E-mail address: <getinfo@haworthpressinc. com> Website: <http://www.HaworthPress.com>]

KEYWORDS. *Literacy, technology, computers, inquiry, process writing, holistic literacy, inquiry and computers, process writing and computers, holistic literacy and computers, integration (of technology and literacy), challenges to using technology*

Elementary teachers have a significant responsibility to foster children's abilities to read and write. By the time children finish elementary school, they are expected to proficiently read and discuss fiction and nonfiction as well as compose with standard spellings, grammatical structures, and conventional markings (e.g., quotation marks, commas). At the same time, technology is increasingly available in schools. Elementary teachers are encouraged to use tool-based technologies such as the World Wide Web, multimedia encyclopedias, and word processors. (These are considered tool-based because they are used as tools to accomplish tasks.) However, tool-based technologies do not inherently develop children's literacy abilities. When the user opens a word-processing document or a Web page, there are no prompts or exercises that require children to work on spelling or grammar, to identify the main idea, or to develop other literacy skills.

The purpose of this study was to understand how literacy instruction and tool-based technologies can be integrated. Such an integration is significant for several reasons. Integration would allow elementary teachers to fulfill their responsibility to foster children's literacy development while concomitantly helping children become proficient with tool-based technologies that are important for high school preparation (e.g., word-processing reports and finding sources for research papers) and workplace preparation (e.g., proficiency with word-processing, databases, the Web, e-mail). Without integration, elementary teachers are faced with the dilemma of how to fit technology into their already full curricula. Such a dilemma may mean that other important aspects of the curricula are omitted or that technology is relegated to something children use when/if they have extra time. Integration also seems appropriate for tool-based technologies that are designed to be tools used to accomplish tasks. Learning to use a tool while accomplishing a task may improve both the task (e.g., reading and writing) as well as learning how to use the tool (Brown, Collins, & Duguid, 1989).

While many findings can be reported, in this paper I focus on the successes and challenges that a teacher had when she tried to integrate literacy and tool-based technologies. Given an opportunity to understand one teacher's successes and challenges may help other teachers replicate similar successes and address similar challenges. So that readers can understand these successes and challenges, I also describe the setting, which includes an explanation of the instructional approaches and theoretical underpinnings the teacher used. Due to the importance of fostering literacy development in elementary schools, the encouragement to use tool-based technologies (which do not inherently encourage literacy development), and the significance of understanding successes and challenges to integrating literacy and tool-based technologies, I used the following question to guide my research: What are the successes and challenges that a teacher might encounter when integrating literacy instruction and tool-based technologies? Interview methods could be used to determine these successes and challenges; however, interview data may be limited to perceived successes and challenges. I wanted to identify both perceived and unperceived successes and challenges. I used ethnographic data collection and analyses techniques to identify both the perceived and unperceived successes and challenges.

BACKGROUND AND PROJECT DEVELOPMENT

Setting and Participants

This project occurred in an elementary school which was located in the southeastern United States in a suburban public school. Eight years prior to this study, a third-grade and a fourth-grade classroom were set up with tool-based technologies. Throughout these eight years, the students in the third-grade technology classroom progressed to the fourth-grade technology classroom. In other words, the students were involved in these tool-based technology classrooms for two consecutive years.

We conducted this study in the fourth-grade classroom which had the following technologies: 35 computers, 10 printers, 2 televisions, 2 CD-ROM drives, 1 cartridge drive (predominately used for capturing video), 1 VCR, 1 videocamera, 1 laser disc player, 1 modem, 1 telephone, and 1 scanner. Each student had a personal computer on his/her desk as well as access to five multimedia work stations in the classroom. In addition, the students could access materials found on CD-ROMs, laser discs, the World Wide Web, videotapes, filmstrips (which often included narrated cassette tapes) as well as textbooks, trade books, and magazines.

The students were selected by a board of faculty members from a pool of applicants. The board purposely selected a representative sample of the school population with regard to race, gender, and academic ability. The class consisted of 26 students: 13 boys and 13 girls. There were one African American boy, three African American girls, and one Hispanic girl. The remaining children were Euro American. Twenty of these students had been in the third-grade technology classroom. The teacher described the class as "average" in ability, citing that no student qualified for special, remedial, or gifted services.

The classroom teacher, Ms. Jones (a pseudonym), was a seasoned teacher with over 20 years of classroom teaching experience. She had received various awards for her outstanding teaching and was considered to be a very good teacher. Interestingly, when I worked with Ms. Jones it was the first year that she had taught fourth grade or taught in a technology based classroom. She became interested in teaching in such a classroom after attending a district workshop conducted by one of the teachers involved in one of these technology classrooms.

Theoretical Underpinnings

With regard to literacy, Ms. Jones wanted to foster (a) collaboration, (b) contextualized literacy skills instruction, and (c) student choice. She valued collaboration because some learning theorists argue that knowledge is constructed by individuals as they interact in social environments (Vygotsky, 1978). Instead of isolating learners, Ms. Jones wanted to promote opportunities for the students to learn from one another (Andrew, & Musser, 1997; Daiute, 1985; Jones & Pellegrini, 1996; Rowe, 1994). Contextualized literacy learning allows children to learn not only the skill itself but also when and how to use the skill (Atwell, 1987; Harste, Short, & Burke, 1988; Routman,

1994). For example, teachers can tell students how to use commas and then provide exercises to practice using commas; however, they may not remember the instruction when they actually need to use commas (Brown, Collins, & Duguid, 1989). Thus, Ms. Jones wanted to observe children as they read and wrote in meaningful contexts, to determine what skills they needed to improve their reading and writing abilities, and to provide instruction to them when they needed it. Ms. Jones also wanted to foster choice. Choice is deemed valuable to literacy development. Harste, Short, and Burke (1988) write:

> Choice is an integral part of the literacy learning process. In many ways choice is the propeller that gets the whole process started. It is in making the decision to read this book rather than that book, or to write this story rather than that story, that ownership of the process occurs. (p. 61)

Ms. Jones wanted to offer students choices whenever she could. Below is a description of how Ms. Jones integrated literacy and tool-based technologies while adhering to these theoretical underpinnings.

Data Collection and Analysis

To capture the events of the classroom, I was a participant-observer in the classroom for several hours each day from January to June. I took extensive observation notes that were expanded each day into more elaborate reflections while watching corresponding videotapes and reviewing collected artifacts. The expanded notes were coded as follows (Corsaro, 1985): descriptions of observed activities and social interactions (field notes), my interpretations of these activities and interactions (theoretical notes), and notes about intrusiveness, shifts in data collection methods, and emergent themes (methodological notes). I also conducted formal and informal interviews with the students and teacher, collected samples of the students' work (e.g., animations, multimedia slide shows, written reports) and sources used by the students (e.g., Web pages, textbook and trade book passages, CD-ROM articles). After becoming familiar with the setting (weeks 1-6), I videotaped the classroom lessons and literacy activities (weeks 7-18). When segments were needed for data triangulation, I transcribed them for further analysis. Also the formal interviews with Ms. Jones were audio taped and transcribed.

Using the constant comparison method (Glaser & Strauss, 1967; Strauss & Corbin, 1990), I analyzed the expanded observation notes to identify successes and challenges encountered while integrating literacy and tool-based technologies. As hypotheses emerged, I interviewed Ms. Jones and the students. These interviews allowed me to refine the hypotheses. I then discussed these refined hypotheses with project debriefers who challenged me to consider alternate explanations and a new round of classroom observations, interviews, and analyses. Lincoln and Guba (1985) recommend that naturalistic researchers debrief with knowledgeable consultants, who are not directly involved in the study, so researchers can acquire impartial feedback; these consultants are called debriefers. My debriefers included two literacy professors (one was a naturalistic inquirer; the other, a specialist in the integration of literacy and technology) and two educational researchers (who were naturalistic inquirers).

Several techniques suggested by Lincoln and Guba (1985) were used to increase the trustworthiness of my data collection and analysis. First, this inquiry occurred over an extended period of time involving more than 400 hours of observation during five months. Second, I triangulated my sources (i.e., teacher, students, participant-observer) and my data sets (i.e., observation notes, videotapes, audio tapes, students' work samples). Triangulation allowed me to confirm my findings in three or more data sources until redundancy was established. Third, during data collection and analysis, I purposely looked for disconfirming information. These data were used to discard or revise the emergent hypotheses. Fourth, I met with four debriefers (Lincoln & Guba, 1985) throughout data collection and analysis. The debriefers and the teacher read a final report about the project and offered further suggestions for revisions (e.g., theoretical perspectives and participants' backgrounds). These revisions were incorporated in all reports of the project. Last, by continually generating, refining, and in some cases refuting hypotheses, I developed a systematic way to analyze the corpus of data. Through this dynamic process, the emerging theoretical constructs were empirically grounded and used to understand successes and challenges that this teacher encountered while integrating literacy and tool-based technologies.

INTEGRATION PROJECT

Ms. Jones organized the integration of literacy and technology around two instructional approaches: inquiry projects and process writing (see Table 1). The inquiry projects started with topics from the district curriculum (e.g., oceans, geometry, poetry, regions of the United States) (see Figure 1).

To begin an inquiry project, Ms. Jones announced a topic and the students silently read their textbooks to identify questions and points of interest. They then formed inquiry teams of classmates who had similar interests. These teams found materials about their topics by searching the Web, videodiscs, CD-ROM encyclopedias, trade books, magazines, videotapes, learning kits with narrated filmstrips, and telephone interviews (usually with parents, sometimes with professionals such as zookeepers). The students completed 11 inquiry projects between January and June. On the average, these projects took six to eight school days with 30 to 120 minutes of work per day. Each day, the teams met to discuss what they had found since the previous day (while at home, the students often read more sources or discussed their topics with their parents). The inquiry projects culminated with the students "teaching the class" what they learned about their topics. In order to teach the class, the students had to figure out how to communicate their topics to their classmates. The teams used technology to develop presentations that typically incorporated bulletin boards (made with computer graphics and captions), newspapers (composed and printed on computers), multimedia slide shows, animations, and skits (composed and revised on computers with multiple copies printed for students in skits).

Ms. Jones incorporated the writing process within the inquiry projects. At the beginning of the year, she discussed how the writing process involved brainstorming, drafting, editing, revising, and publishing. She posted this process on a classroom wall (in the form of a staircase) and consistently announced on which step of the process the students should be working. For example, during a poetry unit, the whole class analyzed poetry and then brainstormed topics for poetry. The students went to their seats and brainstormed their own topics. Ms. Jones circulated the room and discussed the topics with each student. If the students' topics were sufficient, Ms. Jones told them they could begin drafting with their word processors. Before the students were allowed to publish their compositions, they were expected to request feedback from two or three classmates. Ms. Jones discussed with the class that appropriate feedback included at least three positive comments before any suggestions should be made. To culminate the writing process, the

TABLE 1
Synthesis of Daily Schedule

Time	Activity
8:45-9:30	Students entered room: • Students got books and materials they would need from their classroom lockers and put them on their desks • Students began work on whatever assignment the teacher had on the board. These assignments typically included: write a journal entry, work on independent book report and presentation, work on team unit of inquiry, correct assignments returned by the teacher
9:30-9:45	Whole class time: • Pledge of Allegiance and a patriotic song • Review of morning tasks including strategies and materials for accomplishing such tasks • Return and review graded assignments • English lesson based upon what the teacher observed the day before during individual and team work times (i.e., if students needed guidance on how to outline or use commas)
9:45-11:10	Independent projects or team inquiry units: • Independent projects included individual compositions usually representative of a specific genre, and book reports • School library: Select a book for an individual book report or gather materials related to the unit of inquiry • Study Buddies: 45 minutes every 2-3 weeks; a second grade class entered the room with a composition assignment; each second grader was paired with a fourth grader who helped with typing, editing, and revising the composition assignment
11:10-11:20	Whole class time: • Teacher asked students to evaluate their progress during the morning • Teacher announced, based upon students' comments, what they would do after lunch (i.e., continue morning projects or shift to something else). • Teacher gave directions for what the students should do when they returned from lunch
11:20-12:00	Lunch and restroom
12:00-12:20	Odds and ends: This time was used for a variety of activities including: • Finish morning work • Individual or team presentations • Math lesson • Handwriting lesson (1-2 times a week)
12:20-1:00	P.E. and water break
1:00-1:05	Whole class time: • Teacher discussed how they would spend the afternoon
1:05-3:20	Odds and ends: This time was used for a variety of activities including: • Handwriting (1-2 times a week, for about 20 minutes) • Math (about 30 minutes of instruction and activity) • Music (the teacher team taught music with another teacher for about 30 minutes one day a week) • Work on individual or team projects • Individual or team presentations
3:20-3:30	Whole class time: • Reviewed homework • Gathered materials to go home • School announcements

FIGURE 1
Inquiry Process

Initiate Inquiry	Conduct Inquiry	Culminate Inquiry
Based on the district's curriculum, Ms. Jones announced an inquiry unit topic (e.g., oceans, aerospace, geometry, poetry). Students silently read district textbooks to find topics they wanted to investigate. The class met and discussed topics they found interesting and formed inquiry teams based on similar interests.	Inquiry teams (3-4 students on each team) went to the school library to find information about their selected topics (e.g., books, magazines, CD-ROM encyclopedia, and learning kits with videotapes, filmstrips, and photographs). Inquiry teams met with the teacher to share what they found in the library and discuss resources in the classroom (e.g., books, magazines, multimedia CD-ROMS, e-mail, Web, phone, laser discs). Inquiry teams met to discuss their findings and how they would present their findings to their classmates.	Each student submitted a summary of his/her information to Ms. Jones. Ms. Jones reviewed the summaries and either approved them for presentation or recommended further inquiry. Students presented their findings to their classmates by giving each student a blank outline about their topic (for note-taking) and orally presenting their topic with supporting materials (e.g., video, filmstrips, animations, multimedia slide shows, and student-made newspapers, magazines, and books). Using the blank outlines, the class took notes during presentations and asked questions so they could understand the topic and complete the blank outlines. Students took a recall test of the presentations.

students printed out their compositions; in other words, they published their work. These publications were then used during their inquiry presentations, posted on bulletin boards, handed out for classmates to take home (i.e., newspapers), or added to the class library for class-mates to check out (e.g., reports about regions of the United States).

EVALUATION OF PROJECT

Successes

The purpose of this project was to understand how literacy instruction and tool-based technologies can be integrated. I found that the instructional approaches Ms. Jones used were effective in accomplishing this integration. Data analysis revealed that over 70% of the reading and writing activities in this classroom, which at some point included tool-based technology, occurred while the students researched or reported their findings about inquiry topics (which incorporated the process approach). Furthermore, Ms. Jones successfully adhered to her theoretical positions (collaboration, contextualized literacy skills instruction, and student choice).

In order to illustrate this success, I provide the following transcript of Jessica as she revised her story about a robot. Prior to the following dialog, the class completed an inquiry unit about aerospace. Ms. Jones gave the students articles to read about robots (similar to ones the students found in aerospace experiments and rocket construction). Ms. Jones invited the students to write about robots so they could create a class anthology about robots. In this excerpt, Jessica has completed a story about a robot named Ashley who does the household chores for the girl who found her, Chelsey. Before Jessica printed her story to add to the class anthology about robots, she invited two classmates, Chuck and Lisa, to come to her computer and read her story from her computer screen. I enter the discussion while Chuck is reading Jessica's story out loud. Chuck and Lisa take turns reading and making suggested changes. (Italics represent text from Jessica's story.)

> Chuck: *Then* [a girl named] *Chelsey started school. Ashley* [the robot] *started home and cleaned house. A week wented by.*
>
> Jessica: Went by.
>
> Chuck: Went by. You should just cut off that -ed, it should just be, *a week went by.*
>
> Jessica: [edited her text] . . .
>
> Lisa: *Chelsey said, "What do you want to do, Ashley"* You need to um . . . [pointed to the screen]
>
> Chuck: *"What do you want to do"* Oh, put a question mark right there [pointed to the screen].
>
> Jessica: [edited her text] . . .

Lisa: *When they woke up*

Chuck: *When they woke up THOUGH?*

Lisa: *They wached TV*

Jessica: *When they woke up THEY* [Chuck changed "though" to "they"]

Lisa: There is a "t" there [referring to the "t" in watched]

Chuck: Oh yeah, I forgot . . .

Lisa: *. . . played games and went outside, and they played with their friends*

Chuck: . . . that needs to be capitalized . . .

Jessica: *Then after that, they went to the zoos and farms. At one farm they rode the bull. The bull killed Ashley. We was so mad* [although Jessica pronounced 'mad', it was spelled 'made'] *at the bull but I . . .*

Lisa: Made at the bull?

Jessica: [edited "made" into "mad"] . . .

Chuck: It keeps saying "after" [many of your sentences begin with "After"]

Lisa: Why don't you make friends with another robot in the story?

Jessica: Well

Lisa: Make it a happy ending

Jessica: Well, I don't want it that happy . . .

Chuck: That was a very good story . . .

Jessica: OK, so can I read yours next?

Chuck: Yep.

Collaboration occurs throughout this dialog. In fact, the students in this class continually collaborated. When Ms. Jones was asked about the collaboration among students, she discussed a situation in which each student was assigned to write poems:

> I kept stressing, "This is your poem; you are doing it by your-self." What did we find? [Students] congregating, commenting on each other's poems . . . And whenever I say, "Study your spelling," [They say,] "Can we study with somebody else?" I think because we do such a big part of the day with the group work [inquiry projects] that they are so used to interacting. I do not think that they would do that if we had not been spending an hour and a half or two every day doing these group [projects].

The students in this classroom were expected to work with class-mates during their inquiry projects. Ms. Jones noted that the students became accustomed to working with one another and requested to collaborate even during individual activities (e.g., poem writing and spelling).

Literacy skills were successfully contextualized in this classroom. For example, Jessica and her peers discussed the following skills:

1. spelling (i.e., there is a "t" in watched, take the "e" off of made to spell mad),
2. syntax (i.e., take the -ed off of wented), characterization (i.e., why don't you make friends with another robot),
3. plot development (i.e., make it a happy ending), and
4. punctuation (i.e., put a question mark there).

Jessica revised the conventions of her story (e.g., spelling, syntax, and punctuation). However, she decided to leave the plot intact–she pre-ferred her version of the story over what Lisa suggested. Ms. Jones also provided mini-lessons to individuals and small groups as they demonstrated the need for a skill. For example, she observed several students using commas inappropriately while they composed. Thus, Ms. Jones asked these students to meet with her, bring their English textbooks, and review the uses of commas. These students immediately applied their new knowledge to the reports they were word processing.

Choice occurred throughout the inquiry projects and process writing. The students chose their topics (e.g., ocean tides, tidal waves, and the topography of the ocean floor), sources of information (e.g., science textbook, trade books and magazines, CD-ROMs, laser discs, videotapes, filmstrips), and presentation formats (e.g., animation, bulletin boards). Choice also occurred during *individual* projects. Specifically, the students chose which book they wanted to read. They chose which genre they wanted to explore. They chose what format they would use to report to the class about the book (i.e., multimedia slide show, written script and performance of character impersonation, written and oral "sales pitch" for the book). As a consequence, the students appeared to have ownership of the information they gathered and made decisions about how they would present their projects to their classmates.

Challenges

While the integration of literacy and tool-based technologies was successful, the focus of this report is to discuss both the successes and the challenges. During my five months in this classroom, I found that the teacher encountered the following challenges on a regular basis: (a) student inability to differentiate between quality information and "flashy" sources, (b) student ability to create substantive products that are not simply "flashy," (c) student ability to deal with conflicting or inaccurate information, (d) accuracy of what students reported, and (e) privacy to students as they risk developing their literacy abilities. While this is not an exhaustive list of challenges faced by the teacher, it is a list of challenges that were consistent as well as related to integrating literacy and technology.

Analyzing the Quality of Sources. Ms. Jones had to provide ample instruction on how to, as she stated, "find the meat" in various sources. In other words, some sources were "flashy" but had little content to convey. For example, students might spend time viewing animations of the Civil War. However, some of these animations did not explain the battles represented in the animation or give background information about the war. Ms. Jones modeled how to find and outline the "meat" in encyclopedias, textbooks, Web pages, and other sources. The students then became mindful of the need to examine whether they could find information in their sources. In an interview with Jessica, I asked why she read particular sources. She stated she read in order, "to get meat." In an interview with Troy, I asked if he had read about his topic, the southeastern United States. He stated, "Yes, we call information meat." Troy, like Jessica and others, read to find information/meat. When Ms. Jones met with the inquiry teams to discuss their findings, she continually asked what information they found and what they planned to teach the class. Ms. Jones' instruction and continual reminders to find "meat" as they perused sources were successful. It is also a challenge that teachers who use only textbooks may not encounter.

Creating Substantive Products. Ms. Jones and her students had to *develop criteria for examining the quality of products they made in this classroom.* Some students thought that because they created a "flashy" animation or multimedia presentation that they had adequately researched and presented their topics. For example, Jessica's inquiry project was about the evolution of the American Flag. She simply scanned a page of different American flags and considered her work complete. She would be able to show her class a slide show of the different flags. When Ms. Jones asked Jessica about the flags, Jessica was unable to explain why they had different numbers of stars, configuration of stars, or what the stripes represented. Ms. Jones provided instruction about the need to not only *find* meat in commercial products but also to create products that *communicated* meat. If these students had simply created paper-and-pencil products, the teacher may also need to emphasize the need to incorporate substance into the report. However, these students had to consider how to include substance in not only written reports but also animations, slide shows, newspapers, bulletin boards, and other technology products.

Determining Conflicting or Inaccurate Information. Due to the large number of sources available to students, they sometimes found conflicting or inaccurate information. For example, while one student was researching the Himalayan mountains, he found three different heights for the tallest mountain. Ms. Jones then discussed with this student the need for examining the age of information and confirming information through two to three sources. As this example suggests, teachers need to be ready to provide instruction about *how to analyze the accuracy of the information* students find. Although such instruction is a challenge, it is valuable for students to realize that not all sources of information are accurate.

Verifying Accuracy of Student Reports. Because the students had access to many sources of information, Ms. Jones faced a dilemma; she could not verify the accuracy of the information for every topic. (In classrooms where students strictly use the school district's textbooks, the teacher would know where the students got their information and thus be able to assume its accuracy.) To deal with this dilemma, Ms. Jones required students to cite references and be ready to find the information if it was questionable. In other words, in the fourth grade, these students learned how to reference information.

Providing Privacy. Because the students writings were on computer screens, anyone could walk by and read them. *The "publicness" of their writings* fostered collaboration, which resulted in valuable interactions. However, it could also create anxiety for students who do not want their brainstorming or drafts to be open to public scrutiny. For example, when I asked Simon what it was like to have his writings available for anyone to read he stated:

> For visitors it is OK. . . . If journals are on screen, we usually turn off our monitors. . . . It [seeing classmates' screens] gives you a lot of ideas. [For example, if you are writing] a poem and see [a] classmate is writing about hockey, [then] you can brainstorm about other sports.

Simon's comment makes it sound like he word processed without his screen turned on. In fact, if he had a journal file open, he would turn off his screen if he left his seat. In other words, Simon indicated that an audience was so inevitable that he turned off his screen when he was not composing. In such classrooms, the students may need opportunities to compose privately. Ms. Jones dealt with the "publicness" of screens by instructing students to tell an author three things they liked about a composition before they mentioned one or two questions or suggestions. While Ms. Jones established procedures for minimizing negative comments during the writing process, students did not have the privacy necessary for personal journal writing or test taking. If teachers want students to write personal journals or take tests with the computer, they will need to develop such conditions (e.g., study carrels).

CONCLUSION AND DISCUSSION

This report discusses findings from an ethnographic study of a fourth-grade classroom which successfully integrated literacy and tool-based technologies. While the integration was successful, the technology created some challenges that Ms. Jones had to address.

However, upon closer examination of these challenges, they also provided valuable learning opportunities. For example, the students in this class learned that just because an animation or multimedia slide show looks "slick," it may have minimal substance. Conversely, when they use technology to communicate information, they can create animations with many features, but, without substance, they have minimal value. Because the tool-based technologies gave the students access to many sources of information (e.g., Web pages, CD-ROM encyclopedias, laser discs, phone interviews, e-mail), the students had to learn to deal with conflicting and inaccurate information. While Ms. Jones had to help students with this challenge, these students emerged from this class with the ability to confirm the accuracy of information. Due to the vast number of sources, the students also learned how to reference their information. Both verifying information and referencing information are important literacy skills. The technology in this classroom introduced the need for these skills before the grade levels in which they are typically taught as well as provided contextualized opportunities to use these skills. The need for privacy is a challenge of which teachers need to be aware. Ms. Jones established classroom norms that minimized ridicule. Students need to be able to compose without fear of ridicule. If computer monitors are open to public view, teachers need to be mindful of the need for privacy.

In the introduction, I argued that the integration of literacy and tool-based technologies was important for several reasons. I argued that integration would allow elementary teachers to fulfill their responsibility to foster children's literacy development while concomitantly helping children become proficient with tool-based technologies. I found that Ms. Jones successfully accomplished this integration by taking some basic theoretical stances and using inquiry projects and process writing approaches. I argued that integration would mitigate the difficulty of trying to fit technology instruction into the full elementary curricula teachers are already expected to cover. I found that Ms. Jones did not have to eliminate any of her curriculum in order to incorporate technology. Instead, the integration of literacy and technology allowed her to contextualize both literacy and technology instruction.

Other teachers who use similar instructional approaches based on similar theoretical stances may encounter different successes and challenges. However, this report allows teachers to consider the successes and challenges encountered by Ms. Jones and consider whether they want to incorporate similar theories and instructional approaches. This report also allows teachers to anticipate possible challenges and decide how they will address them. While several challenges arose, Ms. Jones found ways to address these challenges and even offer the students important skills that may otherwise not be incorporated into fourth grade literacy instruction.

REFERENCES

Andrew, P. G., & Musser, L. R. (1997). Collaborative design of World Wide Web pages: A case study. *Information Technology and Libraries, 16*(1), 34-38.
Atwell, N. (1987). *In the middle: Writing, reading, and learning with adolescents.* Portsmouth, NH: Heinemann.
Brown, J. S., Collins, A., & Duguid, P. (1989). Situated cognition and the culture of learning. *Educational Researcher, 17,* 32-41.
Corsaro, W. A. (1985). *Friendship and peer culture in the early years.* Norwood, NJ: Ablex.
Daiute, C. (1985). Issues in using computers to socialize the writing process. *Educational Communication and Technology, 33*(1), 41-50.
Glaser, B., & Strauss, A. (1967). *The discovery of grounded theory.* Chicago: Aldine.
Harste, J. C., Short, K. G., & Burke, C. (1988). *Creating classrooms for authors: The reading-writing connection.* Portsmouth, NH: Heinemann.
Jones, I., & Pellegrini, A. D. (1996). The effects of social relationships, writing, media, and microgenetic development on first-grade students' written narratives. *American Educational Research Journal, 33*(3), 691-718.
Lincoln, Y., & Guba, E. (1985). *Naturalistic inquiry.* Beverly Hills: Sage.
Routman, R. (1994). *Invitations: Changing as teachers and learners K-12.* Portsmouth, NH: Heineman.
Rowe, D. W. (1994). *Preschoolers as authors: Literacy learning in the social world of the classroom.* Cresskill, NJ: Hampton Press.
Strauss, A., & Corbin, J. (1990). *Basics of qualitative research: Grounded theory procedures and techniques.* Newbury Park, CA: Sage.
Vygotsky, L. (1978). *Mind in society.* Cambridge, MA: Harvard University Press.

Sharla L. Snider
Jeanne M. Foster

Stepping Stones for Linking, Learning, and Moving Toward Electronic Literacy: Integrating Emerging Technology in an Author Study Project

SUMMARY. *This paper details the integration of technology tools into a third-grade Web-based literacy project. The project included 13 students at the beginning of the school year possessing a wide range of technology exposure and reading experience levels. The students were provided an opportunity to work in small groups–reading works by a selected children's author, researching biographical data and exploring the writer's style, and using of conventions of literary works such as characterization, plot, and setting. Included in the project were authentic purposes for writing; research on the Web and traditional sources; cooperative and collaborative learning opportunities; and planning, designing, and creating finished products in a multimedia presentation. [Article copies available for a fee from The Haworth Document Delivery Service: 1-800-342-9678. E-mail address: <getinfo@haworthpressinc.com> Website: <http://www.HaworthPress.com>]*

SHARLA L. SNIDER is Assistant Professor, Reading and Bilingual Department, College of Education and Human Ecology, Texas Woman's University, Denton, TX 76204. E-mail: f_snider@twu.edu
JEANNE M. FOSTER is Program Coordinator, LINKS Center, College of Education and Human Ecology, Texas Woman's University, Denton, TX 76204. E-mail: g_9foster@twu.edu

[Haworth co-indexing entry note]: "Stepping Stones for Linking, Learning, and Moving Toward Electronic Literacy: Integrating Emerging Technology in an Author Study Project." Snider, Sharla L. and Jeanne M. Foster. Co-published simultaneously in *Computers in the Schools* (The Haworth Press, Inc.) Vol. 16, No. 2, 2000, pp. 91-108; and: *Integration of Technology into the Classroom: Case Studies* (ed: D. LaMont Johnson, Cleborne D. Maddux, and Leping Liu) The Haworth Press, Inc., 2000, pp. 91-108. Single or multiple copies of this article are available for a fee from The Haworth Document Delivery Service [1-800-342-9678, 9:00 a.m. - 5:00 p.m. (EST). E-mail address: getinfo@haworthpressinc.com].

KEYWORDS. *Technology, Web-based literacy, project approach, Web-Quest, multimedia, electronic literacy*

Today's students will be entering a workforce with expectations different from those of the past. This modern work world will require them to know more than how to navigate technology tools to achieve a desired and predetermined effect. They will use technology as a tool to express and share their knowledge and findings. In order to address these changes in our society, schools will implement changes as well. Schools will move away from a traditional linear curriculum model that assumes students will enter the learning arena at a specified point with a benchmarked knowledge base and a prescribed set of skills, proceed through a set course, and emerge at the other end "educated." Use of this type of model, which evolved from the industrial age, is becoming obsolete as we progress further into the age of information. It is being replaced by a model that addresses real-world expectations, allowing students to learn through an integrated approach with opportunities to work collaboratively and cooperatively as well as individually. The emerging model of education includes practical, authentic use of technology as a tool for research and presentation; however, we cannot expect the use of technology tools to revolutionize education on their own. Rather, the key to the impact of technology, and in particular to the use of the Web, is in how effectively it is used in the classroom (Fabry & Higgs, 1997; Coley, Cradler, & Engel, 1997; Owston, 1997; Topping, 1997).

DEVELOPING
THE TECHNOLOGY
INTEGRATION PROJECT

Incorporating a New Model of Education

This article details the integration of technology tools with a third-grade Web-based literacy project. The project, which was implemented at the beginning of the school year, included 13 students possessing a wide range of technology exposure and reading experience levels. The students were provided an opportunity to work in small groups, reading works by their chosen children's author and researching biographical data. As they explored these readings, they developed and articulated an understanding of the writer's style and use of conventions of literary works such as characterization, plot, and setting. Included in the project were authentic purposes for writing; research on the Web and traditional sources; cooperative and collaborative learning opportunities; self-directed tasking and planning and designing and creating finished products in a multimedia presentation. This technology integration project will be described through a foundation emphasizing the nature of the tools utilized, the environment, the role of the teacher and learner, and the scaffold provided for an integrated learning opportunity. The implementation of the project is examined from the perspectives of both the teacher and the learner. An evaluation of the project will be addressed through "lessons learned." Finally, suggestions for taking the "next steps" will be given.

Foundation: Tools

Today's children, in many cases, continue to be taught with yesterday's tools, a method that could leave them unprepared for our rapidly evolving technological society. An emphasis on learning to think and learning to learn is an effective replacement for learning predetermined content in isolation. Haymore, Sandholtz, Ringstaff, and Dwyer (1997) identify the latter as a phenomenon in American schools spawned by accountability systems that relied heavily on raising standardized test scores. These programs for change became commonplace in the 1980s and seem to be on the rise once again. Today, leaders in our nation measure our children against each other and against the children of other nations with norm-referenced scores. As society clamors for higher test scores, schools become more adept at turning students into "better test-takers, but at a terrible cost" (p. 12). Their ability to perform complex tasks suffers as the emphasis in the classroom shifts to "drill and practice of the kinds of skills and disjointed facts" (p. 12) targeted in standardized and norm-referenced tests. As more emphasis is placed on these lower-order thinking skills, it becomes more important to evaluate the total school experience for our children and seek a balance. We must never lose sight of the fact that it is imperative for today's students to be able to think critically about the information presented to them, analyze, dissect, and discover new ways to apply the information and use it as a stepping stone to further learning. Furthermore, it is critical for them to be exposed to the many technological advances that will promote their endeavors–advances such as the Internet and computer-based presentation tools. In a classroom such as this, rather than being taught about technology, the emphasis will shift to learning to use technology in everyday learning. The emphasis will shift from instruction in how to use technology tools, to instruction that uses technology as a tool within a meaningful context for learning. In the former model, technology is an object of study. It is operation-based and important to understanding the tool, but the learning is superficial. In the latter, technology tools are the means to an end–they are incorporated with learning in a fashion similar to utilizing a chalkboard, pencil, and encyclopedia. The learning that takes place incorporates complex thinking skills such as analysis and synthesis because it is application-based, more advanced, and thus more sophisticated.

Prior to this project, technology tools were integrated in this third-grade classroom in a minimal fashion, used primarily for word processing and as a learning center activity. Children were accustomed to using word-processing tools in their original compositions. Some of the software packages they used incorporated clip art, but they had never ventured beyond the basic features included in the software. Learning center activities included educational games and skill-and-drill programs. Additionally, the children had a history of exposure to the campus computer lab for 30-minute weekly skill and drill sessions in math and language arts. This program began in kindergarten and continued through fifth grade.

This integration project grew out of a summer graduate course, "Computers in Reading," which built a strong rationale for using the computer as a tool, based on current trends in educational philosophy. The course introduced the graduate students to a variety of available technologies, including Web-based projects and presentation software. The graduate students were encouraged to become "fearless users of technology" and to extend this attitude to one of "fearless implementers of technology" in the elementary classroom. The teacher in this classroom took this challenge seriously. She felt the integration of technology was even more imperative for her class. An overwhelming majority of these children had little or no exposure to technology outside the classroom, thus failing to expose them to authentic uses of technology could impose an obstacle for them in a society that is embracing technology.

By integrating technology in the classroom, it was felt that students would indeed be exposed to authentic purposes for technology and would become neophytes in a technologically literate society. They would have an opportunity to learn that they could use a computer in their everyday activities and as an extension of themselves, to express what they had to share. This would constitute a major shift in their thinking, since much of their exposure to computers required them to attend to the computer's instructions in a drill-and-practice format. Additionally, with a limited number of available computers, each student would be exposed to using a computer in collaborative and cooperative contexts, becoming an integral member and facilitator on a technology team and recognizing the expertise and resourcefulness of others as well.

Some areas that presented challenges in the integration of technology were availability of hardware, software, and trade books; the children's lack of prior exposure to technology tools; and management of a multi-tasking environment. Some of these challenges were recognized and addressed in the planning stages. Still, others surfaced and were solved as the project evolved and will be discussed in "Lessons Learned."

In the planning stages of the project, the classroom software and hardware were inventoried and needs were identified. The support of the campus technology specialist was enlisted to locate and transfer software already on campus and to identify options for access to additional hardware at crucial points in the project. Many of the trade books needed for the project were located in the campus library and the classroom; still others were secured from the public library.

In order to set the tone for using technology as a tool and to orient the children in this attitude, the daily classroom routine was examined for ways to incorporate technology. Presentation software became a way to deliver direct instruction and organize the morning meetings, replacing the hard copy of the meeting agenda. Children were enlisted to run the agenda presentation and to update it on a daily basis. Basic computer and presentation software skills were taught in context, as needed. In this way, the children became familiar with presentation software and its practical uses in a nonthreatening environment. They began to see the computer as a tool, not unlike the books, pencils, and chalkboard, and had become accustomed to learning new skills on the computer to meet their needs. As the project was undertaken, it was their expectation that what they did not know, they would be taught by their teacher or a classmate, or they would be able to learn through exploration.

Foundation: Environment

Classroom environments have a large part to play in how technology is incorporated in the curriculum. A traditional direct instruction model, which was thought to be effective in delivering predetermined content in isolation, does not prepare students totally for a society that requires a great deal of synergy and nonlinear productivity. Our current thinking in classroom environment design therefore reflects this modern model of society. To achieve a more effective environment, we are embracing a shift in our traditional concept of the classroom and fostering A.C.T.I.V.E. (Grabe & Grabe, 1998) environments. Grabe and Grabe adopted the acronym A.C.T.I.V.E. to describe the ideal setting for a technology-rich classroom: Active, Cooperative, Theme-Based, Integrated, Versatile, and Evaluative. An *Active* environment establishes new learning by encouraging children to cognitively manipulate and interpret concepts. This *Cooperative* environment reflects the shift from competitive learning to cooperative learning, which allows children to draw on peers as resources and as sounding boards for formulating, defining, and defending new learning. According to Crook (1998), these learning situations are most successful when three criteria are met: (a) an existing "communal purpose," (b) an ample supply of resources, and (c) previously established interpersonal relationships (p. 241). Grabe and Grabe (1998) recommend learning that is *Theme-Based* to allow critical connections to the real world. These theme-based projects are *Integrated* across the subjects to teach skills in meaningful contexts rather than in isolation. The environment is *Versatile* to accommodate many skill levels and interests. Finally, *Evaluation* is based on progress, products, and effort (p. 23). A teacher- and student-designed rubric such as the one implemented in this project meets the evaluation criteria necessary for this type of environment.

This project's classroom contained elements of both a traditional and an A.C.T.I.V.E. environment. *Traditional*, for the purposes of this article, is defined as a curriculum and classroom environment driven by the mastery of basic skills. About half the children in this class had been identified as "at-risk for school failure" based on a combination of criteria, including low scores on standardized tests. This being the case, raising the children's standardized test scores had been identified as a goal by the administration. The traditional elements of the classroom were incorporated in an effort to provide the children with the tools necessary to be successful in the testing situation. The A.C.T.I.V.E. elements were seen as a more in-depth treatment of knowledge acquisition and one that would address individual needs and foster higher order thinking skills, and the self-direction and self-motivation so important for the children's sense of ownership in their education.

The environment in this classroom incorporated ongoing thematic study, group and individual responsibilities, and flexible grouping. A thematic approach to instruction was implemented in compliance with the district's scope and sequence. The themes utilized throughout the academic year were organized around broad concepts such as "relationships." Within this broad concept, themes such as "rules and responsibilities," "community and family" and "traditions and celebrations" were explored. The theme chosen for this project focused on the exploration of a favorite author. The goal was to gain an in-depth understanding of the writer's craft, including writing style, recurring themes and characters, mood, and setting. In reading several books by the same author, researching biographical information and author interviews, students would have an opportunity to draw parallels and discover common threads. This exposure would then aid them in developing some degree of insight into the author's motivation and style.

This technology integration project was seen as a vehicle to motivate children to take ownership in the education process as well as an introduction to technology as an important tool for everyday learning. By using presentation software, the children would have access to powerful tools that would enable them to design and create a presentation with quality far superior to their posters and other hand-made products. This would in turn encourage them to see themselves as capable users of technology with aesthetically pleasing presentations that approximate professional multimedia products. Furthermore, by using these technology tools for authentic purposes, many of the state-mandated technology learning objectives were learned.

Striking a balance between the traditional classroom model and the A.C.T.I.V.E. model was a challenge. Other third-grade classrooms were not involved in this integration project, so aligning instruction among the classrooms to ensure comparable coverage of the learning objectives became a focus area in grade-level team planning sessions. In order to align the instruction across the grade level, it was important to examine the goals and objectives identified by the district and determine how they could be incorporated with the project. Planning for the project class became a matter of orchestrating the day in such a way that mini-lessons to address objectives were incorporated into the project whenever possible. When they were not relevant to the project, they were addressed at a more appropriate time in the day.

Foundation: Shifting Roles

A change in environment will necessarily require a change in roles. Haymore et al. (1997) assert the premise that roles must reflect the modern workplace "where problems are solved through conversation, inquiry, trial and error, and constant comparison of one approximate solution against another" (p. 13). In this type of environment, teachers will step down from the podium to relinquish their role as "lecturer" in favor of the role of "coach." There will be a shift from teachers as "lesson planners" to teachers as "instructional designers" (Harris, 1998). As such, teachers will focus on selecting activities and providing materials. The teacher will introduce the activity and assign a task set in a meaningful context with clear goals. The teacher's goal is to facilitate the students' work by making connections between observations made by the students and associated principles or theories. The teacher will interact with students in a variety of situations: whole-group, small group, and one-on-one. Overall, there will be a shift from large-group direct instruction to small-group instruction, which addresses the particular needs of targeted students (Collins, 1991). Students will become active participants, constructing knowledge and taking a decision-making role in their education. In this new role, there is a shift in the child's acquisition of knowledge from primarily verbal content to an integration of visual and auditory elements. The student is no longer a passive learner taking in all that is delivered and reflecting that same learning in much the way it was delivered. In this modern model, the traditional "cookie-cutter" students are transformed into active learners who are inquirers and members of a production team, each with an important, often unique role in the total learning experience of class members.

The role of the learner and teacher in this classroom had already been established within the context of "a community of learners."

Children were expected to take an active role in the daily management of the classroom, with individual as well as group responsibilities. For example, during the morning meeting, individual children were responsible for items on the agenda. Examples of these items included the calendar activities, number of the day, and pattern of the day. As each agenda item was addressed, the child responsible for that item would facilitate the meeting. Prior to the introduction of technology as a common classroom tool, this agenda was in the form of a posted template. Each day a new template was posted, and corrections and additions were handwritten by the children. The infusion of technology tools in the classroom resulted in a PowerPoint presentation of the agenda. Each morning, the children would make their corrections and additions on the Power Point slide show. Initially, the children learned to change the background and add relevant images from the Internet. As the year unfolded, the children began taking more and more responsibility for the slide show, including Internet links for a short "biography de jour."

Finally, the children often worked in collaborative groups, in cooperative groups, in dyads, and in triads. Children were accustomed to peer-conferencing in writing workshop, and buddy reading in reading workshop. Self-selection of reading materials was an integral part of the literacy program as well as one-on-one conferences to assess strengths and implement individualized instruction built on these strengths. The use of a computer within these groups further enhanced learning opportunities. According to DeVoogd (1998) "the use of computers in the classroom transform[s] the social hierarchy and grouping organization to allow students more control over their knowledge and participation" (p. 356). This type of structure provided support for increased and diverse group interaction through the use of a computer.

Foundation: Scaffolding

When children are given support to explore how technology works, they are encouraged to realize their technological potential. They become cognizant of their ability to impact technological products and to express themselves through technological tools (Stables, 1997). The WebQuest as developed by Bernie Dodge (1997b) is an excellent scaffolding tool for young technologists with an emerging role as active participants and decision-makers. "A WebQuest is an inquiry-oriented activity in which most or all of the information used by the learner is drawn from the web" (Dodge, 1998, Online). This information may be supplemented with traditional information sources (e.g., trade books, encyclopedia, dictionary). It is designed to assist the learner in focusing on and using the information provided by the quest rather than looking for the information. This information is in the form of links to Web pages that have been previewed by the teacher or WebQuest designer to ensure their relevance and value to the task at hand. The links take the learner to the targeted information, thus relieving him or her of the burden of searching and sorting through the myriad of information available on the Web. This method is all the more attractive and effective when considering the very real possibility that children will be sorting through information that is objectionable or of little value. The WebQuest is a way of narrowing the available resources in much the way a teacher would narrow library holdings by previewing relevant resources and reserving them for the class.

"The WebQuest is designed to support learners' thinking at the levels of analysis, synthesis, and evaluation" (Dodge, 1998, Online). This is accomplished by offering opportunities that allow the learners to make choices and take control of their project while providing enough scaffolding to ensure success and a sense of direction. In a longer term WebQuest, students might be required to use many higher level thinking skills as they compare similarities and differences, classify by attribute, induce or deduce by inferring generalizations, analyze errors, construct support (proof), abstract key ideas, and analyze differing perspectives (Dodge, 1997a, Online). These are all skills to consider and build on when developing the "process" portion of the WebQuest.

WebQuests may be short- or long-term projects. In a short-term project, the instructional goal is knowledge acquisition and integration. "At the end . . . a learner will have grappled with a significant amount of new information and made sense of it" (Dodge, 1997a, Online). This type of WebQuest is designed for completion in one to three class periods. The instructional goal of a longer term WebQuest is to extend and refine knowledge. "After completing a longer term WebQuest, a learner would have analyzed a body of knowledge deeply, transformed it in some way, and demonstrated an understanding of the material by creating something that others can respond to, online or off" (Dodge, 1997a, Online). This type of WebQuest will typically take between one week and one month in a classroom setting. The WebQuest used for these third-grade students, WebQuest: Amnesia, was a longer term WebQuest.

A typical WebQuest is found on a Web page; but, with newer versions of word-processing software that support Web links, a Web page is not essential to the task. A WebQuest includes an introduction that explains what the WebQuest is about, orients the learners as to what information will be presented, and clearly describes the steps to be taken. The WebQuest includes information that will let the learner know the exact process needed in order to accomplish the task. Additionally, learning advice and information resources in the form of links should be provided as well as resources not found on the Web. Evaluation of the students' work should be able to measure the results of the WebQuest. A rubric devised by the teacher in the design phase of the WebQuest or a rubric devised by the teacher and learners in a collaborative context are authentic methods of evaluation. The WebQuest concludes with a method of sharing the learners' product as evidence of the learning gained by the students. This closure activity serves to remind the learners about the learning that took place and encourage extension of the experience into other domains. Sharing the product may be accomplished via a multimedia presentation to peers and adults and loaded on the Web page to share with the Internet community.

The WebQuest was chosen as a scaffold for this literacy project due to the motivation it provided through the "hook" established in the introduction, the support it offered children in navigating the Internet, and the opportunities to learn about technology in a meaningful context. It was expected that children would learn about important elements of literary works in a way that would be motivating, meaningful, and rewarding, and about authentic uses of technology as a tool. In fact, an identified objective was to shift the children's perception of the computer as a teacher to viewing it as a powerful tool they could control.

The WebQuest was particularly attractive because it opened the door to rich resources beyond the classroom in the form of the Internet, making students consumers of information, yet structuring their searches to provide relevant sites and minimize surfing. Additionally, it incorporated authentic purposes for many basic skills identified as state-mandated technology learning objectives.

Another attractive feature of the WebQuest is the opportunities for self-selection, collaboration, cooperation, and individual choice and responsibility. The open-ended nature of the scaffold allowed the children to learn in personally meaningful ways, offering greater flexibility than the educational software that was available in the classroom. Finally, the WebQuest, by incorporating multimedia presentations as evidence of learning, introduced these children to a state-of-the-art means of communicating their new learning and initiate them in the larger community of technology users.

IMPLEMENTATION OF INTEGRATED TECHNOLOGY LITERACY PROJECT

El-Hindi (1998) asserts that today, literacy is more than reading and writing. It includes the ability to "make sense of and navigate through several forms of information including images, sounds, animation, and ongoing discussion groups" (p. 694). This literacy project focused on El-Hindi's definition and incorporated the use of a WebQuest. It was conducted with a third-grade class of 13 students in a suburban "Chapter One" (as determined by low income) elementary school. These students included one child identified as "gifted," three children served by the school's speech therapy program, one child being tested for learning disabilities, and one identified with Attention Deficit Disorder. Of the five boys and eight girls, there were four African American and nine European American students.

The introduction to the WebQuest stated that a favorite children's author was stricken with amnesia and the task before the learners was to help the author regain his or her memory (Foster, 1998). Children formed groups that varied in size from two to four members and selected an author from the choices provided on the WebQuest. The first task was to select job roles and set tasks for the week. Next, the students brainstormed possible avenues that would help their author to regain his or her lost memory. Strategies employed by the student groups included researching biographical information and reading the author's work to determine the writer's style. Additionally, the group constructed a synopsis of each story, focusing on plot, theme, characterization, and literary elements.

Children learned to use the links on the WebQuest page to research their author's biographical data and the books he or she wrote. They wrote letters to the school librarian and the teacher to enlist their aid in gathering trade books. They accessed the computerized card catalog in the library to locate and secure resources. They created advertising fliers to describe their mission and in the process learned many computer skills, including retrieving an image from the Web and using word-processing software. These fliers were then loaded on the Web page with the WebQuest. As the students collected data, they began to design HyperStudio cards as evidence of their learning. An example card was then used in a group critique session, allowing the children to consider elements such as color, contrast, content, and effectiveness. Throughout the project, the students kept a daily learning log describing their accomplishments, problems and solutions, and plans for the next day. Some of their log entries were in the form of E-mail messages to a participating professor from a local university (see Figure 1). By E-mailing this professor, the students were afforded an opportunity for authentic electronic communication and were provided with another expert source of support. All four groups were able to create a HyperStudio card for their author. As a class, they decided to keep this project as an ongoing experience, adding to and refining their cards with specified deadlines for various elements of their products. The HyperStudio stacks were loaded on the WebQuest: Amnesia page and shared with other classes in the school.

Due to the children's unfamiliarity with the tools and the fact that this was a beginning effort in the use of the Web as a scaffold for constructing student projects, expectations were somewhat flexible.

FIGURE 1
Sample E-Mail Message from Student.

```
From Lindsay:
Today I designed the main summary card . I haven't
    finished it yet but
I will tommorow.Tommorow I'm going to do a Venn
    diagram on the dentist in the Sweetest Fig and
    the guy in The Garden Of Abdul Gasazi !!!!! On
    Friday My group gets to get on hyper studio !!
```

Note. Authentic purposes for writing were included in the project. Children kept a local university professor involved in the project apprised of their progress. The student's original composition was retained.

Therefore, rather than following WebQuest design steps exactly as designed, the instructors did not initially establish a rubric for the children. Instead, students were given an opportunity to use Hyper-Studio and generate the initial card prior to establishing a rubric for the product. This allowed the children to familiarize themselves with the options and limitations of the software and gave them a more informed understanding of the scope of the WebQuest project. With this increased understanding, the children were then able to become active participants in generating a rubric for each group's first Hyper-Studio card. This first rubric was developed in a whole-group brain-storming session and focused on reasonable expectations (see Figure 2). Rubrics for successive cards were then modeled after this initial rubric.

Daily learning log entries helped the students structure their goals and reflect on their progress. These entries also provided evidence of understanding and pointed to possible teaching points that needed to be addressed either individually or in a group setting. Additionally, weekly teacher-student group conferences permitted guidance and fur-ther scaffolding by a "more experienced other" and helped the teacher to establish a timeline for completion of the specific tasks inherent in the project.

FIGURE 2
Rubric for Evaluating Design Elements of Author Multimedia Card.

Rubric for Evaluating the Design Elements of the Author Multimedia Card

Author's Card must include:
- 6 buttons   6 points
- Background   3 points–color coordinated,
                     2 points–somewhat color coordinated
                     1 point–not well coordinated
                     0 points–missing
- Sound   2 points–relevant and audible
- Text Box   3 points–author, group names, text box

E: 14-12
S: 11-9
I: 8-5
N: 4 or less

Through participation in the WebQuest and development of the multimedia HyperStudio stacks, students demonstrated various skill mastery and development indicated in the state curriculum structure related to technology applications for K-12 (TEA, 1999). The skills addressed through this project–categorized by the areas of: (a) Foundations; (b) Information Acquisition; (c) Problem Solving; (d) Communication–are included in Table 1.

In addition to supporting developing technology skills, encouraging the use of various multimedia programs, and helping students to set project goals and evaluate a finished project, designers should consider the roles of student and teacher and how these can be facilitated most effectively. Reflection on the scaffolding provided to the children in the form of links and supplemental sources as well as on

TABLE 1
Basic Technology Application Skills Addressed Through the Project

Category	Skill Addressed
Foundation	The student demonstrates knowledge and appropriate use of hardware components, software programs, and their connections.
	The student uses data input skills appropriate to the task.
Information Acquisition	The student uses a variety of strategies to acquire information from electronic resources.
	The student acquires electronic information in a variety of formats.
	The student evaluates the acquired electronic information.
Solving Problems	The student uses appropriate computer-based productivity tools to create and modify solutions to problems.
	The student uses research skills and electronic communication, with appropriate supervision, to create new knowledge.
	The student uses technology applications to facilitate evaluation of work, both process and product.
Communication	The student formats digital information for appropriate and effective communication.
	The student delivers the product electronically in a variety of media.
	The student uses technology applications to facilitate evaluation of communication, both process and product.

Note. Adapted from Texas Education Agency (1999). *Texas essential knowledge and skills technology application curriculum* (On-line). Available: http://www.tea.state.tx.us/teks/126toc

the clarity and effectiveness of the goals presented in the WebQuest is paramount. All of these factors should be considered in order for an evaluation of the WebQuest to be an effective tool for planning future projects.

Evaluation: Lessons Learned

An important part of the evaluation process demands that the instructors reflect on the effectiveness of the project and use this to plan future WebQuests. As part of the evaluation process, the instructors considered lessons learned in this first attempt at a WebQuest. Prior knowledge of the specific multimedia program used in this project emerged as the primary area of concern. The children had never been exposed to HyperStudio and needed an opportunity to play with the tool as a way of familiarizing and fulfilling a desire to explore. Although this aspect had not been built into the project by design, the children took advantage of the student-directed environment to undertake these explorations. These explorations, at first, seemed to be time-consuming, off-task behavior; however, they proved valuable to the children's understanding of the tools and built foundational skills that were utilized and further developed as the project unfolded. Instructors will want to consider the children's level of expertise and knowledge of the tools being used and allow opportunities for them to explore the tools and validate their explorations.

As this project evolved into a long-term endeavor, it became obvious that additional structure was needed to help students remain focused on the project goals and minimize time wasted on narrow objectives and off-task behaviors. To achieve this goal, deadlines were imposed for various written assignments. These assignments were in addition to the HyperStudio cards (e.g., summaries, character and story webs, and a log of titles with their main ideas). As instructors design their own projects and estimate the amount of time to be spent on the project, they can include related written assignments with due dates.

NEXT STEPS

Teachers and curriculum materials designers may want to further explore Web-based literacy projects by researching examples of Web-

Quests (see Dodge 1999). Many fine examples can be found by accessing this Web page and following the links attached to this page.

Once the designer has exposure to examples and an understanding of the goals and various elements of a good WebQuest, a unit of study should be identified. When choosing goals for the project, special attention should be given to aligning the WebQuest with established curriculum scope-and-sequence guidelines. Student interest can also be used as a determining factor in the formulation of a unit of study. Additionally, the designer will need to locate the necessary software and hardware to ensure that the WebQuest is feasible. Finally, the designer will use search engines to locate and collect relevant Web sites for use in the project. Following these next steps, keeping in mind the lessons learned through this first attempt at a WebQuest, provides a scaffold for teachers wishing to bring authentic uses of technology to their classrooms. In using these ideas as a framework, teachers can provide their students with the stepping stones to walk further down the path of the information age equipped with the tools necessary for today and provide a foundation for the crucial skills needed for tomorrow.

REFERENCES

Coley, R. J., Cradler, J., & Engel, P. K. (1997). *Computers and classrooms: The status of technology in U.S. schools.* Princeton, NJ: Policy Education Center, Educational Testing Service. (ERIC Document Reproduction Service No. ED412893)

Collins, A. (1991). The role of computer technology in restructuring schools. *Phi Delta Kappan, 73*, 28-36.

Crook, C. (1998). Children as computer users: The case of collaborative learning. *Computers in Education, 30*, 237-247.

DeVoogd, G. L. (1998). Computer use levers power sharing: Multicultural students' styles of participation and knowledge. *Computers and Education, 31*, 351-364.

Dodge, B. (1997a). About WebQuests [Online]. Available: *http://edweb.sdsu.edu/courses/edtec596/about_webquests.html*

Dodge, B. (1997b). Building blocks of a WebQuest [Online]. Available: *http://edweb.sdsu.edu/people/bdodge/webquest/buildingblocks.html*

Dodge, B. (1998). WebQuest overview [Online]. Available: *http://edweb.sdsu.edu/webquest/overview.htm*

Dodge, B. (1999). The WebQuest page [Online]. Available: *http://edweb.sdsu.edu/webquest/webquest.html*

El-Hindi, A. E. (1998). Exploring literacy on the Internet. *The Reading Teacher, 51*, 694-700.

Fabry, D. L., & Higgs, J. R. (1997). Barriers to the effective use of technology in education: Current status. *Journal of Educational Computing Research, 17*, 385-395.

Foster, J. (1998). WebQuest: Amnesia [Online]. Available: *http:///venus.twu. edu/~g_9foster/literacy.htm*

Grabe, M., & Grabe, C. (1998). *Integrating technology for meaningful Learning.* Boston: Houghton Mifflin.

Harris, J. B. (1998). *Virtual architecture: Designing and directing curriculum-based telecomputing.* Eugene, OR: International Society for Technology in Education.

Haymore, J., Sandholtz, J. H., Ringstaff, C., & Dwyer, D. C. (1997). *Teaching with technology.* New York: Teachers College Press.

Owston, R. D. (1997). The World Wide Web: A technology to enhance teaching. *Educational Researcher, 26,* 27-33.

Stables, K. (1997). Critical issues to consider when introducing technology education into the curriculum of young learners. *Journal of Technology Education, 8*(2), 1-13.

Texas Education Agency (1999). *Texas essential knowledge and skills technology application curriculum* [Online]. Available: *http://www.tea.state.tx.us/teks/126toc*

Topping, K. (1997). Electronic literacy in school and home: A look into the future [28 pages]. *Reading Online* [Online serial]. Available: *http://www.readingonline.org* (ERIC Document Reproduction Service No. ED 416437)

Donna Matovinovic
Norma Nocente

Computer Technology
in an Authentic Science Project

SUMMARY. *While a constructivist approach to the integration of technology in the science curriculum can enable teachers to educate students on the cyclical nature of the research process and interrelate various scientific concepts, there are several considerations for educators must take to assure that it is done effectively. The authors provide a review of a project that was designed and implemented for high school science students that integrated the use of technology in a constructivist environment. This review summarizes the strengths and limitations of the project and provides educators with further considerations when implementing such a project. As educators become more familiar with what is required to successfully integrate technology in a constructivist environment, the limitations and obstacles that may be encountered can be limited. More research devoted to the use of computer technology to teach science process skills will bring teachers and students closer to harnessing the potential powers of both project-based learning strategies and the computer environment. [Article copies available for a fee from The Haworth Document Delivery Service: 1-800-342-9678. E-mail address: <getinfo@haworthpressinc.com> Website: <http://www.HaworthPress.com>]*

DONNA MATOVINOVIC is Test Developer, Edmonton Public Schools, Edmonton, Alberta CANADA T6G 2G5.
NORMA NOCENTE is Assistant Professor, Department of Secondary Education, University of Alberta, Edmonton, Alberta CANADA T6G 2G5. E-mail: norma.nocente@ualberta.ca

[Haworth co-indexing entry note]: "Computer Technology in an Authentic Science Project." Matovinovic, Donna, and Norma Nocente. Co-published simultaneously in *Computers in the Schools* (The Haworth Press, Inc.) Vol. 16, No. 3/4, 2000, pp. 109-119; and: *Integration of Technology into the Classroom: Case Studies* (ed: D. LaMont Johnson, Cleborne D. Maddux, and Leping Liu) The Haworth Press, Inc., 2000, pp. 109-119. Single or multiple copies of this article are available for a fee from The Haworth Document Delivery Service [1-800-342-9678, 9:00 a.m. - 5:00 p.m. (EST). E-mail address: getinfo@haworthpressinc.com].

KEYWORDS. Authentic science, authentic problem solving, computers in education, constructivism, critical thinking, science education, technology integration

Computer technology can have a tremendous impact on student learning–or so it seems. How could a tool that has revolutionized so many aspects of society not have an effect on education? Yet an examination of the research in technology in education does not leave one impressed with the gains made in student learning. This lack of evidence to support the integration of technology stems mostly from the fact many classroom applications of technology have not taken advantage of the technology's unique attributes. In addition, to make the best use of technology usually requires a shift from traditional teaching practices. Computer technology is a powerful catalyst for school reform. Not only do the new tools force us to re-examine our teaching practices, they also open new learning opportunities that may impact student learning.

With increased availability of computer technology within the schools and the new technology curricular outcomes that educators are expected to meet, concerns regarding the most effective way to ensure a quality education and integrate technology into the curriculum are raised. Although educators across the curriculum are affected, the implications and concerns facing science educators and their teaching practices will be the primary focus of discussion. In order to address three primary concerns confronting science educators when integrating technology into the curriculum, a project was designed and implemented that will be described in detail later in this discussion.

RATIONALE

The project developed out of the need to address a concern regarding the traditionally ineffective integration of technology in the high school science curriculum. Typically students are simply required to use the Internet to conduct research and perhaps use a presentation tool to describe their findings. These attempts to integrate technology into the classroom do not provide students with an opportunity to deepen their understanding of the scientific process nor do they teach students how technology can aid in scientific discovery. Consequently, a constructivist approach was taken when developing the project. This constructivist approach toward learning ensures that students are actively involved in their own learning in a meaningful way, are encouraged to monitor and reflect upon their own learning, and are continually building upon their prior knowledge base (Simons, 1993).

Creating a constructivist environment using technology enables educators to overcome other barriers facing traditional approaches toward the science curriculum such as student misconceptions regarding a scientific method and the presentation of science concepts outside of a relevant context. A concern facing science teachers is the misrepresentation of the scientific method in traditional approaches to teaching. Conventional methods used to teach science and science textbooks used within the classroom perpetuate the idea that scientific inquiry occurs in a sequential manner (Hodson, 1998a). Hodson states that "the actual chronology of experiment and theory is rewritten in textbooks," helping "to sustain the myth that the path of science is certain and assigns a simple and clear cut role to experimental [processes] thereby assisting the perpetuation of further myths concerning experimental processes (1998, p. 57). Hodson supports the theory that working in a less structured manner is the only way for students to experience authentic scientific investigation. A loosely structured approach was therefore taken in the development of the project to impress upon students the cyclical nature of the scientific process.

Using a constructivist approach towards the integration of technology allows scientific concepts to be interrelated and akin to real life situations (Duffy, Fishman, & Honebein, 1993). Traditionally, concepts tend to be taught in isolation, and students generally are the passive receivers of information rather builders of their own knowledge base (Blumenfeld, Soloway, & Marx, 1991). The project-based approach taken towards science education in the study addresses this final concern. According to Abrams and Wandersee (1995) and Lazarowitz and Tamir (1994) "the goal of enhancing understanding of the nature of science, especially how scientists really work, and the associated goals of developing scientific attitudes and interest in science can be best achieved by project work" (p. 109). Through this project-based approach students are able to see the relationship between concepts (Johnson, Lamb, & Smith, 1997). Students also develop a better understanding of the scientific method because they are involved in authentic research. Authentic scientific investigation involves collecting data that are used to shed light on real-world issues (Lebow & Wagner,

1994). Dealing with real-world issues requires the integration of many concepts from many subject areas. When students are involved in authentic situations, the concepts are contextualized and the connections between them are more apparent. According to Lebow and Wagner, students are then able to transfer their learning to real-life situations (1994). Perkins supports the theory that the use of technology in student learning will ensure this transfer of learning (1991). Consequently, the use of communication and information technology is vital for students participating in authentic research. Being involved in authentic situations, also enables the students to have access to real-world data. A large quantity of data and its subsequent analysis in a classroom situation could not be possible without technology. Hodson (1998) believes that computer technologies "have made it possible for learners to investigate thoroughly their own questions about a whole range of things without the constraints imposed by inadequate laboratory facilities, underdeveloped practical skills, insufficient time, lack of materials or considerations of personal safety" (p. 104).

PROJECT DESCRIPTION

This research involved students in an authentic scientific investigation. The project involved a general science course given to two groups of tenth-grade students in a high school with a science and technology focus. Two groups were required since the school runs on a semester system, and the project in which the students were involved was a year-long study. Both groups of students were involved in similar activities but played different roles in data collection. Students in the first semester were high achievers, while students in the second semester were of average academic ability.

A project based approach was used to integrate two units: weather and plant physiology. Typically these units are taught separately through teacher-centered strategies without the use of computer technology. The project-based learning approach used computer technology as a tool to integrate the weather and plant physiology units and to engage students in more student-centered activities.

The students in this research participated in an Internet project called Plantwatch (*http://www.devonian.ualberta.ca/pwatch/*). In various geographic locations, students observed flowering times for spring plants and reported these dates on the Web site. In the first semester, they were required to travel to various outdoor locations to identify various species of plants and tag them. These tagged plants were to be observed in the spring by the second-semester students. Cumulative data and maps showing the variation in flowering times are available on the site. The data collected are used to monitor the effects of climate change and also helps decision-making in fields such as health, farming, forestry, and tourism. For example, the information on spring flowering is used to provide pollen-warnings for allergy sufferers who are then able to take antihistamines prior to the onslaught of pollen. This long-term research also provides baseline data for studies of how living things respond to climatic change. As students gather data to help monitor the environment, they gain an awareness of maintaining biodiversity.

To supplement the data collection activity, lessons were developed to serve as an introduction to the Plantwatch project and to help students conduct their own data analysis. These activities are briefly described along with a rationale for each. The complete lesson plans are available at *http://www.ualberta.ca/~nnocente/scilessons.*

In the introductory activity, students are asked to identify their own knowledge of the scientific method and to compare it with methods used by Nobel Prize winners in the areas of physics, chemistry, medicine, and peace. Students obtained the information from the Nobel Foundation Web site. The purpose of this activity was to draw a more realistic view of research and scientific methods despite the variance in discipline. At the end of the activity, students found that the terms used to describe the events that occurred in a scientific endeavor were similar, but the order of events itself was quite different depending on the area of study. Students also discovered that the scientific method is not restricted to science but rather is a way of thinking. This way of thinking was exemplified by the description of the research of Nobel Peace Prize winners.

In a follow up activity, students exchanged their new understanding of the scientific method with a scientific researcher. An e-mail discussion allowed students to question an expert, clarify their own understanding, and build upon their own knowledge. These initial activities provided students with a basic understanding of the scientific method and the vocabulary used in what one may call authentic "real-world" scientific inquiry.

In a subsequent activity, students worked in pairs to conduct a scientific inquiry. They were not given a procedure of scientific inquiry to follow. Instead, they had to develop a procedure and note the steps in a journal. Students then completed a concept map to illustrate the sequence of events in their scientific inquiry. One pair of students would then critique another pair's procedure through a blind-review process. This captured the essence of what normally occurs in the scientific world when papers are submitted. A rubric was used to assess the peer reviews. Student performance ranged from average to excellent. Students commented on the freedom aspect of the authentic inquiry process and generally enjoyed it more than the traditional "cookbook" approach to science.

The purpose of these introductory activities was to help students develop a better understanding of the scientific process. The Internet connection gave them access to information that normally would not be found in the library. In addition, since the information on Nobel Prize winners was in electronic format, they could do word searches to help them get right to the section that described a particular process. According to Jonassen (1996), activities such as the ones described above help students to develop critical and creative thinking skills. Critical and creative thinking skills are developed when students are required to assess information, determine criteria, recognize fallacies, imagine a process, plan a process, compare and contrast classroom inquiry practices with "real-world" inquiries, and verify conclusions with a scientific researcher. The collaborative process of this project allowed students to share in the construction of ideas and collaboratively reflect and gain understandings. In this process, peers are viewed as resources rather than competitors.

The following activities were planned to help students' gain a better understanding of the concepts found in the science curriculum while developing computational skills. Internet, database, and spreadsheet activities were designed to engage students in information synthesis and data analysis. Students were then required to form conclusions based upon the data analyzed. In the "What do plants do?" WebQuest activity students were provided with ten pre-selected Internet sites and were asked to synthesize information from the sites to complete a series of questions about plant structure and function. They were also required to determine the effects of specific abiotic factors on the structures and/or functions listed. This activity forced students to access a number of resources to obtain necessary content information since no one site contained all the necessary information. Students then entered this information into a database and were able to perform queries.

In the database activity, students worked with the Plantwatch phenology database. Phenology is the study of the seasonal timing of life cycle events: The database records contain the dates of the first and full bloom of eight plant species that leaf out in response to warming temperatures in the spring. These data were also entered into a second database that contained a brief description of the topography of the area where each sample plant was located, the temperature readings at the time of each first and full bloom, and the readings of the corresponding carbon dioxide and ozone levels. Students were then asked to make predictions concerning the effects of carbon dioxide, ozone levels, temperature, and/or the location of the plant sampled on first and full bloom dates. They sorted the data and queried the database to look for trends. Based on the information found in the database, it was intended that students discover the relationship between abiotic factors and the plant structures' response to certain conditions.

In the spreadsheet activity, students formed conclusions based on available data collected in the "What do plants do?" and "Weather Effect Database" activities. They then established an argument to defend the rationale behind their conclusions. Students created a series of graphs that represented particular relationships. These relationships became evident as students queried the databases. Students derived their own understanding of phenology by calculating the averages for different sets of data, constructing graphs to represent the data, and generating conclusions based on the data analysis. In addition, students were engaged in a class discussion regarding the conclusions generated and were asked to comment on the strengths and/or weaknesses of the conclusions drawn, based on the generated graphs. In this activity, students were able to represent on a spreadsheet the various relationships between concepts and their understanding of these relationships.

EVALUATION OF THE PROJECT

The notion of presenting authentic science projects is not new, but because of computer technology these projects have become more feasible. In this situation students are actually contributing to data that will be used by the researcher. In fact the data collected by the students is of primary importance to the researcher. The computer technology used during the project enabled students to form meaning out of the data collected and identify relationships among concepts.

The participating teacher and students provided feedback on the project and the role of computer technology. Students appreciated the ease of data retrieval, the pre-selected sites for Internet research, and the organizational and analytical powers of both database and spreadsheet programs. In this project Web sites were downloaded to create an Intranet, thus ensuring site access and speed.

The teacher commented that the project helped to engage students and enabled them to have access to information normally inaccessible. Students were then able to analyze this information. Students learned new science concepts and at the same time developed computer skills. In addition, these students were exposed to new teaching strategies that promote collaborative learning and reflection. The teacher recommended that the students who were new to using a database be asked to perform a simple sort activity only. This recommendation was especially pertinent to most of the second-semester group.

Although it appeared that the project was successful in achieving its goals, we would not claim it a huge success. Several limitations were experienced during the project. Despite the fact that these students attended a technologically equipped school and many had previously taken an information-processing course, many students lacked simple and basic computational skills. For example, many students did not understand the simple function of a database, even though they could query and sort information. The tension experienced by students when trying to learn computer skills, while simultaneously attempting to understand the courses content, detracted from the overall value of the course content. Students became frustrated with the computer technology, and the technology often acted as a roadblock to the learning process.

Students also experienced difficulties synthesizing information in order to draw conclusions. In order to exercise high-level thinking skills such as problem solving or synthesis of information, students first need guidance to help them make the transition from low to medium to high levels of thinking. Without this initial guidance, many students did not have the skills to solve context-based, real-world problems.

Students were so used to traditional teaching strategies and assignments that they had difficulty adjusting to a constructivist environment. Students must therefore be gradually integrated into a constructivist classroom and taught how to operate within that environment (Simons, 1993). Providing students with mini-lessons conducted within a constructivist framework prior to introduction of an intensive project may be a solution.

The high school structure itself proved to inhibit the growth and effectiveness of the project. Difficulty finding available computer lab space and the students' semester-based timetable proved to be limitations. For example, second-semester students missed the plant data collection because the trees came into bloom over the week-long school spring holiday.

Although contributing to the Plantwatch project involved students in an authentic scientific investigation, it was not particularly meaningful to them. Some students found the information boring and irrelevant to them on a personal level. To be a truly authentic problem-solving situation students need to generate the research questions and methodology.

Many factors such as the instructional design of a particular task and a student's attitude toward computer technology may also influence student achievement. To overcome barriers such as negative student attitudes, long-term implementation is critical. Students need time to become familiar with the computer applications and to learn how to use their thinking skills to manipulate the software in order to address task objectives. In addition, students need to have many positive experiences using computer technology in an educational setting in order to develop a positive attitude toward using computers to achieve educational objectives.

LIMITATIONS OF THE PROJECT

In addition to limitations of available lab space, the lack of high-order student thinking skills, and the lack of student interest in the subject areas studied, the project's success faced still other obstacles. The teacher cited several technical drawbacks of using computer technology in general. In addition to a lack of available computer lab space, time was needed to evaluate what software the network could support. Ensuring that data was always available for student use and the amount of time the teacher spent troubleshooting rather than assisting with student learning proved to be difficulties.

Not only were students ill-prepared in terms of their technical skills, the teacher had to become proficient in the use of the computer software programs that made up the computer components of the activities. This was no easy task and took many hours of reading how-to manuals before the teacher was comfortable enough with the software to integrate it into the project. In addition to understanding the actual software, the teacher had to determine the most effective way to integrate it into the curriculum. The teacher also had to determine the appropriate software to use for each activity.

In addition to the time devoted to project planning, preparation, and software training, it became apparent that the project-based learning strategy would take more instructional hours than the traditional approach.

The accurate assessment of student learning in a constructivist environment also had its limitations. Challenges were faced when designing an assessment tool that measures the knowledge and skills acquired by students throughout the project. Much of what the students learned could not be captured by standard assessment techniques, so new methods of evaluation such as rubric assessment were developed.

CONCLUSION

While a constructivist approach to the integration of technology in the science curriculum can enable teachers to educate students on the cyclical nature of the research process and interrelate various scientific concepts, there are several considerations that educators must bear in mind to ensure that it is done effectively. As educators become more familiar with what is required to successfully integrate technology in a constructivist environment, the limitations and obstacles may be overcome. More research devoted to the use of computer technology to teach science process skills will bring teachers and students closer to harnessing the potential powers of both project-based learning strategies and the computer environment. According to Reil, "New tools alone do not create educational change. The power is not in the tool but in the community that can be brought together and the collective vision that they share for redefining classroom learning" (1990, p. 35).

REFERENCES

Abrams E., & Wandersee, J. (1995). How to infuse actual scientific research practices into science classroom instruction. *International Journal of Science Education*, *17*(6), 683-694.

Bartolo, L., & Palffy-Muhoray, P. (1998). SAM-Net (SCIENCE and MATH on the Net): Connecting students and teachers to scientific research through scientific communication and electronic networking. *Journal of Computers in Mathematics and Science Teaching*, *17*(2/3), 133-147.

Barab, S., Hay, K., & Duffy, T. (1998, March). Grounded constructions and how technology can help. *Techtrends*, pp. 15-23.

Blumenfeld, P., Soloway, E., & Marx, R.A. (1991). Motivating project based learning: Sustaining the doing, supporting the learner. *Educational Psychologist*, *26*(3/4), 369-398.

Duffy, T., Fishman, B., & Honebein, P. (1993) "Constructivism and the Design of Learning Environments: Context and Authentic Activities for Learning." In Thomas Duffy, Thomas Lowyck, and David Jonassen (Eds.) *Designing Environments for Constructive Learning*. Berlin: Springer-Verlag, 87-108.

Hodson, D. (1998). Is this really what scientists do? In J. Wellington (Ed.), *Practical work in school science* (pp. 93-108). London: Rutledge.

Hodson, D. (1988a). Experiments in science and science teaching. *Educational Philosophy and Theory*, *20*, 53-66.

Jonassen, D.H. (1996). *Computers in the Classroom*. New Jersey: Prentice-Hall.

Johnson, L., Lamb, A., & Smith, N. (1997). Wondering, wiggling, and weaving: A new model for project-and community-based learning on the Web. *Learning and Leading with Technology*, *24*(7), 6-13.

Lafer, S. (1997). Audience, elegance, and learning via the Internet. *Computers in the Schools*, *13* (1/2), 89-97.

Lazarowitz, R., & Tamir, P. (1994). Research on using laboratory instruction in science. In Gabel, D.L., (Ed.), *Handbook of research on science teaching and learning* (pp.94-128). New York: Macmillan.

Lebow, D., & Wagner, W. (1994, Winter). Authentic activity as a model for appropriate learning activity: Implications for emerging instructional technologies. *Canadian Journal of Educational Communication*, *23*, 231-244

Liu, X., MacMillan, R., Timmons, V. (1998). Integration of computers into the curriculum: How teachers may hinder students' use of computers. *McGill Journal of Education*, *32*(3), 51-69.

Perkins, D.N. (1991, May). Technology meets constructivism: Do they make a marriage? *Educational Technology*, *13*, 18-23.

Riel, M. (1990 January/February). Building a new foundation for global communities. *The Writing Notebook*, (January/February), pp. 35-37.

Simons, R. (1993). Constructive learning: The role of the learner. In Thomas Duffy, Thomas Lowyck, & David Jonassen (Eds.) *Designing environments for constructive learning* (pp. 291-311). Berlin: Springer-Verlag, 291-311.

Michele Stafford-Levy
Karin M. Wiburg

Multicultural Technology Integration: The Winds of Change Amid the Sands of Time

SUMMARY. *This case study describes how a teacher in a poor border community in southern New Mexico combined technology-based teaching strategies she had learned in a professional development grant with multicultural elements to ensure learning and equitable access to technology for her minority students. [Article copies available for a fee from The Haworth Document Delivery Service: 1-800-342-9678. E-mail address: <getinfo@haworthpressinc.com> Website: <http://www.HaworthPress.com>]*

KEYWORDS. *Multicultural technology, ESL/Bilingual Education and technology, one-computer classroom, professional development, secondary Language Arts tech integration*

MICHELE STAFFORD-LEVY is Teacher/Curriculum Facilitator for Santa Teresa High School and Santa Teresa Middle School in the Gadsden Independent School District, Anthony, NM 88003. E-mail: wrrm@flash.net
KARIN M. WIBURG is Associate Professor and Coordinator of the Educational Learning Technology graduate program, New Mexico State University. She also co-directs the La Clave Professional Development Program in Gadsden, MS-3CUR Dept. of Curriculum and Instruction, Las Cruces, NM 88003. E-mail: kwiburg@nmsu.edu

[Haworth co-indexing entry note]: "Multicultural Technology Integration: The Winds of Change Amid the Sands of Time." Stafford-Levy, Michele, and Karin M. Wiburg. Co-published simultaneously in *Computers in the Schools* (The Haworth Press, Inc.) Vol. 16, No. 3/4, 2000, pp. 121-134; and: *Integration of Technology into the Classroom: Case Studies* (ed: D. LaMont Johnson, Cleborne D. Maddux, and Leping Liu) The Haworth Press, Inc., 2000, pp. 121-134. Single or multiple copies of this article are available for a fee from The Haworth Document Delivery Service [1-800-342-9678, 9:00 a.m. - 5:00 p.m. (EST). E-mail address: getinfo@haworthpressinc.com].

121

Que Barrio?
I hear the vatos say
Que barrio?
As if it makes a difference any way.
My tierra, tu tierra,
What difference does it make?
We are all the misma sangre
When I look into your Indio face.
Que barrio?
What's the fuss all about?
Mi 'mano is you!
But then the homies shout
Que Barrio?
We are all alive and must agree
La raza vive! Let's change history!

–Stafford-Levy

Stafford-Levy (1999) wrote this poem for her students about the battles within the barrios that happen on the border. This border metaphor (Villenas, 1996) also applies to academics and their various battles to keep their identities while participating in higher education and struggling amid different educational philosophies and changing paradigms. Part of this paradigmatic change involves tackling the new technology in the classroom.

As a language arts teacher in a border community, Stafford-Levy tries to inspire her students to become empowered by modeling new teaching practices. In her high school class, her teaching style is radically different from most of what her students have experienced in previous classes. This case study describes how she combines meaningful literature with a project approach to technology integration (Wiburg, 1997).

DANGEROUS DUALITIES
FOR LANGUAGE MINORITY STUDENTS

The high school class in this case study is located in a poor, dusty desert community in southern New Mexico. For the most part, the students here are the children of recent immigrants and are bilingual/bicultural. An enormous duality exists for them in that they speak

Spanish at home and English at school. Wong-Filmore (1991) warns educators that this dichotomy can create an enormous gulf between parents and children, grandparents and grandchildren–even alienation from the family. Moll and Greenberg (1992) studied Latino communities and found vast "funds of knowledge" related to science, mathematics, and social studies; yet these funds of knowledge have gone untapped in the school curriculum (Moll, Arlmanti, Neff, & Gonzales, 1992; Wiburg, 1998).

In this case study, Stafford-Levy integrated technology and culturally responsive pedagogy to ensure equitable opportunities for success for all of her students. The model used for doing this was based on the work of Chisholm (1998), who advocates the inclusion of six elements when integrating technology in multicultural classrooms: cultural awareness, cultural relevance, a culturally supportive environment, equitable access, instructional flexibility, and instructional integration. In her article, Chisholm invited other educators to apply these six elements to the design of learning environments for diverse students. We used this conceptual framework to guide technology integration in Stafford-Levy's classroom. This project was also grounded in technology integration strategies learned from a professional development initiative in the district.

Through a grant from New Mexico State University (Wiburg, Huerta-Macias, Trost, & Lozano, 1999), 36 hours of teacher training on technology integration was provided to teachers, including Stafford-Levy, in a rural border district near the university. Training in the use of technology in culturally responsive and constructivist ways preceded a planned large acquisition of hardware. Thus staff development occurred before the planned purchase of computers for all schools. However, the professional development grant, *La Clave Para Mejorar* (The Key to Improvement) provided Stafford-Levy with two computers for her classroom. Using these computers, she then faced the complex task of integrating the six multicultural elements with constructivist uses of technology in the English literature classroom. Fortunately, the grant also provided information on how to manage technology integration in the one-to-four computer classroom. This case study describes how Stafford-Levy combined the technology-based teaching strategies she had learned in this professional development effort with multicultural elements to ensure equitable access to computers for her underrepresented students.

INJECTING TECHNOLOGY

Teacher training and development are vital for teachers who are transitioning from having been schooled one way and now need to impart the new skills needed for the twenty-first century (Fulton, 1995; ISTE, 1999). Most educators and academics are familiar with the current ideologies that espouse learner-centered classrooms that are collaborative in nature, project-based, and question-driven; however, they have not been assisted in tying these strategies to the use of technology. Nor have they integrated technology from a multicultural perspective. La Clave Para Mejorar is a multi-year systemic initiative designed to build expertise in this district and funded through the Technology Literacy Challenge fund. Wiburg co-directs the La Clave project with the Assistant Superintendent of Instruction, Yvonne Lozano, for the schools in this border district. The project provides teachers opportunities to learn in-depth technology integration within a constructivist and culturally responsive pedagogy. Teams from all 17 schools in the district–six teachers, a curriculum facilitator, and the technology lab person–attend monthly workshops. All of the district's principals also received technology-integration training.

Of all the workshops Stafford-Levy attended she found the information on how to juggle thirty kids and one computer most enlightening and she immediately implemented the project-center approach. There were no computers available for English classes in her high school at the time this case study began, but Stafford-Levy was able to use the two La Clave computers she was awarded. However, she admits that it was very frightening to try out new ideas at first–especially when "I was schooled one way and yet practicing another." She also worried that it might be hard to utilize technology and a project-approach in her field of language arts. "Prior to my training, I simply believed that projects were relegated to the science classes and I thought that English literature didn't lend itself to such a concept."

With the technology strategies learned, the classroom curriculum was another aspect that required scrutiny. Wiburg (1998) noted that our classrooms reflect increasingly diverse populations:

> The curriculum used in most public schools is based on materials and instructional strategies developed in the first half of the twentieth century, when nearly three-fourths of all students were

European Americans (Pallas et al., 1989) and the country's human resources needs were the product of an industrial rather than
information age. (p. 269)

Wiburg goes on to say that the current curriculum is entirely inappropriate for Latino students. Stafford-Levy echoes these sentiments
with the innovative curriculum and classroom management with
which she integrated technology.

INTEGRATING TECHNOLOGY
IN A MULTICULTURAL CLASSROOM

Chisholm's framework for integrating multicultural elements was
connected in the classroom to what had been learned in the La Clave
project. The elements–cultural awareness, cultural relevance, culturally
supported environments, instructional integration, instructional flexibility, and equity–will now be addressed.

Cultural awareness in this study was defined as providing students
with full exposure to technology, including all the potentialities that
using technology implies. In most cases, language minority students
have used technology in limited ways (Wetzel & Chisholm, 1998)
such as for drill and practice rather than for student-directed productive activity. A project-based approach utilizing technology was used
in order to make the state-mandated literature curriculum more culturally relevant for bilingual/bicultural high school students in a Southwest border community. Stafford-Levy used her language arts classroom as the venue for change in the face of adversity, poverty, and
minimal technology infrastructure. She created a culturally supportive
environment by encouraging her students to bring their life experiences into her democratic classroom.

CONSTRUCTIVIST CLASSROOMS
AND INSTRUCTIONAL INTEGRATION

Technology use in any classroom is most powerful if tied to inquiry
learning using the content being studied. In order for this to be
achieved, it is incumbent upon educators to integrate constructivist
designs that allow students to explore, question, and discover. Wi-

burg and Norton (1998) state "constructivist notions of learning start with a simple proposition: Individuals construct their own under-standing of the world in which they live" (p. 29). In this case study, Stafford-Levy integrated a constructivist philosophy in order for her Mexican-American high school students to bridge their rich local experience with an increased awareness of the world through English literature. This is related to one of Chisholm's elements, *instructional integration*, which she defines as the "degree to which technology becomes an integral part of classroom learning, student productivity, and information gathering for all learners across a variety of academic disciplines" (p. 261). This constructivist approach framed within the context of the multicultural classroom creates meaningful experiences for all learners, but especially for minorities and second-language learners.

In this case study, students were required to read literature by the Puritans, the Romantics, and the Realists. They were faced with Hawthorne, Melville, Emerson, Thoreau, and the like. In order for her students to find meaning in what they were reading, Stafford-Levy elaborated on the universal themes in the stories. Nevertheless, it was still difficult to motivate students to connect with the traditional English curriculum. She asserts that technology and the project-based model have helped her address the problem. Prior to having the computers placed in Stafford-Levy's classroom, she admits that the kids sat in rows, reading out of thick literature books, filling out handouts ("dittos"), and writing (by hand) responses to the traditional great works they read.

However, this particular border educator felt that significant pieces of Chicano literature were also an essential read for her students. The project-based use of technology supported the integration of more culturally relevant material including works in Chicano literature such as Cisneros' *House on Mango Street*, Anaya's *Bless Me Ultima*, and (her mother) Lopez-Stafford's *A Place in El Paso*. Students were able to respond to the literature by writing in electronic journals about the meaningful works they read. According to Stafford-Levy, "Meaningful literature coupled with today's technology has changed all the previous monotony for me." She is using a classroom management technique known as the project center approach (Wiburg, 1997) that was modeled for her in the training she received through the university/public school La Clave project. Here is an example of how a project-based approach, utilizing technology, was implemented in her junior literature class.

CENTERS AND ENGLISH LITERATURE

Stafford-Levy claims that,

> After integrating a discovery approach into my class, I created and witnessed the most exciting lessons. Designing them meant a lot of leg work and *preparation*: rifling through my files, bringing in a truck full of books from our school library for extended learning, running off handouts and discussion articles, consulting the teacher's edition for relevant questions. These new lessons lasted two weeks! What a shift in thinking! However, once you lay out the map (by using a Check Sheet), you step back and watch your students' journey of learning unfold. (Field Notes, 1999)

The way the project center is set up provides students with considerable *instructional flexibility*–another one of Chisholm's elements for technology integration in a diverse setting. With the project center approach for the one computer classroom, a check sheet of tasks for each student is provided. Students move through the centers at their own pace. Of course, the idea of "centers" is borrowed from Montessori (1992) who utilized the discovery method by setting up manipulative centers for children to independently explore. An abbreviated example of one of Stafford-Levy's project center Check Sheets is shown in Figure 1.

Teachers who have recast themselves as facilitators remind the learners that the teacher is now the project supervisor. Students relate to the idea of completing tasks in the workplace and gain school to work skills. After visiting each center, students check off the completed task and move to the next center. All tasks are completed at the student's own pace, contributing to a lower affective filter (Krashen, 1973) and increased learning opportunities. The project supervisor/ teacher holds a conference with each student halfway through the centers and at the end of the project for a final check off and evaluation. This classroom strategy facilitates the process of moving toward richer forms of assessment for diverse students. In the next year,

FIGURE 1
Stafford-Levy's Project Center Check Sheet.

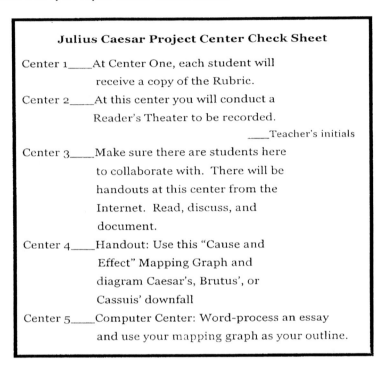

Julius Caesar Project Center Check Sheet

Center 1____At Center One, each student will
             receive a copy of the Rubric.

Center 2____At this center you will conduct a
             Reader's Theater to be recorded.
                                    ____Teacher's initials

Center 3____Make sure there are students here
             to collaborate with. There will be
             handouts at this center from the
             Internet. Read, discuss, and
             document.

Center 4____Handout: Use this "Cause and
             Effect" Mapping Graph and
             diagram Caesar's, Brutus', or
             Cassuis' downfall

Center 5____Computer Center: Word-process an essay
             and use your mapping graph as your outline.

Stafford-Levy plans to have her students help design the rubrics that will be used for center tasks. This exemplifies Chisholm's element of equity. The conference between teacher and student is available to all students and, in Stafford-Levy's classroom, each student has equitable access to the computer as a center.

INSTRUCTIONAL FLEXIBILITY

There are several things Stafford-Levy recommends that should be included in the centers in order to support instructional flexibility. The project center approach can utilize all the different modalities of learning (Gardner, 1993, p. 15). First, there needs to be a writing component for students to word process on the computer, where the computer station serves as a writing center. Second, there should be some sort of art project to supplement the lesson: drawing with chalk, painting, cutting and pasting, creating a *collage* from magazines. Stafford-Levy maintains that all learners enjoy relief from the linear work of reading and writing, and so she incorporates an art center in her language arts class. Third, there should be some sort of communication component integrated into the lesson: giving a speech or presentation, discussing an article, recording a radio show on cassette, or filming on video a dramatic interpretation. Performance is an important component of Stafford-Levy's redesigned classroom lessons. Incorporating all the different discourse forms that support the various learning styles is at the very heart of multicultural education. Stafford-Levy has a variety of project centers–from Poe to Poetry. The following is an example of Stafford-Levy's project center on Edgar Alan Poe.

FROM POE TO POETRY

The most powerful work emerges from students who are inspired to work. They want to work, they write what they know about, and they write about what is meaningful and empowering (Freire, 1976) for them and their community. Stafford-Levy believes that the project center approach for technology integration in the one-to-four computer classroom lends itself to a low-risk, nonthreatening environment. It allows students to think critically at their own pace in a collaborative environment and, more importantly, as independent learners.

Stafford-Levy has created many literature units–Shakespeare, Melville, L'Amour, Cisneros, Bradbury–and an original poetry unit. Her students sit in regular student desks, and they face each other in clusters of about six chairs that serve as centers. In the middle of each cluster is a folder labeled with the center number. The computer center has a host of possible activities: from Internet searches to authoring multimedia presentations. The Edgar Alan Poe project center is an example of the variety of activities one can craft with this approach to learning with technology in the multicultural classroom.

Stafford-Levy usually has her class study Poe around Halloween, and she says that a lot of excitement is generated with this unit.

> For me, the very name of Edgar Alan Poe conjures up images and so by creating an atmosphere in my class, I attempt to set

the stage for this unit. I darken the windows with black plastic tablecloths and project Poe's image on the wall with the aid of an overhead projector and a transparency of him. (Field Notes, 1998)

She teaches how Poe mastered the mystery and how we still use his formula to this day. Students travel from center to center reading his various works: *The Raven, Annabelle Lee, The Fall of the House of Usher, The Masque of the Red Death*. Each work center will have an activity to supplement the learning. For example, there will be a listening center for *The Fall of the House of Usher* where students can listen to a dramatic interpretation on cassette of this great work. Another example involves students designing t-shirts for *The Masque of the Red Death* after they've read this story. At *The Raven* center, they can join the Raven Society by logging onto the Web site. This center allows students to complete certificates of membership after they have read this piece by Poe. At another center students can visit the Web site about Poe, the man. Here, all the rumors of his alleged drug addiction are dispelled. His publicist spread those rumors about him after his death. Stafford-Levy feels it is very important in this day and age to convey to the kids from the barrio that Poe's genius was not drug-induced. Students are encouraged to explore this Web site and take a virtual tour of his home in Baltimore, Maryland. At the end of this two-week journey, the teacher gives the students a chance to play the game Clue for extended learning. By playing this game, students have an opportunity to watch all the elements of the mystery in action.

> The Poe Center is extremely exciting and I handle Julius Caesar by Shakespeare the same way–with all of their studies culminating in a video production of the play. This dramatic interpretation places the play in the barrio and the background music for their play is done to the beat of a Rap tune. I use the project center approach with all of the units that I teach and the students really enjoy learning and I enjoy teaching. (Field Notes, 1999)

After using the Poe center and a center for developing poetry, her students began to increase their writing and communication skills.

Following is an original poem by Stafford-Levy's student Ana Ramirez (age 16):

Across
A fierce river they have
to cross
Risking their lives for a
simple job
Drowning on their way across
What a sad way to die
Once they're over the other
side
some make it others
are caught
Those who are caught
are beaten
Others are sent back
With thoughts of trying again
Others never make it Back
to either side alive

Nevertheless, Stafford-Levy says she has encountered barriers along the way.

RECOMMENDATIONS

As educators, we know that teaching high school can be challenging and that all classrooms have their problems. Some of the dilemmas that Stafford-Levy has reported lie with the various personalities of her students. She claims that some of the students are from different gangs or they hold grudges against one another and will not work with their alleged "enemy." So what this particular educator had to do to help the process along was to place all the folders and materials in a neutral zone–in the middle of the room on a long table. Students came to this table to get the materials they needed and then went back to their permanently clustered seating arrangement.

Another problem that arose was that some students could not handle the freedom that the project center allowed. Stafford-Levy says, "I have to circulate frequently. I make sure that my students are on task. I'll find students chatting about life or what went on over the weekend, but don't all teachers encounter this?" Yet, this teacher finds it easier to get kids back on task when there are a variety of tasks that can be done–many with the support of technology.

Another obstacle that Stafford-Levy had to overcome was the very heavy textbook. She says,

> The cumbersome textbook became a real problem because lockers are a thing of the past and backpacks (with all of those problems) are the current trend at most high schools. I was inspired by the movie *Stand and Deliver* and gave the students a copy of the text for home and made a class set available to them during class time.

This could be problematic for those schools who cannot afford to do this, but Stafford-Levy is fortunate that there are extra books for her students and she claims that this works well for her particular group. She goes on to say, "We don't have much, but books–we've got."

CONCLUSION

Norton and Gonzales (1998) summarily state,

> Technology is a powerful tool to support inquiry-based learn-ing–learning that is constructivist, that values conceptual under-standing over procedural efficiency, that is responsive to stu-dents' prior knowledge and experience, that builds connections to the outside world, that supports development of higher think-ing skills, that prepares for lifelong learning, and that promotes educational equity. (p. 39)

Although this seems like a tall order, Stafford-Levy, with the sup-port of a project that provided continuous professional development in a poor, rural district, has demonstrated that technology can be success-fully integrated in a multicultural high school classroom. Professional development played an important role in that successful integration. Fulton (1996) and Grant (1996) agree that in order to create these successful learning environments for students, teachers need experi-ence with inquiry-based learning. For second-language learners, it is critical. It is evident that ongoing professional development must provide educators with opportunities to actually implement the new skills (Norton & Gonzales, 1998). When used in the context of the multicultural classroom, technology can be used to support and enhance the learning process (Gonzales, 1992). Gonzales asserts that multicultural and language minority classrooms often lag behind in terms of access to advanced technology use. The approach Stafford-Levy has used in her diverse classroom has provided powerful, student-centered uses of technology. Technology helped integrate students' life experiences into the curriculum while also providing students access to the wider world of literature. Through literature students began to know the world. The project approach to technology integration, like all classroom strategies, posed challenges for Stafford-Levy. It is hoped that sharing those obstacles and how they were resolved will help educators to use technology in ways that empower all students. La Pointe (1988) states:

> Technology, if used knowledgeably, can both help provide equal and educational opportunity for all children as well as facilitate high academic achievement. But, before technology can have a real effect, teachers, principals, superintendents, and school boards, etc., must reach a consensus on the details of what we want it to do and how to do it. (p. 32)

As we have seen in this case study, technological integration is being successfully accomplished through a culturally responsive project approach to technology integration. We are sharing this story in the hope that more teachers will use technology to make their classrooms more exciting, democratic, meaningful, and equitable.

REFERENCES

Chisholm, I. M. (1998). Six elements for technology integration in multicultural classrooms. *Journal of Information Technology Education, 7*, 247-268.

Fulton, K. (1996). Moving from boxes and wires to 21st century teaching. *T.H.E. Journal, 24*, 76-82.

Freire, P. (1976). *Pedagogy of the oppressed*. New York, NY: Continuum.

Gardner, H. (1993). *Frames of mind: The theory of multiple intelligences* (10th Anniversary Ed.) New York, NY: Basic Books.

Gonzales, C. (1992). *Technology in multicultural teacher and student development*. Unpublished paper, University of New Mexico, Albuquerque.

Grant, C. M. (1996). Professional development in a technological age: New definition, old challenges, new resources. TERC. [Online]. Available: *http://ra.terc.edu/
alliance_resources_services/reform/tech-infusion/prof_dev/*

International Society for Technology in Education (1999). Will new teachers be
prepared to teach in a digital age? A National Survey on Information Technology
in Teacher Education. New York, NY: Milken Exchange.

Krashen, S. (1973). Lateralization, language learning, and the critical period: Some
new evidence. *Language Learning, 23*, 63-74.

La Pointe, A., & Martinez, M. (1988). Aims, equity, and access in Computer Education. *Phi Delta Kappan, 70*(1), 59-61.

Levy, M. (1999). Que barrio? *Warrior Weavings Literary Magazine (6)*, 25.

Montessori, M. (1948). *The secret of childhood*. New York, NY: Ballentine Books.

Moll, L., & Greenberg, J. B. (1992). Creating zones possibilities: Combining social
contexts for instruction. In L. Moll (Ed.) *Vygotsky and education: Instructional
implications and applications of socio-historical psychology* (pp. 319-348). New
York, NY: Cambridge UP.

Moll, L., Arlmanti, C., Neff, D., & Gonzales, N. (1992). Funds of knowledge for
teaching: Using a qualitative approach to connect homes and classrooms. *Theory
into Practice, 31*(2), 132-141.

Norton, P., & Gonzales, C. (1998). RETA-Regional Educational Technology Assistance initiative–Phase II: Evaluating a model for statewide professional development. *Journal of Research on Computing in Education, 31*, 25-48.

Pallas, M., Natriello, G., & McDill, E. I. (1989). Changing nature of the disadvantaged population: Current dimensions and future trends. *Educational Researcher,
19*(5), 16-22.

Villenas, S. (1996). The colonizer/colonized chicana ethnographer: Identity mar-
ginalized, and co-optation in the field. *Harvard Educational Review, 66*, 711-731.

Wetzel, K. (1998). An evaluation of technology integration in teacher education for
bilingual education and English as a second language education majors. *Journal
of Research on Computing Education, 30*, 379-397.

Wiburg, K. (1997). The dance of change: Integrating technology in the classrooms.
Computers in the Schools, 13, 171-183.

Wiburg, K., Huerta-Macias, A., Trost, M., & Lozano, Y. (1999, April). *La Clave
Para Mejorar*. Paper presented at the annual conference of the American Educational Research Association (AERA), Montreal, Canada

Wiburg, K., & Norton, P. (1998). *Teaching with technology*. Orlando, FL: Harcourt
Brace.

Wiburg, K. (1998). Literacy instruction for middle-school Latinos. In A. Huerta-Macias & M. Gonzales (Eds.), *Exemplary practices for Latinos in middle schools*
(pp. 269-287). Lancaster, PA: Technomic.

Wong-Filmore, L. (1991). When gaining a second language means losing the first.
Early Childhood Research Quarterly, 6, 323-346.

Jacqueline K. Bowman
Hari P. Koirala
Linda Espinoza Edmonds
Marsha Davis

Graphing Calculators: Critical Tools for Actively Teaching Math and Science

SUMMARY. *This article describes how a teacher changed her method of teaching after acquiring knowledge about graphing calculators in a*

JACQUELINE K. BOWMAN is Assistant Professor, Education Department, Eastern Connecticut State University, 83 Windham St., Willimantic, CT 06226. E-mail: bowmanj@ecsu.ctstateu.edu

HARI P. KOIRALA is Assistant Professor, Education Department, Eastern Connecticut State University, 83 Windham St., Willimantic, CT 06226. E-mail: koiralah@ecsu.ctstateu.edu

LINDA ESPINOZA EDMONDS is Teacher, Windham Middle School, 123 Quarry Street, Willimantic, CT 06226. E-mail: edmondsteach@yahoo.com

MARSHA DAVIS is Professor, Mathematics and Computer Science Department, Eastern Connecticut State University, 83 Windham St., Willimantic, CT 06226. E-mail: davisma@ecsu.ctstateu.edu

The authors are thankful to the Connecticut Department of Higher Education for the grant and to NASA for allowing us to use their materials for the workshops. The authors would also like to thank our teachers without whom this project would not be possible. This project was funded by a grant from the Eisenhower Professional Development Program.

[Haworth co-indexing entry note]: "Graphing Calculators: Critical Tools for Actively Teaching Math and Science." Bowman, Jacqueline K. et al. Co-published simultaneously in *Computers in the Schools* (The Haworth Press, Inc.) Vol. 16, No. 3/4, 2000, pp. 135-149; and: *Integration of Technology into the Classroom: Case Studies* (ed: D. LaMont Johnson, Cleborne D. Maddux, and Leping Liu) The Haworth Press, Inc., 2000, pp. 135-149. Single or multiple copies of this article are available for a fee from The Haworth Document Delivery Service [1-800-342-9678, 9:00 a.m. - 5:00 p.m. (EST). E-mail address: getinfo@haworthpressinc.com].

135

professional development program. It describes one particular unit on understanding variables and graph interpretation taught in a seventh-grade science and math class. The use of graphing calculators proved to be effective in increasing student understanding of relationships between variables, graphing, and experimental design. The teacher in our project also found graphing calculators to be effective tools for teaching constructively. Our study implies that math and science teaching can be improved through the use of graphing calculators. [Article copies available for a fee from The Haworth Document Delivery Service: 1-800-342-9678. E-mail address: <getinfo@haworthpressinc.com> Website: <http://www.HaworthPress.com>]

KEYWORDS. *Graphing calculators, technology integration, graphing, variables, math, science, teacher change, constructivist teaching*

The need to help teachers develop their ability to integrate computer technology into the teaching of mathematics and science in schools is well recognized and often reported (Balacheff & Kaput, 1996; Battista & Lambdin, 1994). Other forms of technology, such as the graphing calculator, have received less emphasis, especially in middle schools. In order for the graphing calculator to become a common tool, students must develop facility with its use during their middle school years. Because teachers themselves have not experienced graphing technology supported learning, they have a difficult time using graphing calculators to enhance students' conceptual understanding of mathematics and science. The graphing calculator has only recently become an inexpensive and readily available technological tool, and many teachers lack proficiency in using it in their classrooms. Teachers will be more willing to use new forms of technology in their classrooms only when they have had learning experiences with it (Sarama, Clements, & Henry, 1998).

In order to help teachers increase their use of technology, we developed an Eisenhower project, Integrating Mathematics, Science, and Technology Education Through the Physics of Space. Integration of mathematics and science teaching in middle schools through the use of technology was the main theme of our Eisenhower project. During the course of this project, teachers were provided with the time to develop their expertise using graphing calculators and to develop units in compliance with The National Mathematics and Science Standards (National Council of Teachers of Mathematics, 1989; National Research

Council of the National Academy of Sciences, 1996). The Eisenhower project began in May of 1998 and continued through August 1999. During that time, we offered two week-long summer workshops, two afternoon workshops, and curriculum support throughout the year. One of the major goals of the project was to foster teacher expertise, confidence, and skill in using graphing calculators.

A total of 25 upper-elementary and middle school teachers from area school districts participated in the workshops. Even though these were experienced mathematics and science teachers, only five of them had basic graphing-calculator skills. The other 20 teachers had only heard about graphing calculators but had never used them in their classrooms. One of the teachers in the Eisenhower project, Linda Espinoza Edmonds, was extremely enthusiastic about the possibility of using graphing calculators in her classroom. Her enthusiasm for the use of technology led us to choose her and her classroom for an in-depth study. This paper will describe the effectiveness of graphing calculators in Linda's seventh-grade science and math classroom.

LINDA'S BACKGROUND

Linda Espinoza Edmonds is a knowledgeable teacher with five years of teaching experience. She teaches seventh- and eighth-grade math, science, and Spanish. Since she entered our graduate program at Eastern Connecticut State University in 1996, she has altered her view of teaching from lecture-based to activity-based. Linda now believes in a constructivist approach to learning, in which "knowledge is not simply transferred from teacher to student or from textbook to student. Students build their own explanations and ideas" (Schulte, 1996, p. 26). Her beliefs have led her to adopt a hands-on approach to teaching that includes the integration of technology. One of her fundamental beliefs is that middle school students need to develop a deep understanding of science process skills (Rezba, Sprague, Fiel, & Funk, 1995). She is a risk-taker and firmly believes in the right of students to understand math and science concepts through exploration and discovery.

Linda taught at an urban/suburban school in eastern Connecticut. For the purpose of this study we examined her seventh-grade science class. The class consisted of 22 students, most of whom were average and above-average academically. Three students in this class were identified as students with special needs. Sixteen of these students were also in Linda's math class, which provided her an opportunity to observe the same students in a different setting.

METHODOLOGY

In developing the study we began with a series of informal interviews with Linda conducted before, during, and immediately after the first workshop in the summer of 1998. We continued informal interviews during the following school year. After the school year, we conducted a more formal interview with Linda about her views on how using graphing calculators affected her teaching and student learning. Linda also reflected in writing on salient features of her teaching during the school year.

We provided classroom support to aid Linda in integrating the use of graphing calculators into her science and math classes. The classroom support included frequent consultations about math and science activities, graphing calculator technical support, classroom observation, and model teaching by one of the researchers.

In addition to examining Linda's teaching, we studied student learning. Students were observed, their work was collected and analyzed. One above-average, one average, and one student with attention deficit hyperactivity disorder (ADHD) were interviewed at the end of the school year. All interviews including Linda's were recorded, transcribed, and then analyzed.

DEVELOPMENT OF THE INTEGRATED PROJECT

For the purpose of this study we are focusing on one particular project called the "Bouncing Ball Experiment." The bouncing ball experiment is a classic science education experiment on elasticity and Newton's laws. It involves having students collect data on how high a rubber ball bounces after being dropped from a variety of heights (Gabel, 1993). Since Linda had already tried this activity without graphing calculators in her eighth grade classroom during the previous school year, the selection of this project gave us an opportunity to compare her teaching with and without the use of graphing calculators.

Linda adapted this activity from its original form so that students could experiment using their own personal experiences and the graphing calculator to develop their understanding of experimental design, including the use of manipulated (independent) and responding (dependent) variables. Another goal of the activity was to improve students' abilities in interpreting graphs. Because of the speed with which data analysis can take place when working with the graphing calculator, students should be able to spend more time interpreting graphs and less time in the tedious task of constructing the graph (Wilson & Krapfl, 1994). Linda assumed that this would result in an increased depth of understanding about variables and their relationships.

The use of graphing calculators in this project was consistent with Linda's beliefs about teaching. Linda is a firm advocate of constructivism, and her primary intent was to perform as a facilitator of student learning (Schulte, 1996). Linda also believes in cooperative group work and she expected this project to be useful in enhancing student-student interaction and learning.

PROJECT OUTLINE

The first goal of the project was to increase student knowledge of experimental design, including manipulated and responding variables. Another goal was to improve student abilities to interpret relationships between variables through graphing.

Linda began the project by talking about the bouncing behavior of balls. She and the class discussed how a variety of balls, such as basketballs, volleyballs, playground balls, tennis balls and hard rubber balls, bounce differently. From this discussion she and the class developed an experiment involving hard rubber balls, because including many different types of balls in the experiment would have introduced too many variables and would have made the results difficult to interpret. Students then determined that their manipulated variable would be the height from which the ball was dropped and decided how they would measure the responding variable, the bouncing of the ball. As shown in Figure 1 the students chose a variety of methods of measuring this variable.

On the second day students divided into four groups, were given their hard rubber balls, and began collecting their data. Balls were dropped several times near the wall and the height of the first bounce

FIGURE 1
Table Used by Students in Linda's Class in Conducting "Bouncing Ball Experiment"

Height from which ball was dropped (cm)	Prediction: Height of first bounce (cm)	Height of first bounce (cm)	Hang Time– Time between 1st & 2nd bounce (sec)	Total number of bounces	Total time bouncing (sec)
10					
20					
40					
50					
57					
75					
100					

was marked and measured. Results were averaged. This process was repeated for hang time, the time between the first and second bounce, the total number of bounces, and the total time bouncing. Students found the classroom environment crowded and asked Linda if they could use the hallway and gym for collecting their data. Linda allowed them to do this. Since each student had a TI-83 graphing calculator, all data was entered into lists.

On the third day students reported their results. All of the groups agreed that the hang time was too difficult to determine and decided to drop that measurement from their interpretation. An example of student data is shown in Figure 2. Height from which the ball was dropped is shown in $L1$, the predicted height of the first bounce in $L2$, and the actual height of the first bounce in $L3$. After a brief introduction to graphing using the calculator, students began data analysis by creating graphs on their own calculators. Within their own groups, they began discussing the types of relationships that they saw. One of the first graphs that they looked at was the relationship between their prediction of the height of the first bounce and the actual height of the bounce. See Figure 3 for an example. Most of their predictions were fairly accurate. All of the groups predicted that the relationship between the two variables was direct. In other words, increasing the height of the drop would increase the height of the bounce.

Students discussed general trends in their group's graphs using the following focus questions: Did the points on their graphs slope upward or downward? Was there a relationship between the variables?

FIGURE 2
An Example of Student Data as Displayed in a TI-83 Calculator

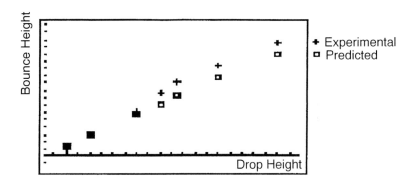

FIGURE 3
Predicted versus Experimental Height of the Bounce

How would they describe this relationship? After discussing relationships within their groups, they moved to a whole-class discussion on
which method of measuring the responding variable would be the best
one to use. Students decided that the bounce height seemed to be the
best because both total number of bounces and total time bouncing
produced graphs that were all scrunched up (little or no variation in the
variable).

On the fourth day, students began examining the data from the
different groups. They expected all of their graphs to be very similar in
appearance, but to their astonishment they were not. The students

found not only that using different surfaces produced different results, but that some of the groups who used the same surface had different results. As shown in Figure 4, dropping the ball on the gym floor consistently produced better bounces than using the carpeted hallway. Differences between groups using the same type of surface occurred because different students had different ideas about what the term "drop the ball" meant. Some groups of students believed that dropping included some degree of tossing the ball. This led to a discussion on the importance of operationally defining terms.

Finally, students summarized the science and math concepts that they were able to explore and understand through this experiment. Their understanding of variables–manipulated, responding, and controlled–was enhanced, because students were actively engaged in doing science with the calculators and did not get bogged down with the mechanics of constructing data tables and graphs. Similarly, student discussions indicated that students had developed a deeper understanding of linear relationships and the connection between mathematics and science. Since Linda also taught math, she was able to refer to the experiment in her math class, especially when teaching variables, slope, proportion, and graphing.

PROJECT OUTCOMES

Our belief that technology integration would improve the project was evident in the outcomes. Integrating graphing calculators with this

FIGURE 4
Bounce Height on Gym Floor versus Carpeted Floor

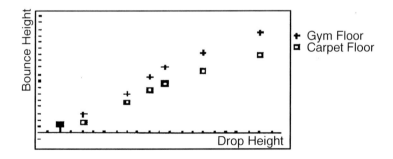

project produced a high interest level among students, increased time for experimentation and data analysis, enhanced higher order thinking, improved cooperation between group members, and provided improved opportunities for teacher facilitation.

The high interest level among students was evident from the interview with Linda when she said, "Using the graphing calculators held the students' interest. They were willing to work harder and work more. They would walk into class and ask, 'Are we using the graphing calculators today?' They were interested, they were engaged." The interviews with the students also indicated a very high interest level. For example, Dan, an average academic student in the class, stated that "I liked them very much cause they made it a lot easier to understand . . . how to compare things and variables." Alan, a student with ADHD, also found the calculators very interesting, because data from his calculator could be sent to a viewscreen calculator that projected everyone's data on the wall. He also liked the fact that he could press the buttons and immediately see the graph on the calculator. Another student, Carl, liked the calculator because it helped him to understand math and science concepts. His enthusiasm for the graphing calculator can be seen in the following interview transcript between Linda and Carl.

> L: How did you like using graphing calculators in math and science class?
>
> C: I liked a lot. It was very exciting.
>
> L: Why do you think it was exciting to use the graphing calculators?
>
> C: Why? Because we were used to just hard books and just facts–and like now it's actually fun to learn math and science instead of just like no explanations. And it made it easier to understand the hard concepts.

According to Linda's report and our field notes, the use of graphing calculators was exciting and enjoyable for almost all students in the class. They all found the graphing calculator a useful tool, because it provided immediate feedback.

The graphing calculator also proved to be a valuable time-saving device, which increased the time available for experimentation and data analysis. Linda had conducted the same experiment with her eighth grade class the previous year. Compared to the previous year, Linda and her class were able to broaden the experiment by examining additional variables, collecting more data, and doing more types of data analysis. This is clearly evident in the following transcript with Linda.

> To have this class graph three sets of data and calculate an average and do it would probably take me almost a week, four to five classes. That's just the graphing that's not collecting the data. A day or two to set up the experiment to collect the data. We're talking about 40-minute periods. We were able to do the experiment, collect the data, share the data, and graph it in three days. So we're comparing six to seven days with three days. Which allows me to go and do a second experiment to see if they've internalized the concepts and if they can use it now.

Remarks from students also indicated their belief that doing it long-hand would increase the amount of time the experiment would take. For example, the following dialogue between Linda and Carl illustrates this point.

> L: So you actually looked at five or six different variables including your prediction. How long do you think it took you to put that data in and make those graphs with the calculator?
>
> C: 'Bout a week.
>
> L: We spent about a week on the project?
>
> C: Well, less than a week.
>
> L: What if we had to do all those graphs on paper?
>
> C: [Laughs] We would have wasted a lot of class time, and it would have taken like twice as long.

Because the graphing calculator saved time, it increased the amount of time available for work on higher order thinking. Surprisingly, some students were drawing conclusions and began to initiate additional data gathering to help validate their conclusions. Linda made it clear in her final interview that:

> When I taught graphing I was able to do more and clarify more of the misconceptions and misunderstandings because they could graph it, push the button, and see it. If it didn't work, they got an error message. Then they could figure out what they had done wrong. I found that a lot when we did tables and did experiments. We could easily do an experiment and have several groups going on and doing the same things, compile the class results, and look at several graphs superimposed upon each other and then determine the trend and why did we not get the same results. And they could begin looking at other variables and other things that impacted . . . I had the students . . . design an experiment within a ten-week period. They had to come up with a question, design their own experiment, carry it out, and write a lab report with a short abstract, a short definition of the variables, talk about the relationship–whether it was a direct or indirect relationship between the variables. I don't think they could have done that without the ease of the calculator. Being able to put data in as we did with preliminary experiments and see the results immediately.

It was not only Linda who thought that the graphing calculators enhanced higher order thinking but also the majority of the students in this seventh-grade class. Carl, for example, stated that they could enter data, make tables and graphs, interpret them, and understand hard concepts, which would have been difficult to comprehend just by reading books. His view is best illustrated in the following transcript:

> It helped me to relate it to real life, and like because in the ball drop experiment. Like we could actually understand it and we could see how the data turned out on from a table to a graph. And in that experiment in the tables we had like on the graph we plotted the different tables. And first we predicted how high the ball was gonna bounce, and then we put the actual data in, and then we had put in different numbers like total bounce time from bounce 1 to bounce 2, and then total bounce time like all the bounces, and then we had total number of bounces and so we

converted that to a graph and we could actually see how the data turned out.

It was not surprising for us to hear from Carl that he was able to understand math and science concepts using the graphing calculator because he was a good student in the class. What was surprising to us was that Alan (an ADHD student) also stated that the graphing calculators not only helped his understanding of math and science concepts but also to see these two different subjects integrated through using calculators.

The use of graphing calculators also improved student-student interactions within cooperative groups. Students did not become frustrated by the mechanics of constructing graphs longhand, and relations between group members were more sociable. Doing the graphs with the calculator also allowed students for whom graphing by longhand would be nearly impossible to keep pace with the other students. Linda mentioned this in her final interview.

> And even my students who were very concrete learners, and making a graph would be very difficult for them, they could put the data in and they could stay up with the rest of the class and not fall behind. And ordinarily they would have needed special help. They were able to work better cooperatively in a group because their peers could show them where they needed to go and direct them.

Her conclusion was that students were able to work better together in cooperative groups and were able to offer support to students who traditionally had difficulty doing experiments. Graphing on the calculator allowed students who normally would have fallen behind to keep up with the class, allowing them to feel successful and building their confidence.

The teacher was surprised to find that her ability to facilitate was improved. Two key factors were involved in this improvement, the increased time availability and the improvement in cooperative group work. Since students concentrated more on experimentation, Linda found that:

> I truly was able to become a facilitator in the classroom. As we used the calculators in various experiments, I found that I was able to ask questions like the following: What other variables

could you look at? Why do you think the results turned out like that? Why is that a problem? What is the relationship between your two variables?

The answers students gave to Linda's questions allowed them to become more involved in learning. As students were actively engaged in the construction of their own knowledge, they began asking questions, and she found herself developing experiments based on students' questions and interests as opposed to following a set curriculum.

IMPROVEMENTS TO THE PROJECT

Linda suggested the following improvements. She would have individual students write brief paragraphs describing the procedures their group followed, a description of the relationship between the manipulated and responding variable of their choice, a comparison of their prediction with their actual results, any modifications to the experiment that would make it "scientifically better," and the graph developed by their group. This would allow the teacher to assess individual student understanding of the experiment and the experimental process.

Linda would include time for a discussion about a range of different types of graphs. In particular, she wanted students to be able to identify which graph is most appropriate for a given set of data. She would also incorporate more time for discussing direct and indirect proportionality in her classroom, which would increase students' depth of understanding of both math and science concepts.

CONCLUSIONS

The integration of graphing calculators with the bouncing ball project proved to be highly successful. The project had a strong impact on student learning, which included a deeper understanding of graphing and the relationships between variables in a scientific experiment. The teacher was not only able to see students' higher order thinking improve related to science concepts, she was equally able to use these ideas in her math class to improve students' knowledge of variables, ratio, proportion, equations, graphing, and slopes.

Due to these positive changes, Linda emerged from this project with an enthusiastic attitude about using graphing calculators. She was particularly impressed with the increased amount of time for more experiment and analysis that could be used to explore concepts more deeply by using this form of technology. Since Linda had taught similar classes in the past, she was certain that the depth of knowledge that her students acquired from this project was not possible without the use of graphing calculators.

IMPLICATIONS

This project has important implications for teachers. Even though the teacher we worked with was extremely interested in integrating technology into her curriculum, she probably would not have done so without the classroom support we were able to provide through our Eisenhower-funded project. At the end of the first workshop, she indicated her interest in using graphing calculator technology in her school, but doubted her ability to use the technology, because of her own unfamiliarity with technology integration. Through the grant, we were able to do model teaching in her classroom, which allowed her to observe the reactions of her students to the use of graphing calculators. This implies that in order for technology integration to be successful, teachers must be provided with adequate classroom support. This finding is consistent with that of Hope (1997), who states that the success of an innovation is largely influenced by the amount and type of assistance that teachers receive.

Graphing calculators are relatively inexpensive and widely available, costing less than $100 each. This low cost makes it much easier for a school to purchase a classroom set or for a parent to purchase one for their student. In schools that use cooperative groups, this number could be reduced to one calculator per group. Graphing calculators are also highly portable, making it very easy for students to take one home with them and to use them out in the field. Graphing calculators, therefore, are a relatively easy way for schools to integrate technology.

Given the low cost of graphing calculators and their high acceptance rate in high schools, it is surprising that they are not more widely used at the middle school level. While the teacher involved in this project was knowledgeable and confident in her subject matter, she had had little or no experience with using technology in the classroom. By the end of this project, Linda believed:

> I think, as educators, we have the responsibility to become famil-iar with the technology. That can be a fearful thing for teachers who haven't used it. But when you use it and you gain some experience with it, you can do just about anything.

We must remember that even teachers who are willing to integrate technology must have the necessary support to allow them to take this risk and make a successful transition.

REFERENCES

Balacheff, N., & Kaput, J. J. (1996). Computer-based learning environments in mathematics. In A. J. Bishop, K. Clements, C. Keitel, J. Kilpatrick, & C. Laborde (Eds.), *International handbook of mathematics education* (pp. 469-501). Dor-drecht, The Netherlands: Kluwer Academic Publishers.

Battista, M. T., & Lambdin, D. V. (1994). Calculators and computers: Tools for mathematical exploration and empowerment. *Arithmetic Teacher, 41*(7), 412-417.

Gabel, D. L. (1993). *Introductory science skills* (2nd ed.). Prospect Heights, IL: Waveland Press.

Hope, W. C. (1997). Resolving teachers' concerns about microcomputer technology. *Computers in the Schools, 13*(3/4), 147-160.

National Council of Teachers of Mathematics. (1989). *Curriculum and evaluation standards*. Reston, VA: Author.

National Research Council of the National Academy of Sciences. (1996). *The nation-al science education standards*. Washington, DC: National Academy Press.

Rezba, R. J., Sprague, C., Fiel, R. L., & Funk, H.J. (1995). *Learning and assessing science process skills* (3rd ed.). Dubuque, IA: Kendall/Hunt Publishing.

Sarama, J., Clements, D. J., & Henry, J. J. (1998). Network of influences in an implementation of a mathematics curriculum innovation. *International Journal of Computers for Mathematical Learning, 3*(2), 113-148.

Schulte, P. L. (1996). A definition of constructivism. *Science Scope, 20*(3), 25-27.

Wilson, M.R., & Krapfl C. M. (1994). The impact of graphics calculators on stu-dents' understanding of function. *Journal of Computers in Mathematics and Science Teaching, 13*(3), 251-264.

Karen Dutt-Doner
Marty Wilmer
Cathy Stevens
Lisa Hartmann

Actively Engaging Learners in Interdisciplinary Curriculum Through the Integration of Technology

SUMMARY. Global Warming: A Heated Debate *is an interdisciplinary WebQuest project developed to target science and technology content standards in the State of Maine Learning Results. By implementing this interdisciplinary, technology-based group research project, we hoped that students would become more interested and involved in their learning, better understand and practice research skills, be able to retrieve more current Internet information for their research projects, support each other in their learning, and have a better understanding*

KAREN DUTT-DONER is Assistant Professor, University of Southern Maine, Coordinator of the undergraduate teacher education program TEAMS (Teachers for Elementary and Middle School), Department of Teacher Education, 504 Bailey Hall, Gorham, ME 04038. E-mail: karend@usm.maine.edu
MARTY WILMER is Teacher, Scarborough Middle School, 44 Gorham Road, Scarborough, ME 04074.
CATHY STEVENS is Math & Science Teacher, Scarborough Middle School, 44 Gorham Road, Scarborough, ME 04074.
LISA HARTMANN is Technology Specialist, Scarborough Middle School, 44 Gorham Road, Scarborough, ME 04074.

[Haworth co-indexing entry note]: "Actively Engaging Learners in Interdisciplinary Curriculum Through the Integration of Technology." Dutt-Doner, Karen et al. Co-published simultaneously in *Computers in the Schools* (The Haworth Press, Inc.) Vol. 16, No. 3/4, 2000, pp. 151-166; and: *Integration of Technology into the Classroom: Case Studies* (ed: D. LaMont Johnson, Cleborne D. Maddux, and Leping Liu) The Haworth Press, Inc., 2000, pp. 151-166. Single or multiple copies of this article are available for a fee from The Haworth Document Delivery Service [1-800-342-9678, 9:00 a.m. - 5:00 p.m. (EST). E-mail address: getinfo@haworthpressinc.com].

151

of reliable and unreliable Internet resources. This paper outlines our project in trying to implement technology into our teaching. We reflect on our experiences as well as provide suggestions for others. [Article copies available for a fee from The Haworth Document Delivery Service: 1-800-342-9678. E-mail address: <getinfo@haworthpressinc.com> Website: <http://www.HaworthPress.com>]

KEYWORDS. *Interdisciplinary curriculum, research, Internet, active learning, cooperative learning, technology integration*

BACKGROUND

Global Warming: A Heated Debate is an interdisciplinary project that has been developed as a result of a mini-grant awarded by the Scarborough (Maine) School Department. These grants support teachers in developing assessments that measure student progress in meeting the State of Maine Learning Results (K-12 performance standards) (*http://www.scarborough.k12.me.us/middle/quest/resourc.htm*) and/or promote the use of technology to meet the Learning Results. This project is based on the instructional model of a WebQuest, the development of which originated with Bernie Dodge, a professor at San Diego State University. WebQuests are designed to effectively use the learner's time. In addition, the goal of a WebQuest is to extend and refine knowledge about a topic.

In this project, students take on roles as members of various groups testifying before a special subcommittee whose task is to recommend whether or not the U.S. Senate should ratify the Kyoto Protocol, an international agreement that outlines varying target levels for reductions in greenhouse gases for industrialized nations. A lot of controversy exists regarding the topic of global warming–scientists have generally agreed that it is happening, but the extent to which it is being caused or accelerated by human activity is not so certain. Mandated reductions in greenhouse gas emissions will almost certainly have economic impacts on many industries and consumers (e.g., in the form of higher fuel taxes and material costs, decreased consumer choice, lost jobs, etc). So what should we do if we are not sure of the causes or the outcomes of a problem? Can we afford to wait and take our chances with the outcomes until more is known, or should we act now, even if that action is costly? Students use various resources, many of them online, to prepare a presentation for the subcommittee, giving the point of view of their interest group. In being asked to consider how some of the other groups may rebut their arguments, students are also able to see how the same scientific and economic data may be slanted or used differently by groups of differing points of view.

This project is targeted at middle school science curricula, but also involves social studies and language arts. It could also be modified and implemented at the high school level. We implemented the project in two classrooms: in a multi-age, grades 6-8 mainstreamed classroom that was team-taught and in a seventh-grade science class. The driving force behind the design of this project was to target the science and technology content standard in the State of Maine Learning Results entitled "Implications of Science and Technology": "Students will understand the historical, social, economic, environmental, and ethical implications of science and technology" (p. 77). In addition, the students will demonstrate their ability to meet "Inquiry and Problem Solving" standards, "Civics and Government/International Relations" standards, "Economics/Economic Systems of the United States" standards in the social studies, and "Research-Related Writing and Speaking" standards in English language arts. Specific middle grades performance indicators that we feel this activity addresses are that the students will be able to:

1. Use search engines and other Internet resources to collect information for research topics.
2. Work, write, and speak effectively when doing research in all content areas.
3. Assess the ways in which the United States government has attempted to resolve an international problem.
4. Identify how the fundamental characteristics of the United States economic system (e.g., private property, profits, competition, and price system) influence economic decision making.
5. Explain how personal bias can affect observations.
6. Construct logical arguments.
7. Research and evaluate the social and environmental impacts of scientific and technological developments.
8. Describe an individual's biological impact and other impacts on an environmental system.

9. Give examples of actions that may have expected or unexpected consequences that may be positive, negative, or both.
10. Explain the connections between industry, natural resources, population and economic development.
11. Discuss scientific and technological ideas and make conjectures and convincing arguments.
12. Access information at remote sites using telecommunications.
13. Identify and perform roles necessary to accomplish group tasks.

WHY DID WE TRY SOMETHING NEW?

The topic of global warming was not a new one in our teaching. Prior to WebQuest, a more traditional approach was used to teach this topic. Classroom lecture along with students completing research projects on various topics using library resources (including encyclopedias, journals, and CD-ROM resources) served as the means for learning about global warming. While some students used Internet access at home as a resource, many were unable to discriminate between reliable and unreliable sources.

We found that students often relied on frequently outdated information using this form of research, and most of the information was provided by the teacher in a didactic format (i.e., discussing graphs; presenting formulas, theories, and models, etc.). Since this approach did not allow for the students to truly become active participants in their learning, we sought a more constructivist approach to student learning.

These limitations, along with the efforts of our school to better integrate the Science and Technology State of Maine Learning Results into our teaching and curriculum, suggested the integration of technology into our teaching. As a result of our efforts, we received a small grant to design and implement a Webquest project that focused on the topic of global warming (*http://www.scarborough.k12.me.us/middle/quest/teacher.htm*)

PROJECT DEVELOPMENT

There are many underlying principles that guided our work in developing this project. First is the notion of active learning based on a constructivist model. There is a great deal of research, not surprising to teachers, that suggests students learn more and retain more when they are actively engaged in their own learning (Meyer & Jones, 1993). Participating in real-life simulations not only provides students with an authentic task in which to demonstrate knowledge and skills, but it gives credibility to the task. Students also can better understand the purpose for a project that has real-life implications. When students are guided using a constructivist model (Brooks & Brooks, 1993; Forman & Kuschner, 1977), the teacher, and possibly peers, help them develop a deeper understanding of content and skills. In addition, a teacher interacting with students using a constructivist model focuses on each individual child, building on the student's strengths to over- come areas of weakness. Second, and related to the first, is the notion of collaborative group work. The research in this area suggests that students are academically stronger working with others than they are alone (Johnson, Johnson and Holubec, 1990; Slavin, 1990). In addi- tion, the teacher can structure classroom activities in such a way that students support one another with the guidance to truly learn new information. Johnson, Johnson and Roy (1984) point out the impor- tance of working in groups: "More elaborate thinking, more frequent giving and receiving of explanations, and greater perspective in dis- cussion material seem to occur in heterogeneous groups, all of which increase the depth of understanding, the quality of reasoning, and the accuracy of long-term retention" (pp. 27-28). Third, the research on multiple intelligences suggest that there is "a wider family of human intelligences" than once believed (Gardner, 1983). Gardner proposed that each person has one or more inherent intelligences that should be developed in order for him/her to reach full potential. Teachers need to provide more opportunities for students to share their knowledge in different ways so that we can tap into their different intelligences. Finally, in recent years, the implementation of an interdisciplinary approach to teaching has taken root in schools across the country (Willis, 1999). The ever-expanding curriculum and the standards movement has made it necessary to consider ways to integrate content knowledge. Research has found that interdisciplinary learning pro- vides opportunities for students to apply skills, retrieve information faster, gain depth and breadth in learning, have more quality time for curriculum exploration, and learn important information by truly un- derstanding concepts and underlying structures (Lipson, 1993).

By implementing an interdisciplinary, technology-based group research project we hoped that students would (a) become more interested and involved in their learning, (b) better understand and practice the use of research skills, (c) be able to retrieve more current information for research projects from the Internet, (d) support one another in their learning (about using technology, about the in-depth content of global warming), and (e) have a better understanding of reliable and unreliable Internet resources.

Even more specifically our goals for the project included that the students should:

1. Gain experience exploring resources and learn how to use them to complete a research assignment.
2. Gain experience using evidence to construct and present logical supporting arguments for an assigned point of view.
3. Learn how economic, as well as societal and scientific, factors influence national and international political decisions.
4. Gain insight into how (what appears to be) a given set of scientific and/or economic facts can be used to support differing points of view.
5. Gain new background knowledge and insights regarding the greenhouse effect, global warming, and related science and social studies content.

Once the grant proposal had been accepted, we had the tedious responsibility of putting up the WebQuest site with all its necessary details on the Internet. As we were developing our project, we first had to choose a topic. While this should not have seemed to be such a daunting task, it quickly became one. As we were considering the topic, we needed to ensure that there would be enough current information for our students to use on the Internet to support their research projects. In addition, we needed to ensure that we were covering appropriate content as it related to our district curriculum and State of Maine Learning Results. Once we chose global warming as a topic, we then struggled with finding model sites to support varying points of view and to ensure that these model sites were quality sites. As we were developing our WebQuest site, a number of people became involved–including our technology specialist within the school, the two teachers implementing the project, and a district technology specialist–to get the Web site up and running on the school's Web page. We needed to ensure that the site included enough detail and support for the students. We also needed to include information for other teachers who may want to implement the project, so we created a teacher's page. We logged over 100 hours in doing the preliminary work of getting the site ready for implementation.

THE WEBQUEST PROJECT

Assuming about 45 minutes of science class time involved daily, the project (group preparation and presentations) took from four to six weeks. Because the project was an interdisciplinary one, pulling in the resources/time of the language arts and/or social studies classes, the overall span of time was shortened.

To begin the WebQuest, our school's technology specialist held a series of classes to teach the students the necessary information and assess their understanding of the Internet and our school policies in order for the students to earn their Internet licenses. An Internet license is required of all students at the middle school in order to use the Internet as a resource. Only those students whose parents signed a permission slip could earn the license. For a variety of reasons (no parent signature, absenteeism, and a new class member), 5 of the 37 multi-age students did not earn a license.

Before starting the Global Warming WebQuest, the teachers needed to provide the students with some background information. Commencing with a brainstorming session, students listed everything they "knew" about global warming and the greenhouse effect, without any feedback from the teachers as to the veracity of their statements. Their first homework assignment was to come up with three questions that they would like to answer about these topics. These questions were compiled by topic area into one list, including global warming causes, gases, treatments, and effects; ozone depletion causes and effects; and general effects (related to global warming and the greenhouse effect).

In the next class, a graph from the GEMS (Great Explorations in Math and Science; Lawrence Hall of Science, University of California at Berkeley) unit showing there were several ice ages over time was discussed. The teachers explained that the ozone layer depletion is not actually related to global warming, which was a common misconception held by many of our students. Students were then given two packets per cooperative group, Chapters 1, "Clues to Past Climate," and 3, "Current Global Climate Change," from the National Science Teachers Association book, *Forecasting the Future: Exploring Evidence for Global Climate Change,* along with a sheet of background questions. These questions were:

1. What is the greenhouse effect?
2. What is global warming?
3. What gases contribute to global warming?
4. Where do these gases come from? (Most will have more than one source.)
5. How do these gases contribute to global warming?
6. What can be done to prevent global warming from getting worse, or to make the situation better?

The students could work on the questions together within their groups. Some chose to have one student read while they all listened for the answer to one of the questions, which seemed to be the best method for obtaining the most complete answers. Other groups split up the reading and skimmed for answers, but they often got only part of an answer for most questions. Students had about three class periods (42 minutes each, with a break in the middle for lunch) to work on this activity. Answers were corrected and graded for completion and accuracy.

Then students were introduced to the WebQuest site in order to ensure an understanding of the project: (*http://www.scarborough.k12.me.us/middle/quest/teacher.htm*). Teachers walked students through the site, explaining how to access the WebQuest, how to get to the different pages, and the expectations for the activity. (See Appendix A for Web page introduction.) The next day, students were given their assignment to their specific group. (See one of eight detailed WebQuest assignments in Appendix B.)

Each group was given a folder in which to keep notes, plans, etc., so that the absence of any one student would not hold up the group. Each group was responsible for researching their assigned point of view, and giving an oral presentation, with visuals, as if they were presenting to a Senate subcommittee who would then recommend whether or not the United States should ratify the Kyoto Protocol. Guidelines to help support the students in their project were provided on the WebQuest site and included background information for each group, focus questions, team responsibility assignments, guidelines for planning the required PowerPoint presentation, and project requirements (*http://www. scarborough.k12.me.us/middle/quest/process.htm*).

Three individual assignments were required. First, each student was required to maintain a dated log, explaining what they did during that class period, what sites they visited or resources they used, what they learned, and what they planned to do during the next class. This log was checked periodically to assure that students were entering adequate information, and was collected at the end of the project. A summary of one resource was also required. This included providing an accurate citation, a detailed summary, and an explanation of how this resource supported their group's point of view. The summary was collected about one week prior to the oral presentations. Third, each student needed to respond to the United Nations question, which basically asked, when the effects of something are not clear, should one take action now or wait and see what happens in the future? Responses were collected about two weeks after the introduction to the WebQuest. Students were given a hard copy of the two scoring rubrics that indicated how the three individual assignments and the group presentation were going to be graded. We were hoping that the students would use the rubrics as guides for their work (*http://www.scarborough.k12.me.us/ middle/quest/grouprbr.html* and *http://www.scarborough.k12.me.us/middle/ quest/indivrbr.html*).

In order to support the group research project, the class was assigned to the computer labs for as many days as it was available, approximately three to four times per week for four weeks. Sometimes we had one lab available; other times we had two. Lab One had about 15 computers available for student use, while Lab Two had 10. Students could work with a partner at a computer, which allowed more than half to be on the Internet on lab days. We also had four computers in our classroom, two student and two teacher computers, that students could use when they were in the room. Students were not allowed to print out copies from the Internet since we wanted to assure that they would go online to complete the project! They needed to record the URL where they visited and take notes for each site. Because of the limited class time devoted to the project, during class students were also required to visit only the sites that were linked to our WebQuest (*http://www.scarborough.k12.me.us/middle/quest/resourc.htm*). They could explore the Internet on their own, during study halls, or at home, if they felt this was necessary. We spent days finding the best sites, and we wanted to assure that the students checked them out before they went looking elsewhere.

Students who were not able to work on a computer had a few options. First, these students worked in our school library, with teaching partners, the first couple of days. However, they had trouble locating appropriate resources. Finally, we selected books and made them available in our classroom, which also allowed more kids to access a computer during the period. Each group also had a copy of each of the other chapters from *Forecasting the Future* to keep in their folder. Once a group felt they had enough information for their required PowerPoint presentation, they could start planning their visuals. We required a fairly explicit storyboard before any group could start working on a PowerPoint presentation. As the culminating project activity, each group was given approximately 10 minutes to present their point of view, which we filmed. For all PowerPoint presentations, students were required to submit a printout of their slide show as well. The presentations were evaluated using the rubric for group presentations as a checklist and recording any other pertinent information on the sheet. We then discussed each group's presentation and came to a consensus on a grade for each group and for each individual's participation in the group. For example, one student talked to others during her group's presentation, so we gave her a slightly lower grade for this piece.

POSSIBLE VARIATIONS OF OUR WEBQUEST

Of course, there are many other possible variations to our approach. Here are a few suggestions.

1. Invite community members and/or parents into your classroom for the presentations; have them take the roll of U.S. Senators and actually vote on the treaty–or let the whole class assume the Senate roll.
2. To make the experience more authentic, a social studies class could have each student assume the identity of a senator from an assigned state; the student would then need to consider how his/her state's interests would be affected by the treaty, and vote accordingly.
3. At the time of this writing, the deadline for nations to ratify the Kyoto Protocol was March 1999, but the Senate vote has not

been taken. It is therefore quite possible that U.S. ratification will have been decided by the time you would be ready to use these project plans. If so, they can still be used in several ways. The easiest approach would be to ignore the result of the Senate vote; present it to the students after their own presentations have been made and a classroom "vote" taken. If students are aware of the results already, change the scenario, increasing the amount of the reduction in greenhouse gases being mandated. Would this change anyone's thinking?

4. We limited the number of presenting groups to eight, both for logistics purposes as well as to attempt to keep a balance of probable points of view.

5. If desired, more detailed content knowledge could be incorporated into the project by adding more (or more specific) interest groups to the presentation plan. For instance, a team of oceanographers could be added that could explore in-depth the unfolding knowledge of the role of the oceans as a carbon sink in the greenhouse effect. Nuclear and renewable energy industry representatives could be added to increase a focus on the pros and cons of various types of energy sources.

EVALUATION OF THE WEBQUEST PROJECT

After this experience, it was clear to us that students learned more about global warming using the WebQuest approach. Upon reviewing student reflections on the project, it became clearer that the WebQuest not only taught them about the issues surrounding global warming but also encouraged them to understand the real-life implications. One student reflected:

> I learned how global warming affects us and what can happen. Our group thought we should ratify the treaty. It doesn't matter to me if it's signed. I do want to try to stop global warming, but after watching other presentations I don't like the idea of prices going up and people losing jobs.

The questioning and reflecting that this project encouraged had a much greater impact on students than simply learning factual information. Utilizing varying resources on the Internet that represented varying viewpoints provided the students with an opportunity to consider this issue from all sides. In addition, students were required to demonstrate their technology skills through use of the Internet and creation of Powerpoint presentations. Students worked well in their collaborative groups by sharing their expertise and developing effective PowerPoint presentations. The Internet proved to be a better way for students to obtain current information. Students were interested and deeply involved in the project activities. A couple of groups presented at a statewide conference entitled "Global Climate Change in Maine–The Risks and Opportunities" as a result of this project.

We came across three stumbling blocks, probably not uncommon to teachers who have made efforts to use the Internet in their teaching. First, students presented some factually inaccurate information that they found on the Internet. Second, as with all teachers, we found computer access difficult to manage with many students working on the same project. Third, there were a number of logistical problems that occurred as we were implementing this project for the first time. Rather than each teacher trying to reinvent the wheel, we offer the following suggestions from our classroom experience that should help maximize student focus and work quality.

1. Have a file for each group that contains a printed copy of their group "Information Kit," "Process Page," etc. Students not working on the computer did not have their group questions and identity in front of them unless they had taken their own notes.
2. As a pre-project activity, have students complete a "scavenger hunt" of selected sites from the Resource Page. This will require students to visit a variety of sites so that they are aware of the information available in the linked sites. (see A Virtual Tour of the Greenhouse Effect, *http://www.scarborough.k12.me.us/middle/quest/weblesson.htm*)
3. Require that the "summary of a piece of evidence" be due midway through the project, not at the end of it. You might also want to require each group member to summarize a different source to ensure that the group is accessing a variety of resources.
4. Carefully consider the level and experience of your class before starting the project; if this is their first research experience, you may want to cut down the individual project requirements.

5. Some background knowledge about the carbon cycle and green-house effect would help assist middle-level students to more eas-ily and quickly make sense of the various terms and resources they encounter; a good way to obtain some of this background would be with some of the early activities in the GEMS unit, Global Warming and the Greenhouse Effect (1990: Lawrence Hall of Science, University of California at Berkeley–*http://www. lhs.berkeley.edu/GEMS/GEM322.html*). Another resource is *Fore-casting the Future: Exploring Evidence for Global Climate Change* (1996: National Science Teachers Association, Arlington, VA–*http:// www.nsta.org/pubs/special/popular.htm*). This curriculum and activ-ity guide includes many readings you may duplicate for students, as well as hands-on activities to increase each student's knowledge base.

BACK TO THE KEY QUESTION, WHY DO WEBQUEST?

It seems through all of this detail about our project, it is important to revisit the reasons why a teacher should consider taking the plunge into WebQuest. For teachers, it provides an opportunity to integrate technology into an existing curriculum. In addition, it utilizes the learner's time, focusing on using information rather than looking for it. Finally, the project supports the learner's thinking in-depth at the levels of analysis, synthesis, and evaluation.

For students, using the Internet as a research tool allows current access to information that may otherwise be inaccessible. In addition, students can share information found through the use of the Internet. Finally, students become more familiar with technology and learn how to find quality information on the Internet.

REFERENCES

Forman, G. & D. Kuschner. (1977). *The child's construction of knowledge.* Belmont, CA: Wadsworth Co.

Gardner, H. (1983). *Frames of mind: The theory of multiple intelligences.* New York: Basic Books.

Johnson, D.W., Johnson, R.T., & Holubec, E.J. (1990). *Circles of learning* (3rd ed.). Edina, MN: Interaction Book Co.

Johnson, D.W., Johnson, R.T., Holubec, E.J., & Roy, P. (1984). *Circles of learning* (2nd ed.). Alexandria, VA: Association for the Supervision of Curriculum Development.

Lipson, M., Valencia, S., Wixson, K., & Peters, C. (1993) Integration and thematic teaching: Integration to improve teaching and learning. *Language Arts*, *70*(4), 252-264.

Meyer, C., & Jones, T.B. (1993). *Promoting active learning*. San Francisco: Jossey-Bass.

Slavin, R. (1990). *Cooperative learning: Theory, research and practice*. Englewood Cliffs, NJ: Prentice-Hall.

Willis, S. (1999, Summer). Crossing discipline lines. *Curriculum/Technology Quarterly*, *8*(4), 1-2.

APPENDIX A

INTRODUCTION

A team of experts sponsored by the United Nations published a report in 1995, which concluded that humans are influencing the climate of the earth. But how much? Even after many years of study, this Intergovernmental Panel on Climate Change (IPCC) was not able to decide how significant that human influence is. They think that at least another decade of research will be required to answer that question.

So what do we do in the meantime? How urgent is the need for action? These are the most hotly debated questions.

Meanwhile, an international conference on climate change was held in Kyoto, Japan, in 1997. There, the industrialized nations of the world agreed to reduce their emissions of heat-trapping "greenhouse gases," within 15 years, by an average of 5.2% (below 1990 levels) by the year 2012. The United States agreed to a 7% reduction. Even though the U.S. agreed to these reductions at the conference, the "Kyoto Protocol" is really an international treaty. In order for the U.S. to enter any treaty, the Senate must first "ratify" it.

SOME BACKGROUND

Scientists estimate that life has existed on Earth for four billion years, and in that time, the climate has fluctuated many times between periods of tropical heat and ice age. Now the earth appears to be getting warmer again–but why? One thing that scientists know is that since the time of the Industrial Revolution, atmospheric carbon dioxide levels have risen by about 25%. Another thing that has been demonstrated is that during periods of rising global temperatures, carbon dioxide levels in the atmosphere also rise. However, scientists are not sure if the rising temperature causes the carbon dioxide to increase, or if increased carbon dioxide causes the temperature to rise.

The "Kyoto Protocol" mentioned above will "enter into force" on the international level only after two conditions are met:

1. Fifty-five (55) countries must sign and ratify the treaty.
2. Those countries must represent at least 55% of the greenhouse gas emissions from industrialized nations.

Since the U.S. represents such a large proportion of the worldwide emissions, these conditions make it difficult (but not impossible) for the treaty to take effect without being ratified by the U.S.

APPENDIX B

To help the United States Senate decide whether or not to ratify the treaty, a special sub-committee has been formed by the Senate to study the issues involved. To do this, the sub-committee will be calling for presentations by various interest groups that may be affected if the treaty goes into effect–or doesn't go into effect. You have been chosen to be part of a team that will represent one of these groups!!

Insurance Industry Lobbyists represent companies, which insure property against damage from floods and other natural catastrophes, such as hurricanes.

Environmental Lobbyists represent groups concerned with protecting the environment, such as Sierra Club, World Wildlife Federation, Greenpeace, Rainforest Action Network, and Friends of the Earth.

Forest Industries Lobbyists represent companies that produce tree-based products such as lumber and paper.

Transportation Industries Lobbyists represent a variety of companies that are in some way related to transporting people and goods from place to place, including auto manufacturers and gasoline/oil producers.

Consumer Advocates represent a variety of groups working to protect the well-being of consumers of all ages and income levels, such as the National Consumer Coalition, Consumer Union, AARP, and the Cooler Heads Coalition.

Ambassadors of a Coalition of Third World Nations mainly represent poor agricultural countries, which have not been asked to limit greenhouse gas emissions because they do not have large developed industries. Many of them are small island nations.

Food Producer Lobbyists represent farmers and livestock producers who are concerned with supplying food to a growing international population.

Scientific Advisory Panel has been given the responsibility to factually summarize scientific data and theories on global warming and greenhouse gas emissions to the scientifically illiterate sub-committee.

Your task in this "Global Warming WebQuest" is to become a member of one of the interest group teams described above. You and your teammates will work together to create a presentation to the Senate sub-committee that will summarize the point-of-view of your interest group with regard to the issue of the United States being required to reduce greenhouse gas emissions. (*http://www.scarborough.k12.me.us/middle/quest/teachers.htm*)

Susan (Gay) Gallagher

Collecting and Manipulating Weather Data: Using Technology Tools in a First-Grade Classroom

SUMMARY. *This case study describes the integration of technology into a first-grade classroom. Integrating computer software and Internet resources enhanced the visual displays and lesson objectives. Students collected weather data during the school year and created a variety of graphs to represent their data. The lesson resulted in creating a high, sustained, student interest level in the project as well as graphing and map skills experiences for first-graders. The successful project also served as a catalyst for the teacher's continued use of technology tools in her classroom lessons. [Article copies available for a fee from The Haworth Document Delivery Service: 1-800-342-9678. E-mail address: <getinfo@haworthpressinc.com> Website: <http://www.HaworthPress.com>]*

KEYWORDS. *Technology integration, visual display of information, computers, graphing, elementary lesson plans*

This case study describes a technology integration project conducted in a first-grade classroom in a small community school district

SUSAN (GAY) GALLAGHER is Assistant Professor, Professional Teacher Education Department, University of Nebraska at Kearney, 2024 Founders Hall, Kearney, NE 68849. E-mail: gallaghers@unk.edu

[Haworth co-indexing entry note]: "Collecting and Manipulating Weather Data: Using Technology Tools in a First-Grade Classroom." Gallagher, Susan (Gay). Co-published simultaneously in *Computers in the Schools* (The Haworth Press, Inc.) Vol. 16, No. 3/4, 2000, pp. 167-175; and: *Integration of Technology into the Classroom: Case Studies* (ed: D. LaMont Johnson, Cleborne D. Maddux, and Leping Liu) The Haworth Press, Inc., 2000, pp. 167-175. Single or multiple copies of this article are available for a fee from The Haworth Document Delivery Service [1-800-342-9678, 9:00 a.m. - 5:00 p.m. (EST). E-mail address: getinfo@haworthpressinc.com].

167

of a rural Midwestern state. The data collection for this case was conducted in a field setting during the 1997-98 academic year. Observations, interviews, and e-mail were used in the data collection process. The identity of the school district and teacher are protected and a pseudonym has been used to protect the confidentiality of the participant.

Mrs. Sheridan is a veteran teacher who had very little experience with computers in the classroom. She had one computer located on her desk in the classroom and used it only for messages on the school network. Mrs. Sheridan did not feel comfortable and was not confident using the computers with her 15 students. She felt that there were not very many resources that were grade-level appropriate for first grade and had not actively pursued the integration of any computer resources into her curriculum. Most of the computer software and Internet sites she had viewed required reading skills above the first-grade level. It is fair to say that Mrs. Sheridan was skeptical about the effectiveness of using computers in the first-grade classroom.

The classroom lesson described in this case study focused on collecting weather data. Prior to using technology tools in this lesson, the students would get the temperature reading at their school each morning and record the temperature by assigning it a color from a temperature scale that was posted on a bulletin board. After checking the temperature, the students returned to their desks and colored in the day with the appropriate color on a calendar. The lesson was designed to connect a science and math lesson in the curriculum. Integrative curriculum opens possibilities for critical analysis, problem solving, and questioning that might not occur in a traditional curriculum (Beane, 1993). The National Council of Teachers of Mathematics (1989) advocates learning and using mathematics as important aspects of the entire school curriculum. The first-graders were focusing on numbers, the daily weather, and reading the color scale of the different temperatures to determine the correct color for the day. The color-coded weather chart was also used to teach the students how to count by 2 and 5 using the scale on the chart.

The activity was limited in several ways. Students did not have any visual image to look at to determine the temperature. It did not offer much variety for students with different learning styles. All students were recording exactly the same information for the same location. The activity was a routine every morning for the students, but did not generate much interest or discussion beyond the day's weather on the way to school. Once the students had colored in their calendars, the activity ended and the students did not do anything further with the colored calendars or the information contained in the calendars. The lesson had been taught in this format during September and October of the school year.

Beginning in November of this school year, a grant project was implemented in Mrs. Sheridan's first-grade classroom. The grant project provided five student computers, software for each machine, a color printer, Internet access, an LCD projector, and the support of an instructional technology trainer/consultant to help model teaching strategies and to assist in developing technology-based curriculum materials. Given the nature of the data being collected, it seemed that using the computer to provide visual displays of the information the students were gathering might help them understand more about their data and the patterns that resulted in the data. Resnick (1987) asserts that cultivating aspects of thinking, normally defined as higher order skills, is important to students at all developmental levels. The use of a color-coded temperature scale was the only visual aid in the lesson activity. The colors on the scale resembled the colors used on surface temperature maps. A surface temperature map illustrates the location and spatial patterns of the temperatures in addition to providing the color-based temperature information. With the addition of computer access for the students, using an Internet Web site would provide an inexpensive visual resource for the class. Also, the computers would enable the students to graph the data they were collecting and allow them to manipulate and view the data in several different formats. A graphing program designed for early elementary students would help integrate math concepts into the lesson.

INTEGRATION PROJECT DEVELOPMENT

The weather data lesson evolved quickly as Mrs. Sheridan and the instructional technology trainer/consultant discussed how best to integrate the new computers and Internet access that was available in the classroom. Since weather data are spatial in nature, locating an image of a current weather map on the Internet would allow the children to look at the location of the data and compare it to other regions where the weather was different. A color weather map would not require reading skills and would be easy for the students to use independently each day. The emphasis on this being a student-directed activity and not a teacher-managed activity was important to the design. The ideas for the lesson continued to evolve based on other uses of the computer to visually display data.

Since the children were practicing counting and simple math operations, adding a graphing component to the lesson seemed to be a natural fit. Graphing the data would provide an additional activity beyond simply recording the data. The students continued coloring the color of the day, but on graph paper instead of on a calendar. The use of a graphing program allowed the students to create several different types of graphs to display their data. The students did not have the time or expertise to create each type of graph by hand on paper, but they could easily and quickly graph the same data in different formats on the computer. The computer became a useful tool for students to use to perform tedious tasks (Ploger, Klingler, & Rooney, 1997). By using different graphs, students might understand one type of visual graph of the data more easily. Dockstader (1999) noted that the value of integrating computers is greatest when the task furthers content comprehension. The challenges were to find the weather map and a graphing program that were grade-level appropriate for first-graders. Limited or no reading required, ease of use, and reliability were all considerations in finding technology resources for this project. Mrs. Sheridan reviewed several graphing software programs and selected the Graphers software program by Sunburst. This program was easy to use and included icons for navigation that allowed the first-grade students to work independently on their graphs.

THE INTEGRATION PROJECT

A Web search on "land surface temperature maps" yielded a link to a site at Ohio State University that displayed a daily temperature *map* (*http://twister.sbs.ohio-state.edu/text/wximages/us/ustemp.gif*). The colors used on the map image matched almost perfectly with the color-coded scale already being used in the class. The map also had a 10-degree scale that allowed the students to practice counting by *10* on the map in addition to the counting by *2* and *5* that the students were already doing on the color-coded temperature scale in the classroom. The weather map included state boundaries drawn in over the top of the color display. This allowed for another extension or curriculum connection to be added to the lesson. Students were each assigned a different state to record weather data for, and Mrs. Sheridan continued to record the daily weather data for the "home" state.

The 15 students were assigned to the five student computers in the classroom to check the weather map Web site. Mrs. Sheridan bookmarked the weather map Web site in a Web browser, which eliminated the necessity of any keyboarding or spelling skills by the students. The students could open the Web browser, select the bookmark to go to the site, look at the map, find their state, and record the daily temperature without assistance from Mrs. Sheridan. The students would record their information by coloring squares to represent their observations of the temperature for the day. At this point, the weather data lesson began to evolve in two ways.

First, the Web site displayed an outline map of the United States over the color temperature image and allowed the teacher to assign a state to each student. This helped the children learn how to identify the shape of a different assigned state and record the data. Mrs. Sheridan selected a variety of states in various climate zones and assigned each student in the class one to look at and record the temperature information daily. She tried to match students with a state that they had a connection to based on prior travel, the location of relatives, or the location of a favorite sports team. At first, Mrs. Sheridan was concerned that the first-grade students might have trouble identifying their state on the image. Isobar lines indicating pressure fronts were also displayed on the map, adding some complexity to identifying the states by outline shapes. The students first practiced identifying their assigned state on the map and within the first week became proficient at identifying their state despite the extra lines on the map.

Secondly, the students were given graph paper instead of a calendar on which to color in the daily temperature color. They colored the temperature data in a linear format on their graph paper for each month. In order to help the students compare and contrast the patterns between their states at the end of the month, Mrs. Sheridan displayed the colored strips of data on a piece of poster board next to each student's name and state. This collective graph allowed the students to compare differences in temperature for their state on any given day. Mrs. Sheridan aligned the states according to the latitude of the states, with the northernmost states being at the top of the graph and the southernmost states being at the bottom of the graph. Aligning the states according to their latitude helped the students make some generalizations about the temperatures in their state in relation to other states. The students also compared the temperatures in their state with the home state that Mrs. Sheridan was graphing each day.

At the end of each month, the students were able to use the Graphers software to enter their weather data for the month and create a variety of graphs to represent their data. The software package allowed the students to choose colored squares that correlated with the color-coded temperature scale being used in the classroom. The total number of days was displayed on the graph, and the students could count the number of colored squares on their graph paper to be sure they had entered the correct number of days for each color. The students could then choose from an icon menu to select the type of graph to view. In addition, they could change the visual display by clicking on the pie graph icon to see the colors represented as part of the whole month. Mrs. Sheridan asked them to decide which color had more or less days during the month and who had the most different colors of days on their graph. The students participated actively in these summary discussions and often initiated the class discussion from their observations of their data and graphs. Additional options, such as a data table, were added to the graphic display and were helpful to some students. Finally, the students printed out their monthly graphs on the color printer and added them to the collection of each month's weather data for their assigned state. The students collected the printouts of their monthly graphs for the remainder of the school year.

EVALUATION OF THE PROJECT

Mrs. Sheridan felt the integration of technology while doing this lesson was responsible for several major changes in her students. The lesson evolved to include math, geography, and science objectives for the students. Students were excited about being responsible for gathering the information about "their state." Mrs. Sheridan was surprised by a sustained, high interest level in the project during the course of the school year. She observed a high level of ownership by the students for their state and the data collection process. Mrs. Sheridan identified the student-initiated conversations regarding comparisons or explanations for the differences in the colors as examples of high student interest in the project. Students compared the colors in their states and often asked questions about why some states seemed to change very little while other states had days with many different colors. Students reported information they had heard about their state from television or radio weather and news reports.

Mrs. Sheridan also noted very subtle observations the students were making during the project. They began forming generalizations about the colors in their state and were quick to notice exceptions to the established patterns. They used the surface temperature map image extensively and started asking questions about why their home state was sometimes warmer or colder than other states located next to it. They began to notice that the colors on the map generally moved from one direction across the map. Mrs. Sheridan was pleased with the level of student-to-student conversations that developed while students were drawing conclusions about the patterns and relationships in the weather data displays. The lesson added visuals to help the students develop a spatial concept of the United States. This is something that had previously been very difficult for most of her first-grade students. She felt that the lesson continued to be flexible and was easily directed toward the students' interests and questions.

Mrs. Sheridan gained a great deal of confidence in using the computers with her students through this lesson. The students were introduced to the Web browser at a very basic level. The surface temperature map Web site was very reliable, and Mrs. Sheridan thought this reliability was critical to the success of the project. There were very few days that the Web site was not updated with the exception of certain days that seemed to correspond to national holidays when their school was in session. The technology tools were effective because they provided the students with the information and did not consume a great deal of the teacher's instructional time. The students learned the graphing program very quickly and could enter their data quickly. They could navigate using the icon buttons needing little assistance to create and print their graphs. Mrs. Sheridan thought this was also very important so that the lesson was truly a student activity and not something that the teacher did for the students.

Mrs. Sheridan also noted that having the computer stations located in her room contributed to the success of the project. In the past when she took her students to the school's computer lab, the children were often excited and distracted by the "new" environment and did not seem to stay on task. Once the computers were in her classroom, it became routine for the students to use the computers to get their weather data and to complete their graphs at the end of each month. The students were able to focus on the assignment.

Mrs. Sheridan felt the simplicity of the two technology resources used in the project was very important. She was very skeptical in the beginning about how the technology would work. By keeping the design simple, she felt the lesson had a much greater chance of being effective. Using one Web site was manageable since the children did not have to wait for screens to load over the network. Once the weather map was up on the screen, all of the children could get their data for the activity without waiting for the Web browser to load additional images. Mrs. Sheridan reported the ease of use for both the instructor and the students as compared to the benefits the students received as one of the most important factors in judging the success of the lesson. Using one Web site and one graphing program might appear to be an under-utilization of the vast resources available on the Internet. However, Mrs. Sheridan viewed this limited use as an effective strategy for the developmental level of her first-grade students. The students were not overwhelmed with information and were self-sufficient when completing the activity each day. By limiting the number of Web sites and software programs used, Mrs. Sheridan reduced the number of possible glitches that might emerge during the lesson.

The success of integrating technology resources and tools into the weather data lesson was instrumental in providing a frame of reference for Mrs. Sheridan to design additional technology integration lessons for her first-grade classroom. The lesson offered students visual displays of information and the ability to manipulate their own information, which was not possible with her former traditional approach. The lesson created a successful experience for both the classroom teacher and the students, which in turn encouraged the teacher to generate additional classroom lessons that incorporated technology tools in the instruction. Creating the vision for how technology can improve student achievement and comprehension in the classroom is an essential step for teachers to develop new teaching strategies that use technology tools and resources effectively in instruction.

REFERENCES

Beane, J. A. (1993). Problems and possibilities for an integrative curriculum. In R. Fogarty, (Ed.), *Integrating the curricula* (pp. 69-83). Palatine, IL: IRI/Skylight Publishing.

Dockstader, J. (1999). Teachers of the 21st century know the what, why, and how of technology integration. *T.H.E. Journal, 26*(6), 73.

Graphers [Computer software]. (1996). Pleasantville, NY: Sunburst Communications.

National Council of Teachers of Mathematics. (1989). *Curriculum and evaluation standards for school mathematics*. Reston, VA: Author.

OSU Weather [Online]. (1997). Available: *http://twister.sbs.ohio-state.edu/text/wximages/us/ustemp.gif*

Ploger, D., Klingler, L., & Rooney, M. (1997). Spreadsheets, patterns, and algebraic thinking. *Teaching Children Mathematics, 3*(6), 330-5.

Resnick, L. B. (1987). *Education and learning to think*. Washington DC: National Academy Press.

Rachel B. Gerstein

Videoconferencing in the Classroom: Special Projects Toward Cultural Understanding

SUMMARY. *This article presents a case study of a pilot program implemented with San Franciscan and Taiwanese fourth graders. The project utilized videoconferencing technology to create a collaborative cultural exchange in which students from both cities saw an art exhibit,* The Splendors of Imperial China, *and participated in a dialogue addressing the content of the exhibit, as well as their own cultural backgrounds. The program proved to be a great success based on the students' improved ability, increased knowledge, and changed attitudes toward technology in learning. Videoconferencing has been shown to have great success in classroom collaborations such as this one in educational institutions around the world. [Article copies available for a fee from The Haworth Document Delivery Service: 1-800-342-9678. E-mail address: <getinfo@haworthpressinc.com> Website: <http://www.HaworthPress.com>]*

KEYWORDS. *Videoconferencing, cultural exchange, computer technology, virtual technology*

THE PROJECT

When the internationally acclaimed art exhibit, *The Splendors of Imperial China*, toured the United States several years ago, one of its

RACHEL B. GERSTEIN is Technology Integration Specialist, Arts Educator, Sage Ridge School, Reno, NV 89509. E-mail: gerstein@scs.unr.edu

[Haworth co-indexing entry note]: "Videoconferencing in the Clasroom: Special Projects Toward Cultural Understanding." Gerstein, Rachel B. Co-published simultaneously in *Computers in the Schools* (The Haworth Press, Inc.) Vol. 16, No. 3/4, 2000, pp. 177-186; and: *Integration of Technology into the Classroom: Case Studies* (ed: D. LaMont Johnson, Cleborne D. Maddux, and Leping Liu) The Haworth Press, Inc., 2000, pp. 177-186. Single or multiple copies of this article are available for a fee from The Haworth Document Delivery Service [1-800-342-9678, 9:00 a.m. - 5:00 p.m. (EST). E-mail address: getinfo@haworthpressinc.com].

177

stops was in San Francisco. Several local organizations decided upon collaboration that would enhance the content of the exhibit for local students as well as put it into a much broader geographical and cultural context. Two San Francisco arts organizations offered a cultural exchange between a group of fourth-grade students in San Francisco and Taipei. It was felt that a project of this design would promote a deeper understanding of the art of China and the traveling exhibit by increasing students' direct involvement with the art and culture, while at the same time exposing students and teachers to new technologies for global communications.

The students in each group made a video of their preparations to visit *The Splendors of Imperial China* exhibition at the Asian Art Museum in San Francisco and the National Palace Museum in Taipei. The students then exchanged their videos and each sent the other a Treasure Box inspired by actual pieces of art from the exhibition, but filled with riches meaningful to the students, such as toys, hand-made jewelry, small books, cartoons, political propaganda, and artwork.

The students at each site prepared a production that would be presented during a one-hour videoconferencing session as the finale of the project. The San Francisco students worked with their teachers and a professional storyteller to prepare a puppet show based on their own original modern adaptation of an ancient Chinese fable. The students in Taipei learned a repertoire of both traditional American and Taiwanese music.

Finally, as the culminating event, the children from these two Pacific Rim nations performed the presentations during a live videoconference. The videoconference provided an exciting opportunity for the two classrooms to meet face to face to discuss their cultural similarities and differences and present an artistic production to one another.

This project was responsive to the needs of students and teachers to advanced technological resources while helping them to see museums as a living resource for education and pleasure.

SUCCESSFUL PLANNING

Planning ahead is essential in organizing an undertaking such as this. The planning process began several months before the actual dialogue transpired. It is important to leave plenty of time to plan all the minute details, no matter how trivial they may seem. There are limitations and obstacles in carrying out a videoconferencing exchange, but they can nearly all be overcome with some careful forethought. Most arrangements during the planning process were made via fax or e-mail between partnering sites in San Francisco and Taipei. E-mail is probably the best, easiest, and most affordable form of communication for this purpose.

If geographical distances are great, then the time difference may prove a complicating factor. It is therefore important to take the time difference into consideration and always do at least one test call (at the same time of day at which your real call is planned) to insure that both systems are functioning properly and can communicate easily at the desired times. There is nothing more frustrating than spending several months planning and waiting only to have everything ruined at the last minute because of a technical oversight. Again, it is essential to allow extra time for all communications where major time differences exist. For example, San Francisco faxes reached Taipei in the middle of the night, so there was a full day of lapse time in between exchanges. One major obstacle impeding the success of this project was the organizing of both groups to be at an appropriate time and place simultaneously. Because the time difference was so large, it was important for both groups to be alert and engaged (ready, not sleepy) at the time of the exchange. This was achieved through meticulous planning and organization.

It is a good idea to do one test run several weeks prior to the scheduled date, and one again the day before. The earlier test will provide enough time to make alterations if anything major needs to be changed. The latter will let you know that all systems are ready for your actual event. It is important to note that, once a system has been initially installed and configured, there may not be the need to perform so much testing prior to a scheduled activity.

Key among the details is making sure the partnering videoconferencing equipment is compatible with the host site equipment. This may often prove more complicated than it seems and holds the potential to destroy an otherwise seamless project. It is probably a good idea to enlist the aid of a trained technician to configure both systems initially. Once the systems have been programmed to "speak" to each other, communications can be quite simple. Insuring that all equipment functioned and was in the best operable condition required energy and organization. It is far better to be more attentive to these details than to unintentionally ruin an exchange.

Finding equipment and insuring that there was an allotted amount of money to cover the cost of the actual call time also proved difficult. One can easily research this in advance to approximate the charge. Remember to look at the origination of the call, as well as the length and start and end times. There are many local sources to turn to for support in this area. Most universities have a videoconferencing facility of some sort and hopefully a kind technician who will help. Satellite offices of hardware or software companies that are located in your community may also be good resources. They may have equipment or may be able to refer you to others in your city that do. The local phone company is also a good resource for support, either by in-kind support of your connection time or a small grant. Granting organizations are eager to support pilot projects that utilize innovative uses of new technologies. Take advantage of this unique place in time and seek out some of these grant opportunities. Organizations such as the International Society for Technology in Education (International, 1999) and Classroom Connect (Classroom, 1999) provide monthly listings of grant and project opportunities.

Finally, preparing the students for the actual videoconference is essential. Explaining how the connection works and what to expect in the way of language issues, lag time, video quality, personal appearance, and manners is important for a seamless exchange. Technical information about lighting and audio transmission is not only helpful for students to comprehend, but once they understand how these factors operate in the final product, they can take charge of running them during the actual videoconference.

EDUCATIONAL AND ARTISTIC GOALS

Primary source learning is more reliable than any other form. What better and more engaging method of learning than from the actual origin, live! Videoconferencing is so engaging because it is real time, live-action education. While educators can provide exciting and stimulating resources in the classroom, there is nothing that compares to information gathered from the source. Two-way exchange also allows students to become content experts, a more motivating way of engaging them in the learning process. With these objectives in mind, it was believed that the videoconferencing experience would foster a more efficient learning experience. Project goals included:

1. To develop a greater awareness of multimedia technology as a tool for the classroom and studio environments.
2. To develop effective methods of communication utilizing new technologies.
3. To learn to use art and story as models of communication.
4. To develop an appreciation for art and what museums have to offer to the educational community.
5. To develop the ability to convey our different feelings, experiences, and beliefs through art and story.
6. To develop an appreciation for the culture in which an artwork was created.
7. To develop an awareness and appreciation for different ways of looking at the world.
8. To find or create connection in difference.

A caveat applies here, and that is to insure that there is indeed an exchange or active dialogue taking place. Otherwise, the students may as well be watching a video. Teachers or moderators can support this exchange by planning an active experience and avoiding yes/no questions, lengthy readings or lectures, and single-direction transmissions.

OLD METHODS, NEW OPPORTUNITIES

There are several models for an undertaking such as this one. Traditionally a project of this nature would probably be carried out using written documents and utilizing the pen-pal model, in which students communicate and reciprocate ideas and information through a written exchange. While this method of exchange has always been a fruitful and effective one, it is limited in the nature of the communication that takes place and the effect on the students outside of the actual written documents.

A step beyond the older model would be the utilization of e-mail. In this type of exchange, students are basically communicating in the same way as with the older method of written correspondence, with the addition of speed and more instant response and gratification. Whereas in the first model students must wait days, weeks, or in some cases even months to get a response, e-mail allows for an immediate and sometimes even live communication process.

Videoconferencing enhances the two earlier models in its audiovisual capacity. Videoconferencing is the actual live transmission of compressed audio and video from one location to another. As this transmission is accomplished across phone or network lines, it is almost instantaneous and can go anywhere that these connections are already established. The visual and auditory interaction that transpires not only addresses the needs of more types of learners, it is also an integral part of developing a relationship or sense of connection among participants.

ABOUT VIDEOCONFERENCING

The first videoconferencing took place at the World's Fair in New York in 1964 (PictureTel, 1995). At a cost of millions of dollars, videoconferencing was expensive, clumsy, and not yet ready for the educational arena. A lot has changed since then.

Videoconferencing technology today involves two or more people in separate locations who share audio and video, and can additionally collaborate utilizing shared computer applications (Reed, 1997). There is great potential in this new communication technology, as it offers previously unheard of possibilities for educational programming. Pioneers in the videoconferencing field have already incorporated the technology into distance learning (Heller, 1999) guest appearances in classrooms by scientists, authors, and politicians; collaborations between schools, museums, and artists; professional development opportunities for teachers; and broadcasting of community events.

Among the many benefits of incorporating videoconferencing into classroom instruction are the ways in which it opens the classroom to the world outside. Videoconferencing can, virtually, take students out of the classroom and bring experts and mentors in, while never physically moving anyone. Many organizations, nationally and internationally, are beginning to understand the broad appeal of videoconferencing and the huge enhancement that it can enable in an educational setting. Institutions such as the Cincinnati Zoo, the Museum of Tolerance in Los Angeles, the Monterey Bay Aquarium on the California Coast, the Liberty Science Center in New Jersey, NASA, the Exploratorium in San Francisco, and the Jerusalem Museum in Israel already have regular videoconferencing programs established to work with teachers and to provide expert ideas, opinions, and communications to young people in schools around the globe (Pacific Bell, 1999).

The opportunities for enhanced learning are as broad as the imagination. Students studying marine ecosystems can get answers to specific research questions directly from scientists at the Monterey Bay Aquarium. Students can witness nocturnal or off-hour activities at a science center that would normally be inaccessible to the public (Dove, 1997). A history unit focused on World War II can take on new life and emotional depth as students can ask questions directly to a war veteran. A live museum tour, transmitted via videoconference, can send an exhibit out for students to experience and enjoy, regardless of where they live. A geography lesson becomes a virtual fieldtrip, as students are able to see the landscape in remote parts of the world and ask their peers about the look and feel of the region. The possibilities are endless. It is, of course, important to remember that, while the technology makes these events possible, it is the creativity and organization of the teacher and the participation and enthusiasm of the students, guests, and educational institutions that make successful lessons incorporating videoconferencing work effectively. Videoconferencing experiences in the classroom have had a positive impact on student outcomes in the following areas:

Increased Student Motivation

1. The introduction of technology into the classroom provides an added level of thrill surrounding each project or activity, increasing student motivation and interest. In the same way that TV and computer-based learning often prove to be more engaging to students, videoconferencing is an enticing and motivating medium for learning.

2. The simplicity of videoconferencing (once it is established–set up can be tricky) makes it a truly empowering tool for student use. By taking students outside of the physical classroom, their sense of pride and accomplishment is increased and each student's desire to work toward a higher level of achievement is enhanced.

3. Videoconferencing has shown great success as a tool toward second language acquisition. The live communication with native

speakers has proven to be highly motivating for student success (Mosby, 1997).

Enhanced Communication and Presentation Skills

1. Students are more conscious of their appearance and oral communication when there is a guest present. While videoconferencing, guests are actually at remote sites; students retain this increased sensitivity to language and decorum.
2. Planning a videoconferencing session requires focused organization and attention to detail. Participation in this process provides students with an increased awareness of organizational skills and a more cognizant realization of how language skills are used and perceived by others.
3. Over the course of a project, students' dress, posture, and behavior may change in response to the fact that they are able to view themselves as others view them, and are more acutely aware of their own behavior (Reed, 1997).

Increased Geographical and Cultural Connections

1. Meaningful connections can be developed between groups that would otherwise be completely isolated due to geographic and financial restrictions.
2. Participants are automatically exposed to multiple perspectives on a given subject in a way that might not be possible through the simple use of a textbook-style education.
3. Videoconferencing events provide students and teachers with an opportunity to establish significant relationships with children, specialists, and educators from a variety of cultural and socio-economic backgrounds.
4. Students have the opportunity to create a true community between schools, classrooms, and professional organizations while learning about human knowledge, interests, and diversity.

Expanded Degree of Learning

1. Students are involved in an experiential learning situation and develop better and more creative thinking skills. For example,

students quickly learn to ask more complex questions, as a simple yes/no inquiry elicits a quick and boring response during a videoconferencing session.

2. The authentic learning that takes place when a student communicates with an actual scientist or professional often promotes a deeper level of understanding of the information being discussed, as intelligent questions and discussions are expected to be formulated.

3. Knowledge is obtained directly from the source (artist, scientist, specialist, or real person) as opposed to a filtered view in a textbook. It is, of course, always essential to educate students to evaluate the validity of any source, live or otherwise.

4. Lessons often require more development time from the teachers and students, and the level of engagement nearly always leads to an increased understanding of the subject matter.

THE RESULTS

Although there was only one actual face-to-face videoconferencing meeting between the fourth-graders in San Francisco and Taipei, there was so much build up during the course of the project, that the final event was very exciting and rewarding for all involved.

While we were fortunate to have access to a high-end videoconferencing system, the interface was such that the students easily manipulated it on their own, dialed the call, and ran the system during almost all of the hour-long session. The sense of accomplishment among the class was large and clear. They had taken ownership of the project all along the way, and orchestrating the actual call was the final icing on the cake!

The interaction among the children was quite amusing. There were some surprising answers to the questions they asked, and they made very clear connections and distinctions between the two groups.

The project was assessed in the form of a follow-up survey that was completed by students, teachers, and facilitators involved with the videoconference. The results confirmed what the program directors had predicted. The cultural exchange had been more engaging and the information retention more complete than with a traditional classroom experience. Students remembered more detail about the experience and were eager to discuss and share what they had learned. Teachers, especially, noted the students' incredible enthusiasm, energy, and eagerness to repeat the activity.

There are many sites nationally and internationally that are interested in participating in a cultural exchange. Additionally, cultural and educational institutions worldwide are installing the necessary equipment to send and receive educational transmissions. A wide range of affordable systems are now available for use in schools and classrooms. One of the best resources for anyone interested in videoconferencing is the very comprehensive Knowledge Network Explorer Web site (Pacific Bell, 1999). This site is a great starting point and provides information on contacts, equipment, costs, and directories of schools and organizations with which to collaborate. Videoconferencing provides an exciting and engaging new medium for learning, and it is imperative that educators take a pivotal role in the further development of this technology so that it can be customized to the needs of the classroom.

REFERENCES

Classroom Connect (November 1, 1999) by [Online]. Available: *http://www.classroom connect. org*

Dove, K. (May 21, 1997). Available by e-mail: *kdove@lsc.org*

Heller, F. (August 12, 1999). *Basic curriculum over videoconference.* Available by *global@gwi.net*

International Society for Technology in Education (November 1, 1999) [Online]. Available: *http://www.iste.org*

Mosby, J., & Woodruff, M. (February 10, 1997). *Videoconferencing in the classroom and Library* [Online]. Available: *http://www.kn.pacbell.com/vidconf*

Pacific Bell Knowledge Network Explorer (June 21, 1999) [Online]. Available: *http://www.kn.pacbell.com/vidconf*

PictureTel Corporation. (1995). *Videoconferencing 101: How does videoconferencing work?* [Brochure].

Reed, J. (May 22, 1997). *Summary. Impact of videoconferencing on learning* Available by e-mail: *jreed@mail.sdsu.edu*

Bruce O. Barker
David J. Whiting

Teaching and Learning in World Wide Web-Connected Classrooms

SUMMARY. *Use of the Web as an instructional tool is growing rapidly as the nation's classrooms increasingly come online with high capacity bandwidth. To optimize the use of the Web as an instructional tool, the traditional roles of students and teachers must shift to that of an "engaged model" of teaching and learning. This article presents strategies for effectively teaching and learning on the Web and introduces SURWEB as an Internet-based multimedia resource for engaged learning. [Article copies available for a fee from The Haworth Document Delivery Service: 1-800-342-9678. E-mail address: <getinfo@haworthpressinc.com> Website: <http://www.HaworthPress.com>]*

KEYWORDS. *Web-based instruction, engaged learning, multimedia tools, SURWEB*

Of the technology-related initiatives issued by federal and state education agencies in recent years, the most pronounced is to connect

BRUCE O. BARKER is Dean, College of Education, Southern Utah University, Cedar City, UT 84720. E-mail: barker@suu.edu
DAVID J. WHITING is Assistant Professor, Educational Technology, College of Education, Southern Utah University, Cedar City, UT 84720. E-mail: whiting @suu.edu

[Haworth co-indexing entry note]: "Teaching and Learning in World Wide Web-Connected Classrooms." Barker, Bruce O. and David J. Whiting. Co-published simultaneously in *Computers in the Schools* (The Haworth Press, Inc.) Vol. 16, No. 3/4, 2000, pp. 187-196; and: *Integration of Technology into the Classroom: Case Studies* (ed: D. LaMont Johnson, Cleborne D. Maddux, and Leping Liu) The Haworth Press, Inc., 2000, pp. 187-196. Single or multiple copies of this article are available for a fee from The Haworth Document Delivery Service [1-800-342-9678, 9:00 a.m. - 5:00 p.m. (EST). E-mail address: getinfo@haworthpressinc. com].

187

schools and classrooms to the ubiquitous resources of the Internet and the World Wide Web. Of the U.S. Department of Education's top seven priorities, the one dealing with technology states: "Every classroom will be connected to the Internet by the year 2000 and all students will be technologically literate" (U.S. Department of Education, 1997). In July of 1998, U.S. Secretary of Education Richard Riley reported that while 78% of public schools had Internet connectivity only 27% of classrooms were connected (Riley, 1998). By the time this article is published, that number will definitely have increased, but it is highly unlikely that all classrooms will have Internet access until early into the first decade of the twenty-first century. Yet Nicholas Negroponte (1995) predicted that the Internet would be the telecommunications technology having the greatest impact on education in the coming years.

The promise of Internet connectivity and high capacity bandwidth with rapid access to the World Wide Web empowers teachers and students to more fully integrate technology as a regular part of classroom instruction. Through access to the incomprehensible amount of resources on the Web, teachers in Web-supported classrooms are able to:

1. take students on electronic fieldtrips;
2. clarify and expand new information learned each day in the classroom;
3. design lesson plans and enrichment materials in support of local and national learning standards;
4. arrange for students to participate in collaborative projects with students from other schools across their state, from out-of-state, or in foreign countries; and
5. provide students access to the massive collections of informational resources regularly being added to the Web.

THE CHANGING ROLE
OF TEACHERS AND STUDENTS
WORKING ON THE WEB

Contemporary education has evolved beyond the philosophy of the teacher being the all-knowing disseminator of knowledge and students as passive recipients. Internet connectivity brings to schools the dynamic of cyberspace, with teachers and students now able to access resources and databases far beyond the confines of the classroom (Garrett & Weiner, 1998; Barker, 1998).

Teachers who hope to optimize the instructional potential of the Web must employ new skills and learning strategies in their teaching that will help students accept increased accountability to learn on their own and in cooperative groups and to draw meaningful conclusions from such inquiry. New teaching/learning methods researched in recent years as successful strategies for increasing student accountability focus on a model of "engaged learning" promoted by the North Central Regional Educational Laboratory (NCREL). Researchers at NCREL define engaged learning as "learning that involves more student interactions, more connections among institutions, more collaboration among teachers and students, and more emphasis on technology as a tool for learning" (Jones, Valdez, Nowakowski, & Rasmussen, 1992, p. 2).

Learning how to learn and doing so over a lifetime are at the heart of engaged learning. The engaged learning model centers on the use of information and communications technologies as tools to assist teachers in helping students take responsibility for their own learning, become knowledge explorers, and collaborate with others to find information and to seek answers to problems. In an engaged learning model, teachers move beyond the role of knowledge dispensers and are seen as facilitators, guides, and co-learners with their students. They mediate, model, and coach their students. While making use of electronic databases and information resources beyond traditional textbooks and chalkboards, teachers and students periodically change roles–that is, students may become "teachers" and teachers may become "students." As engaged learners, both teachers and students become "technonauts," knowledge explorers who use technology tools to find, exchange, and analyze digital information (Barker & Dickson, 1999; Jones et al., 1994).

STRATEGIES FOR TEACHING AND LEARNING ON THE WEB

Web-connected classrooms empower teachers and students to form learning communities. These virtual communities of learners emerge wherever a group of learners (possibly in different locations) carry on public discussions with sufficient human interaction to form learning relationships in cyberspace. Teachers and students in virtual learning communities use words and images on screen to exchange greetings, engage in intellectual discourse, conduct meetings, share knowledge, offer emotional support, make plans, brainstorm ideas, learn about other cultures, and otherwise broaden horizons. In fact, they do much of what others do in traditional classrooms, but they do it online and thereby extend the community of the classroom to the community of the world (Norton & Wiberg, 1998).

Using the Web as a teaching/learning tool permits interactive and nonlinear navigation by students through learning materials that activate the senses of sight, sound, and cognitive reasoning. And, via the Web, students and teachers can access hypermedia online learning resources at anytime, day or night. Hypermedia learning activities might include informational searches, electronic process writing, sequential creations, parallel problem solving, virtual gatherings, simulations, social action projects (Harris, 1995), or multimedia production projects. The use of Web-based resources and multimedia production tools further allows teachers and students to participate in a variety of activities that enhance the educational process.

SURWEB:
AN INTERNET-BASED RESOURCE
FOR ENGAGED LEARNING

The exponential growth of the Internet with its equally rapid developments in digital media capabilities is increasingly making it easy for teachers and students to work with video, animation, music, text, still pictures, and 3D graphics for local production of hypermedia learning projects noted above. One excellent example is the SURWEB multimedia tool and resource database available free on the Web at (*http://www.surweb.org/*). SURWEB is the State of Utah Resource Web initiated in 1995 by a consortium of public and private agencies including Utah's K-12 educational service centers, institutions of higher education, WestEd Regional Education Laboratory, museums, state and national parks, and Native American tribal councils and agencies. The $3.3 million project is in its third year of a five-year grant funded by Federal Technology Challenge monies (Spendlove, 1999).

SURWEB has K-12 applications far beyond the borders of Utah. Its growing archives presently include over 22,000 images with related text files. The project initially focused on national parks and monuments, geological formations, native cultures, and wildlife of western America but has since expanded to topics across the school curriculum. Its growing database provides teachers with hundreds of media shows, electronic fieldtrips, and standards-based learning units. Furthermore, the tool enables students and teachers to create and produce multimedia presentations for interchange with other students or for delivery in their home schools. A media basket function, standards-based test bank, and an online tutorial are a few of SURWEB's features. The media basket allows students or teachers to capture images from anywhere on the Web (or from SURWEB's own database of images), add text, and thereby produce their own media shows. A sampling of student/teacher produced media shows include:

1. The Golden Spike National Historical Monument
   http://www.surweb.org/surweb/images/gsn/coverpage/gsn.htm

2. Navajo Rugs
   http://www.surweb.org/surweb/images/nvr/coverpage/nvr.htm

3. The Old Spanish Trail
   http://www.surweb.org/surweb/images/OST/coverpage/OST.htm

4. Dinosaur National Monument
   http://www.surweb.org/surweb/images/dnm/coverpage/dnm.htm

5. Zion National Park
   http://www.surweb.org/surweb/images/zio/coverpage/zio.htm

6. Mountain Men Rendezvous
   http://www.surweb.org/surweb/images/mtm/coverpage/mtm.htm

7. The Desert Tortoise
   http://www.surweb.org/surweb/images/DTS/coverpage/DTS.htm

8. Native Plants and Medicine
   http://www.surweb.org/surweb/images/npm/coverpage/npm.htm

9. Ancient Egypt
   http://www.surweb.org/search/view_custom_show.asp?msid=354

10. Man on the Moon
    http://www.surweb.org/search/view_custom_show.asp?msid=557

11. Fractals: The Art of Mathematics
    http://www.surweb.org/search/view_custom_show.asp?msid=1542

Media shows either have been or are being added in each of the following curriculum categories: agricultural, business, career guidance, dance, family and consumer science, foreign language, health science, health education, information technology, language arts, library media, marketing, mathematics, music, physical education, school-to-work, science, social studies, technology, theater, and visual arts.

SURWEB helps teachers go beyond the textbook. It allows teachers to research and archive a wide range of information. Students become knowledge explorers by organizing and prioritizing their information with the media basket tool while simultaneously reflecting on cognitive connections within their research.

EXAMPLES OF SUCCESSFUL
CLASSROOM INSTRUCTION

New teacher skills: *mediate, model, coach.* New approaches to facilitating learning require new perspectives. Teachers at Mt. Logan Middle School in Paradise, Utah, had the opportunity to experience these new roles and put aside the fear of change as well as the fear of all the ways technology can go wrong in the classroom. Students were assigned a cultural research project where students took on the role of tourist consultant, with instructions to put together an Internet slide show using the SURWEB media basket. Upon completion, shows were published on the Web. The main objective was for students to find out what there is in our state to see and do. And they achieved that goal. I had a lot of surprised kids say, "Oh wow, you mean that's in Utah? We want to go there!" (Tyner, 1998). By using SURWEB to engage students, this teacher was able to change the learning approach from "teacher director" to "student explorers."

Learning how to learn. In order to be successful in facilitating student projects on the Web, teachers must help students set goals, self-monitor, define problems, reflect and ask questions, and evaluate self and others (Fine, 1998). Lindsey, a seventh-grade student, described how she met her goals: "Instead of doing a poster, we used SURWEB to do our project. I am not a computer pro, but I do use computers. I chose the pictures that showed the arch, or the plants, or the soil, or something that I wanted to talk about." Lindsey was able to organize her images in the order she wanted. At the same time, Lindsey was able to gather information about Web resources and use that information to describe her project. She reported: "I took notes of what was there and then I totally re-wrote it in my own words. Then I published what I wrote on SURWEB. I learned a lot."

As Lindsey used online tools to clarify and expand her learning objectives, she met social studies and language fluency standards. Since the work was archived on a remote Web database, she was also able to complete work outside of school and perform her work for an authentic audience at home:

> At first I thought it would be really easy. But it was a little bit harder to learn SURWEB than I thought at first. But towards the middle, I got it. I didn't get completely done here [at the school lab], so I went to my cousin's house because they have a computer that's hooked to the Internet. And it was nice, because I knew how to use SURWEB without a teacher being there. I could show it to my cousins and my mom. She thought it was cool. (Tyner, 1998)

Students as knowledge explorers and as knowledge producers. In Brigham City, Utah, students were able to explore Web resources even without the latest and fastest machines. Several teachers downloaded SURWEB content and had students build reports in HyperStudio. Their work included: "Medicinal Plants of Utah," a multi-curricular report about frontier medicine.

Students were also able to experience immediate authorship and publication. Kathy Olds, a third-grade teacher in Brigham City, developed a learning segment with her class about the Jensen Historical Farm, a working agriculture museum. Students planned a fieldtrip, assisted in photography, and selected the pictures they would upload. They also collaborated on the "expert text" that would go with each picture. All this was done in spite of only having one non-networked 286 computer in the classroom.

What this class actually accomplished was the development of ordering and sequencing, and of narrative and language fluency higher order thinking skills, all within the context of meeting science and social studies standards. Kathy Olds later said: "They used multimedia in a way that challenged all of their senses and took advantage of each child's distinctive learning preferences. If I can use SURWEB, anybody can. Where else do they get to apply these skills in such a rigorous fashion except in SURWEB?" (Tyner, 1998).

EVALUATION OF SURWEB PROJECTS

Students will value their own work as they realize the audience is live. More needs to be done to assist all teachers to conduct authentic education and research activities such as those in the examples. Students appreciated that they had the ability to access, work with, and generally show off their work, and to do so from any location with Web connectivity. As more teachers participate in similar activities, a broader array of student activities will be possible. In addition to online fieldtrips, lesson enrichment, and archiving of Web resources, through SURWEB students can also begin to use this database as the catalyst for online collaboration activities such as parallel problem solving, virtual gatherings, and sequential creations.

USING THE WEB

Successfully managing student learning in Internet-connected classrooms requires extra attention and planning on the part of teachers to assure that students maximize learning activities. Some suggestions for successful practice include (Cotton, 1998, pp. 66-67):

1. Develop a rationale or purpose as to why the lesson or unit is important and why it's important to use the Internet. This is important for both your students to know and for their parents.
2. Create lessons that use a variety of resources such as (off-line) books, encyclopedias, dictionaries, journals and magazines, atlases, as well as the Internet. We are preparing these students for the future where they will have to know many different ways to access information.
3. Have clear objectives for each unit of Internet-based instruction and discuss them in detail with your students prior to starting.

4. Demonstrate the lesson to your class before you send them off to work online. This will clear up any confusion that might occur, as well as reduce the amount of wasted online time that can happen when folks are not clear what they need to do.

5. Along the same lines, discuss each aspect of the lesson in detail so that your students know what to expect and what they have to do in order to learn the content.

6. Have your students develop a "Web Site Log" telling about the Web sites they have visited and what they learned from them. They can also copy/paste URLs for future referencing.

7. Create lessons that have a "set" at the beginning and "closure" at the end. The set creates extra interest in the lesson; the closure allows for some type of "product" to be shared with the group.

8. Include authentic activities and performances that can be conducted both on and off line. Interactivity in computer use encourages more active participation.

9. Bookmark three to five URLs for each lesson beforehand so that your students will have an idea of where they are expected to go on the Web.

CONCLUSION

While some skeptics may criticize the computer as a form of depersonalized learning, Internet-connected computers actually do more to provide learners with creative tools and put them in contact with other learners than any other telecommunications medium available. Web-connected computers promote the concept of a community of learners not only in traditional classrooms but also beyond the classroom in virtual learning communities with global connections.

As educators move into the year 2000 and beyond, our nation's students need to develop skill and expertise in accessing, exchanging, and analyzing digital information resources if they hope to be successful in the world and work place of the future. Without doubt, they need exposure to today's telecommunications tools in order to master the knowledge and the technology that will make them prosper. If the technology of the printing press and resulting books revolutionized learning in the fifteenth century, it is the technology of the computer and the Internet that will revolutionize learning in the twenty-first century. As the Internet continues to evolve and as students and teachers master skills in navigating through its databases, tools, and services, the information of the world will truly be at their fingertips and before their very eyes.

REFERENCES

Barker, B.O., & Dickson, M. W. (1999, Spring). Engaged learning: The changing role of teachers and students in a technological society. *Eastern Education Journal, 28*(1), 17-20.

Barker, B.O. (1998, Winter). The case for technology literacy in education. *The Utah Journal of Reading and Literacy, 3*(1), 20-29.

Cotton, E.G. (1998). *The online classroom: Teaching with the Internet.* Bloomington, IN: EDINFO Press and the ERIC Clearinghouse on Reading, English, and Communication.

Fine, C. (1999). *Learning with technology: Participant's manual.* Oak Brook, IL: North Central Regional Educational Laboratory.

Garrett, L.N, & Weiner, B.J. (1998, October). Learning on the Internet. *Teaching for Success, 10*(7), 4-5.

Harris, J. (1995, May). Educational telecomputing activities: Problem-solving projects. *Learning and Leading with Technology, 22*(8), 59-63. [Online]. Available: *http://lrs.ed.uiuc.edu/Mining/May95-TCT.html*

Jones, B., Valdez, G., Nowakowski, J., & Rasmussen, C. (1992). *Plugging in: Choosing and using educational technology.* Oak Brook, IL: North Central Regional Educational Laboratory.

Negroponte, N. (1995). *Being digital.* New York: Random House.

Norton, P., & Wiberg, K. (1998). *Teaching with technology.* Orlando, FL: Harcourt Brace.

Riley, R. (1998, July 29). Technology and education: An investment in equity and excellence. Speech presented at the National Press Club, Washington, D.C. [Online]. Available: *http://www.ed.gov/Speeches/980729.html*

Spendlove, C. (1999, January 22). SURWEB update and future development. Presentation at the Southwest Area Technology Team Strategic Planning Retreat, Kanab, UT.

Tyner, C. (1998). *The 1998 SURWEB evaluation* (Southeast Utah Regional Web). San Francisco, CA: WestEd Regional Education Laboratory.

Patricia McGee

Persistence and Motivation:
A New Teacher's Path
to Technology Infusion

SUMMARY. *This case study examines a new teacher's beliefs and perceptions about how and why technology can and should be used to support student learning. A middle school science teacher reflected upon her preparation for and applications of technology in her classroom. Data were generated through e-mail exchanges over the course of several months. Qualitative analysis identified themes including a nontechnology focus, expectations, rationale, impact, and beliefs and learned lessons. Findings suggest that for this teacher persistence was critical to learning in absence of pre-service or in-service learning opportunities in the effective application of technology to support learning. It is recommended that technology-oriented staff development incorporate theory, guidelines, models, and illustrations for effective and meaningful applications. [Article copies available for a fee from The Haworth Document Delivery Service: 1-800-342-9678. E-mail address: <getinfo@haworthpressinc.com> Website: <http://www.HaworthPress.com>]*

KEYWORDS. *Technology, computers, professional development, K-12 education*

PATRICIA MCGEE is Visiting Assistant Professor, University of Texas at San Antonio, 6900 N. Loop 1604 W., San Antonio, TX 78249. E-mail: pamcgee@tenet.edu

[Haworth co-indexing entry note]: "Persistence and Motivation: A New Teacher's Path to Technology Infusion." McGee, Patricia. Co-published simultaneously in *Computers in the Schools* (The Haworth Press, Inc.) Vol. 16, No. 3/4, 2000, pp. 197-211; and: *Integration of Technology into the Classroom: Case Studies* (ed: D. LaMont Johnson, Cleborne D. Maddux, and Leping Liu) The Haworth Press, Inc., 2000, pp. 197-211. Single or multiple copies of this article are available for a fee from The Haworth Document Delivery Service [1-800-342-9678, 9:00 a.m. - 5:00 p.m. (EST). E-mail address: getinfo@haworthpressinc.com].

197

Technology tools are increasingly infiltrating America's K-12 class-rooms. And yet teachers are not always prepared, interested, or convinced that these tools can actually support learning or justify replacing traditional, non-technological approaches to teaching. How and why do teachers choose to use technology in their classroom? In this area research has focused on the process of adoption for in-service teachers (Mandinach & Cline, 1996) and the inadequate preparation of pre-service teachers (ITRC, 1998; US Congress, 1998). The literature about beginning teachers reveals that most new teachers are concerned about managing their classrooms and tend to see computer integration as ancillary (Hunt, 1994; Novak & Knowles, 1991). Rather than attempt to determine why teachers do not use technology, this study considers why a new teacher would choose to do so. In an attempt to think more deeply about the transition from pre-service to in-service teachers, this case study looks at the experiences of a beginning middle school teacher and her reflections about how and why she chose to use technology in her classroom.

METHOD

A qualitative approach to inquiry was chosen to better investigate the experiences of a beginning teacher without presumptions. Oftentimes educators generalize research findings to practical classroom experiences in ways that may not be applicable to specific contexts and teacher understandings. This study focuses on the motivations, perceptions, and beliefs of one novice teacher rather than her abilities, skills, or frequent use of technology in the classroom. The intent is to describe experiences rather than label or quantify them. This intrinsic case study (Stake, 1994) examines the unique nature of one teacher's experience rather than represent that of many.

Mary, a middle school science teacher with two years of teaching experience, was chosen as the study informant for several reasons. As a first-year teacher she had used technology without specific or directed training. She chose to use technology, was interested in appropriate applications, and had reflected, and continues to reflect about how and why she uses technology to support instruction. She also has been acknowledged for her use of technology both within and outside of her school. The purposeful sample (Patton, 1990) provides a unique teacher who had succeeded in her decision to use technology in contexts not unlike those of other novice teachers. How she accomplished this when many new teachers do not is the key question for this study.

Data were generated during the summer over a two-month period through e-mail. Collecting data when Mary was not teaching gave her time to reflect and consider her actions and beliefs, a situation that supports deeper thinking and analysis about practice (McGee, submitted; McGee, 1998). Reflections about perceptions require time and a trustworthy, open-ended dialogue; Morgan calls such an interaction "reflective conversation" (1983, p. 374). The ongoing dialogue among researcher and informant provided a broad and comprehensive body of information from which themes began to emerge. Throughout the course of the study, data were analyzed and new questions posed. The constant comparison of data directed and informed the researcher in noting patterns (Erlandson, Harris, Skipper, & Allen, 1993) within Mary's statements. As the study narrative was being written, drafts were sent to Mary for her input. She was asked to correct, amend, or add to what was being reported. In this way author and informant co-constructed their understanding of the study focus.

Mary's experiences and processes about using technology are unique and may be best told as a story (Mishler, 1986).

MARY

Mary teaches eighth-grade earth science in a middle school in which 31% of the student population is disadvantaged, 47% are Hispanic, 41% are Caucasian, 9% are African American, 3% are Asian, and 3% are from other groups. The school is located in a lower middle-class neighborhood in the sixth largest school district in Texas. Notably, the school has been recognized for academic achievements for the past two years.

As soon as Mary finished her elementary certification with a concentration in biology, she immediately began work on a master's degree in curriculum and instruction with an emphasis in technology. There was no technology course in her certification program but she eventually took four technology courses as part of her graduate program during her second year of teaching. At the time of the study she had completed her second full year of teaching and was preparing for her third year. When she was hired, her principal was "clearly looking for someone who would not only use the technology but be a leader and teacher of others." Mary has written and received technology grants, including Earth and Beyond from NASA, two school district grants for technology development, G.L.O.B.E. Eisenhower monies, and the South Texas Coalition of Science Teachers Grant.

Mary's class size is "usually around 30" of which about one-fifth are special education students. Typically, male students slightly out-number female students. Mary estimates that 54% of her students are of Hispanic heritage, 43% Caucasian, 1% African American, 1% Asian, and 1% from other backgrounds. She does have one section of gifted and talented students for whom the curriculum is condensed and topics extended. It is important to note that most of her students "don't have computers at home but have used one at a library that is within walking distance from the school." The students are required to take one semester of computer science in the seventh grade that is offered in the school computer lab.

Mary used technology in different ways. The following section describes several projects she implemented in her second year of teaching.

PROJECTS

Climate

Climate is always a topic of conversation in South Texas and, fortu-itously, the beginning of the school year coincides with hurricane season. Mary knew that "the Internet was an excellent technology tool from which to inquire as to current hurricane activity." Using a tool called Presenter Plus™, she fed a live Internet connection into a televi-sion monitor for large group viewing. Using Weather Underground (*http://wunderground.com*), the class was able to "gather sunrise, moonrise, moonset, moon phase, and current hurricane activity in the Atlantic and Pacific."

The class also participated in the G.L.O.B.E. project sponsored by the National Aeronautics and Space Administration (NASA) (*http://globe.fsl.noaa.gov*). In this program "students collect real data and send it to NASA, via the Internet, to a real scientist." Over the course of the project, "students have the opportunity to pose questions [that are] related to protocols they take measurements from." Mary notes that "students generally find the questions when they sense the data doesn't seem right or we are working on putting in a new protocol and run into problems." This provided a unique opportunity for problem solving. Mary recounts what happened when the class was inquiring "about elevation changes that seem to occur from the Global Position Satellite (GPS) unit that we used to take longitude and latitude readings to verify" their exact location on Earth.

> We were getting weird readings one day and did an inquiry and found out the false readings were intentional from the US government as a security protection from unfriendly countries. The system is not always on and that is why we hadn't encountered this war time policy.

This incident "lead to a discussion of peace time policies versus war time policies" as students investigated how and why these policies were in place, especially in peace time.

As part of the study of climate, students are required to "go outside and draw the clouds that are present prior to any formal study" as a precursor to learning cloud types. The G.L.O.B.E. project "has a tutorial for learning cloud types" that is connected to the "University of Michigan and has real photos (some live) of the ten basic cloud types [Mary] requires [her] kids to learn." The G.L.O.B.E. site has come in handy when the Texas clouds "just evaporate" and then so does the lesson! This tool allows for individualization so that students can practice and take a "tamper-proof quiz" for which scores can be printed and used as part of learning assessment. Mary has used these scores to create "scientist teams."

> The students that pass the quiz first are my first G.L.O.B.E. scientists [who lead] a team of four students that go outside to take data during the warm up part of my class. . . . I change this team each week so all students get an opportunity to be a G.L.O.B.E. scientist for a week.

This project illustrates some instructional underpinnings that have helped shape Mary's classroom structure. Student questions drive part of the curriculum as students work in teams to find answers, working much the same way as scientists work with technology and one another. Student-driven inquiry and curriculum reflect constructivist practices in which students are provided opportunities to pose and find answers to their own questions as opposed to focusing on pre-ordained curriculum (Fosnot, 1996).

Geology

Geology is a major focus in the study of Earth science since geology is "always in the news, whether it is floods, hurricanes, tornadoes, earthquakes, mudslides, forest fires . . . the face of the earth is constantly changing and the Internet provides a way to explore these ideas on a moment by moment basis."

Earthquakes are one phenomenon particularly supported by Internet resources. Mary uses the U.S. Geological Survey site (*http://quake.wr. usgs.gov/QUAKES/CURRENT/quicklook.html*) "to access the most recent earthquakes." Students record data "on world maps using latitude and longitude and the depth of the quakes" which "helps when we get to Earth history and examine Alvarez's Theories of Impact Craters and look at plate movement and active volcanoes" (*http://www.volcanoeworld. gov*).

Mary's class also uses technology in the study of rocks. As a new teacher her "rock collection is still very much" growing, so she uses WWW sites that examine local geological formations (*http://uts.cc.utexas. edu/~rmr/*). She feels that "virtual fieldtrips are better than none" and uses these to "motivate students for extra credit, since the whole area is rich in geological history."

Another tool Mary uses to support learning is a program called GETIT ™ (*http://cambriansystems.com/getit.htm*), a product which she has been field-testing. This CD-ROM contains a virtual museum with a "library, note pad, inquiry simulation [through which] students can save work to a database and add to it as we work." Students are able to explore and collaborate in a virtual space that replicates an authentic work environment.

As students "learn about the different layers of the Earth," they are given options about assignments that involve technology. They can create a PowerPoint ™ presentation or a "travel brochure, journal or story that describes a journey through the Earth to its center which is creative but scientifically accurate." Students analyze and apply their learning as they reorganize information they have collected.

Through the G.L.O.B.E. site, the class has also explored 3-D images of the "Mid-Atlantic Ridge and compared it to the Pacific plate and

Hawaii in terms of how the rate of plate movement is so different." This tool "provides depth not available with models," that are prohibitively expensive.

Space

Mary uses several NASA CD-ROMs, such as *Our Solar System* and *The Ocean Planet*, and her "district has a space lab that is a portable planetarium." This tool allows the class to see "stars, planets, and other satellites" and even includes "folk tales about how the constellations were named." A subtler tool is the classroom computer's "screen saver that tracks extraterrestrial space noise that is new." Students can access a myriad of Web sites with pictures of space objects and phenomena in real and recorded time.

Mary's curriculum clearly centers around student engagement and the natural integration of technology, an approach supported by the Apple Classrooms of Tomorrow (ACOT) research (Sandholtz, Ringstaff, & Dwyer, 1997). Throughout our conversations about technology-infused projects, Mary was forthright and passionately determined to point out the critical issues she feels are paramount to effectively using technology to support learning. The following sections represent themes that emerged over time and reveal helpful insights for both new and more experienced teachers.

TECHNOLOGY WAS NOT A FOCUS

For the most part, Mary observed that technology is not a focus for teacher preparation programs, schools, districts, or practitioners. Although principals questioned her about her technology skills during job interviews, they did not appear to have a deep understanding of technology applications. She feels that "part of the problem is that the districts do not seem to have much vision as to how [to develop] a technology infrastructure," particularly when it comes to teacher support. She observes that "the district's idea of integration is to put the responsibility in the hands of the individual teachers and place a computer facilitator on campus and hope integration happens." Mary feels this attitude may reflect administrator-level understanding and perhaps professional use of technology.

Fellow teachers also did not see technology as a focus. She feels that "many teachers are afraid of breaking the machines and couldn't believe [Mary] would put a student on [her] 'brand new' machine and worried about what the 'Internet' and inappropriate sites" would do to her students. Rogers (1995) might identify these teachers as laggards who are resistant to adopt new innovations and are suspicious of change.

Mary feels that her teacher education program did not stress technology integration or skill development methods. During her student teaching practicum, she was expected to know how to use a grading software but the instructional use of computers was not addressed or modeled for her and "everything was pencil and paper." Although Mary felt that she had the technical skills to use technology, "as far as how a student would use technology with instruction, I had no base." This is not an uncommon perception for pre-service teachers who often experience a discrepancy between their preparation in disciplinary pedagogy and technology pedagogy (Strudler, McKinney, & Jones, 1999; Office of Technology Assessment, 1995; Office of Technology Assessment, 1988).

Mary identified several barriers that she believes perpetuate this lack of focus. The beliefs and prior experiences of other people may be barriers. Some teachers, she knows, have had "negative experiences with technology" and are resistant to adopting new tools. School resources and configurations can also be problematic. At one point in her school, four of the science teachers had computers in their classroom with Internet connectivity, but the library was not online, limiting Internet-based activities for students. The school computer lab was reserved for computer science classes, and so Mary had to make do with the one computer in her classroom. These barriers have been well documented in research about technology integration (Office of Technology Assessment, 1995); and, while they do not reveal any new information, it is important to question why educational communities have not dealt with them.

EXPECTATIONS

Mary found that everyone has expectations about using technology, and particularly as it relates to their role as an educator. She believes that new teachers are perceived to be knowledgeable in technology integration and she "got the impression" that the administration saw her "as a resource rather than offering her help." Mary had little expectation that the district would provide her with support or learning opportunities.

Mary also thought that the students would come to her with "at least a year of computer literacy" and that the school would have designed the curriculum so that students would have computer learning "every year, with skills added as developmentally appropriate." She found, however, that students came to her class with a wide range of computer abilities, and she learned that she had to take responsibility for training students.

RATIONALE

For Mary, the decision to use technology came after instructional goals had been determined. She notes that "technology is just one component and not always the best tool for the job." Technology does provide the students with variety and helps her to develop her own skills. She uses technology because she can make revisions easily and immediately, it can provide feedback to the user, and it allows students to gain "insight into a topic."

She does not always choose to use technology, either because appropriate technology resources are not available or learning is not enhanced. Her unit on density is hands-on because she knows of no software or hardware that measures or simulates the relationship among mass and volume.

Mary purposefully uses technology in her classroom. She feels that "integration isn't one isolated task any more . . . it is a decision to utilize a tool to maximize learning for students." She knows that it motivates students and helps them accomplish things that they might not be able to without technology. It has allowed students to pursue answers to questions they have generated. This element of self-determination (Fosnot, 1996; Deci, Vallerand, Pelletier, & Ryan, 1991) is motivational for students and in turn motivates the teacher, not an unusual occurrence when technology is used (Office of Technology and Assessment, 1995).

IMPACT

The impact of technology in the classroom is clear to Mary. She has found it to be an invaluable tool in many ways, although she has difficulty "conceptualizing what technology does do to students." She knows that it provokes enthusiasm from students, facilitates equity, and can require that teachers re-think their instructional approaches.

It seems that, when students use technology, it "motivates [them] to revise, rework, and otherwise modify work they would be reluctant to do if it is traditionally done." She has found that students who have access to computers at school or at home are "much more receptive to feedback and make the necessary changes to their projects." She adds that,

> In my first year teaching, a [special education] kid qualified to go to the state science fair and it wasn't that he was gifted in science, it was because he was very teachable and had the ability to change and improve his project much easier than someone without technology.

Part of the outcome described by Mary may be her own feedback to her student, which is intentional and thorough although this type of feedback may not be typical of all teachers.

Technology, Mary says, can "level the playing field for all students." She thinks that "many students who don't tend to engage in academic things tend to work if a computer, probeware, graphing calculators, etc., are available to them."

She understands that "technology requires teachers to be much more flexible in their teaching methods." When technology fails the teacher must "always have plan B available." She has no doubt that when teachers use technology "the role of the teacher shifts to the role of a mediator or coach and the student becomes much more involved in the ownership of their learning." Mary suggests that it is this role shift that has prevented more and quicker adoption of technology, as she notes that "teachers don't want to give up the stage." She knows that, in teacher-centered classrooms, students "don't really have the opportunity to use the computers to explore the value of how computers can be used as a resource." The shift in roles that Mary describes is not only a reflection of constructivist teaching practices (Fosnot, 1995) but also a common attribute of teaching with technology (Sandholtz, Ringstaff, & Dwyer, 1997).

Since she has increasingly used technology to support instruction, Mary has seen a change in "the overall flavor of the classroom."

BELIEFS AND LESSONS LEARNED

Mary has clearly articulated beliefs about strategic use of technology, the need for support, and for her development as a teacher. She has learned how to select tools that not only support student learning but also appeals to students. When selecting Internet sites she looks for "sites that have clear direction cues and information that would be helpful or interesting" and avoids sites that "take a long time to download." CD-ROMs, the Internet and probeware have provided variety for student activities and help keep students on task and interested. She allows students to make some decisions about what software to use and is careful to "not endorse one product over an other" but rather "show various examples of what can be used." She helps students consider what software "most closely matches the product they are trying to create."

Limited technology resources in her classroom have helped Mary become a better problem solver, not only of technical problems, but also curricular ones. After realizing that her students did not have the software skills she expected them to, she took "three days to train my kids on how to use the Internet, send paperwork home, and officially license my kids to use the Internet." To have a license, students had to pass a "scavenger hunt" skills test, print a certificate, and have certain paperwork returned and signed by their parents. This strategy stressed the importance of acquiring these skills and informed parents about classroom activities.

Mary sees technology as a motivational tool that can help students make connections to the outside world. She notes that computers perform computations that are "tedious and free up time for deeper inquiry into the unknown."

Mary sees support as a critical issue in the adoption of technology, in training, technical support, curriculum design, and instructional approaches. Research clearly indicates that support in all of these areas is necessary for effective and long-term adoption of technology (ITRC & SEIR•TEC, 1998; Office of Technology Assessment, 1995). She would prefer that the school "have some sort of scope and sequence of classes in place at all grade levels" so that teachers and students have a clear picture of what is to be learned at designated times.

Mary feels that adopting new tools has helped her become a better teacher. She believes she now plans "better for future lessons and has improved her problem-solving abilities. She wonders why teachers often "give up so soon on new things." She explains that, "if I couldn't get a microscope to work one day, I wouldn't just say, ok, that is it, I'm not going to use them again in a lesson!" Since using technology is expected of her, she feels obligated to do so and that includes being "the techie, the teacher, and the advisor." Mary has unintentionally learned about different aspects of teaching through her intentional integration of technology into her curriculum (McGee, submitted; McGee, 1998).

Mary believes that "technology works best in collaboration with others" (e.g., group work and project based learning). This is in direct contrast to what she sees as the traditional approaches that she sees many of her colleagues using. At first she "had to resist using technology just because it was available." She thinks it is "kind of scary to think about how little reflection is really given on the impact it has on student learning." Mary notes that none of her school or district training has addressed technology and student learning. Her first introduction to this information came in her graduate courses, perhaps at a time when she sought out more theoretical answers to the practical dilemmas she encountered in her first years of teaching.

Mary's acquisition of knowledge about technology integration suggests many considerations for teachers and those working to support teacher development.

IMPLICATIONS

In-service teachers may or may not receive extensive or meaningful preparation in using technology. Many pre-service programs isolate technology training rather than infusing strategies across the curriculum (ISTE/NCATE, 1997). This omission of modeling in teacher preparation programs no doubt contributes to limited applications in beginning teachers' practices. Field-based experiences, as Mary notes, may not provide the modeling or discussion about how technology can be most effectively used. Modeling, mentoring, and on-site professional development have been recommended for new teachers (Wasley, 1999) but, as illustrated in Mary's case, they are not always available.

Mary's understanding and adoption of technology as an instructional tool came from her own initiative and persistence. She took it upon herself, spurred by spoken and unspoken encouragement, to become a leader in her school. Despite less-than-enthusiastic colleagues as well as limited support systems, Mary was not discouraged. Persistence is a key to contextually relevant teacher learning (Joyce & Showers, 1995) and requires time and motivation. Mary had to figure out ways to find the time, to learn new skills, to discover the best practices, and to write grants to accomplish her instructional goals. The knowledge necessary for her to accomplish these tasks is not part of teacher education programs or, typically, in-service development opportunities.

Most pre-service technology coursework focuses on procedural skills as do typical in-service staff development offerings. There appears to be a belief that teachers will readily transfer their technical learning, most often acquired off campus, to their own classrooms without any consideration of how or why it can be used purposefully. Contextually relevant training increases the likelihood new skills will be used (Darling-Hammond, 1998). Unlike other initiatives and mandates for improving learning, currently illustrated by the literacy focus, teachers are not typically provided with clear models, illustrations, or rationales for the appropriate integration of technology.

Joyce and Showers (1995) discuss the concept of the reflective practitioner as a basis for teacher learning. They contend that the reflective practitioner thinks about his or her current practices, conducts a conscious and personal inquiry in order to investigate alternatives, and from this reflection develops new and more effective skills. Clearly Mary underwent this process which was facilitated by her persistence and motivation.

CONCLUSION

McKenzie (1991) notes that staff development in the information age must come from teacher interests and concerns. The self-directed and self-motivated adult learner who is engaged in meaningful learning that directly relates to classroom experiences is more likely to alter his or her practices (Butler, 1992), as illustrated in Mary's knowledge acquisition. For other teacher's like Mary, we must consider how best to nurture similar venues of professional growth and, more importantly, provide tools and opportunities for teachers like Mary to model and mentor the successful integration of technology for peers.

REFERENCES

Butler, J. A. (1992). *Staff development* (School Improvement Research Series: Close-Up #12). Portland, OR: Northwest Regional Educational Laboratory.

Darling-Hammond, D. (1998). Teacher learning that supports student learning. *Educational Leadership, 55*(5), 6-11.

Deci, E. L., Vallerand, R. J., Pelletier, L. G., & Ryan, R. M. (1991). Motivational education: The self-determination perspective. *Educational Psychologist, 26*(3/4), 325-346.

Erlandson, D. E., Harris, E. L. Skipper, B. L., & Allen, S. D. (1993). *Doing naturalistic inquiry.* Newbury Park: Sage.

Fosnot, C. T. (1996). Constructivism: A psychological theory of learning. In C. T. Fosnot (Ed.), *Constructivism: Theory, perspectives, and practice* (pp. 8-33). New York: Teachers College Press.

Hunt, N. (1994). Intentions and implementations: The impact of technology coursework in elementary classrooms. In J. Willis, B. Robin, & D. Willis (Eds.), *Technology and teacher education annual, 1994* (pp. 38-41). Charlottesville, VA: Association for the Advancement of Computers in Education.

Instructional Technology Resources Center (ITRC) & Southeast and Islands Regional Consortium (SEIR•TEC). (1998). *Integration of technology pre-service teacher education programs: The southeast and islands regional profile.* Orlando, FL: SEIR•TEC.

Joyce, B., & Showers, B. (1995). *Student achievement through staff development: Fundamentals of school reform* (2nd ed.). White Plains, NY: Longman.

Mandinach, E. B., & Cline, H. F. (1996). Classroom dynamics: The impact of a technology-based curriculum innovation on teaching and learning. *The Journal of Educational Computing Research, 14*(1), 83-102.

McGee, P. (1999). *Collaboration and unintentional teacher learning in telementoring contexts.* Unpublished manuscript.

McGee, P. (1998). *Unintended professional development in curriculum-based K-12 telementoring projects.* Unpublished dissertation, The University of Texas at Austin, Austin, Texas.

McKenzie, J. (1991). Designing staff development for the information age. *From Now On: The Educational Technology Journal, 1*(4). [Online]. Available: *http://fromnowon.org/fnoapr91.html*

Mishler, E. G. (1986). *Research interviewing: Context and narrative.* Cambridge, MA: Harvard University Press.

Morgan, G. (1983). Toward a more reflective social science. In G. Morgan (Ed.), *Beyond method: Strategies for social science research* (pp. 308-376). Beverly Hills, CA: Sage.

Novak, D. I., & Knowles, J. G. (1991). Beginning elementary teachers' use of computers in classroom instruction. *Action in Teacher Education, 13*(2), 43-51.

Office of Technology Assessment. (1995). *Teachers and technology: Making the connection (OTA-EHR-616).* Washington, DC: U.S. Government Printing Office.

Office of Technology Assessment. (1988). *Power on! New tools for teaching and learning (OTA-SET-379).* Washington, DC: U.S. Government Printing Office.

Patton, M. Q. (1990). *Qualitative evaluation methods* (2nd ed.). Thousand Oaks, CA: Sage.

Rogers, E. M. (1995). *Diffusion of innovations* (4th ed). New York: The Free Press.

Sandholtz, J., Ringstaff, C., Dwyer, D. C. (1997). *Teaching with technology: Creating student-centered classrooms.* New York: Teachers College Press.

Stake, R. E. (1994). Case studies. In N. K. Denzin & Y. S. Lincoln (Eds.), *Handbook of qualitative research* (pp. 236-247). Thousand Oaks, CA: Sage.

Strudler, N. B., McKinney, M. O., & Jones, W. P. (1999). First-year teachers' use of technology: Expectations and reality. *Journal of Technology and Teacher Education, 2*(2), 115-129.

Wasley, P. (1999). Teaching worth celebrating. *Educational Leadership, 56*(8), 8-13.

David M. Marcovitz
M. Khalid Hamza
Vicky R. Farrow

Students and Support for Technology in the Elementary Classroom

SUMMARY. *This paper explores the roles of students supporting technology in elementary classrooms. Students' primary role in the classroom is not to support teachers, but with technology, teachers take advantage of support in many forms. This paper classifies the ways in which students were found to support technology in the classroom, taking advantage of their expertise to help the teacher and other students. In some cases, students' efforts provided positive benefits to the teacher and other students, and in other cases, the students' efforts caused more problems than they solved. [Article copies available for a fee from The Haworth Document Delivery Service: 1-800-342-9678. E-mail address: <getinfo@haworthpressinc.com> Website: <http://www.HaworthPress.com>]*

DAVID M. MARCOVITZ is Coordinator of Technology in the Educational Environment, Education Department, Loyola College in Maryland, 4501 N. Charles Street, Baltimore, MD 21210. E-mail: marco@loyola.edu
M. KHALID HAMZA is Assistant Professor, Department of Educational Technology & Research, Florida Atlantic University, 2912 College Avenue, Davie, FL 33314. E-mail: ayah1@concentric.net
VICKY R. FARROW is Assistant Professor, Professional Pedagogy Department, Lamar University, Education Building, P.O. Box 10034, Beaumont, TX 77710. E-mail: Vrfarrow@aol.com

[Haworth co-indexing entry note]: "Students and Support for Technology in the Elementary Classroom." Marcovitz, David M., M. Khalid Hamza, and Vicky R. Farrow. Co-published simultaneously in *Computers in the Schools* (The Haworth Press, Inc.) Vol. 16, No. 3/4, 2000, pp. 213-225; and: *Integration of Technology into the Classroom: Case Studies* (ed: D. LaMont Johnson, Cleborne D. Maddux, and Leping Liu) The Haworth Press, Inc., 2000, pp. 213-225. Single or multiple copies of this article are available for a fee from The Haworth Document Delivery Service [1-800-342-9678, 9:00 a.m. - 5:00 p.m. (EST). E-mail address: getinfo@haworthpressinc.com].

213

KEYWORDS. Support for technology, ethnography, student roles

Support for technology in schools comes from a variety of sources. One area that is often overlooked is the support that teachers get from their students. While students' primary purpose is not to give support to teachers, students do support teachers in a variety of ways that can be beneficial to both teachers and students.

Some support that students give is small help, such as answering a question for another student or the teacher, who is stuck in a program. However, students can give more extensive help when they are paired up with other students for the express purpose of helping them.

When the computer is used in a laboratory setting, the teacher cannot be with every student; and, when the computer is in the classroom as one activity among several (such as for science centers), the teacher cannot direct all the activities at the same time. Knowledgeable students can fill the gap in informal ways, such as answering questions as they arise, and in more formal ways, such as being assigned to teach other students.

While students helping other students can be useful to both the student being helped and the helper, it can be problematic as well. Students do not always know how to give adequate help to their peers. Sometimes the helper just wants to play with the computer, ignoring the needs of the other students, and sometimes the helper does the work himself while the one being helped just sits and watches. Students are always close at hand, but they are not always there to be helpers, and they do not always know how to help.

The case study presented here looked at a public elementary school in the Midwest. It focused on three teachers for parts of two school years (all of the names in this paper are pseudonyms to protect participant anonymity):

1. Sarah–a teacher who has been using computers in her classroom for a few years
2. Cindy–a teacher who has been using computers in her classroom for nearly a year
3. Jennifer–a teacher who has just started using computers in her classroom this year

While these three teachers do not cover the entire range of computer use in schools, this variation provided understanding of support from the perspectives of three teachers who seem to be at different places on Hall and Hord's (1987) levels of use and stages of concern scales. In addition to the three primary participants, other classes in the school were observed and other teachers were interviewed informally (including Nora, a third- and fourth-grade teacher).

All three of the teachers taught both third and fourth grades. Jennifer taught only fourth grade during the first school year of the study, and she taught only third grade during the second school year of the study. Sarah and Cindy taught mixed third- and fourth-grade classes.

Each of the three classrooms had one color Macintosh LC II or LC III computer, and all the computers were attached to the school's local area network, which has Internet access.

RESEARCH METHODOLOGY: ETHNOGRAPHY, CASE STUDY AND SITUATED-EVALUATION

This paper is based on a larger study that combined methods of ethnography, case study, and situated-evaluation, incorporating interpretations of the experiences of the participants to build an understanding of what was observed and how it relates to support for innovation. In parts of two school years, the investigator spent several hours each week at an elementary school observing classes, talking informally to teachers, interviewing teachers, and attending school and district technology committee meetings. The study was an exploration of the culture of the school, how technology fit into that culture, and how various members of the school supported technology.

The qualitative methodology was shaped by situated-evaluation (Bruce, 1993). In *situated-evaluation*, innovations are viewed as part of existing situations. Instead of viewing the innovation, or support in the case of this study, as a separate entity, it was viewed as a part of the existing social system.

In reality, the innovation is but one small addition to a complex social system. Instead of seeing it as the primary instrument of change, it is better to see it as a tool that is incorporated into ongoing processes of change. (Bruce, 1993, p. 17)

Situated-evaluation is an important way to look at support because it helps us understand why support does not always meet its objectives. A situated-evaluation approach might find that the support was inadequate because the designers of the support did not account for the contexts and constraints of the situation, or it might bring about a better understanding of how the situation and the support interact to provide different, not necessarily better or worse, support than what was originally intended.

RESEARCH PROCEDURES

In this ethnographic study, new models for support and innovation were developed by looking closely at support for technology and the use of technology in three third- and fourth-grade classes. Most of the time was spent with these three classes and their teachers: Sarah, Jennifer, and Cindy. Data were collected from four sources: interviews of teachers, informal conversations, observations of classes, and observations of meetings.

Interviews provided the opportunity to discuss some of the issues in detail. Each of the main participants was interviewed once at the beginning of the study to understand her situation and at least once more as topics came up that required more in-depth discussion than informal conversations allowed. Informal conversations allowed the opportunity to discuss issues as they arose, keep informed about events, and maintain an ongoing relationship with the informants. These took place regularly throughout the study, often during recess or other class breaks. Observation of classes provided the opportunity to observe the teachers' issues and needs in action and observe students in their various roles. Each of the classes of the three main participants were observed on average once per week. Other classes using the computer laboratory were also observed. Meetings on the school and district level allowed the opportunity to observe teachers interacting with one another, discussing their needs, and in some cases, acting upon their needs. All the sources of data also provided the opportunity to observe students in their various roles.

Detailed notes were taken during observations. These notes were expanded each day. Notes were analyzed and coded for emergent themes and patterns. The importance of student support emerged from this analysis, and this led to the categories of student support described below.

CATEGORIES OF STUDENT SUPPORT

The multiple observations of students giving support were combined into the following categories: playing, sharing, reading, small help, becoming expert, teaching, other. Reading, small help, and teaching involve direct support from a student to either a student or a teacher. Sharing and becoming expert involve indirect support that students give. Playing includes times that the elementary students offered support in order to play.

Playing

Elementary students spend a lot of time playing, and many of them like to play on the computer. Often the help they offer is an attempt to play rather than to help.

> After a couple of minutes, the [Macintosh] LC III group quit, and Jason got onto the LC III and started playing with the EcoExplorer. He played with the simulator trying to keep the plant alive for a couple of minutes. Then he went to the song composition section. He couldn't figure out how to make a song. He needed to drag the sounds from a menu on the left into his workspace on the right for them to be added to his composition. He was just clicking on them (not dragging them) so the sound would play, but it was not added to the composition.
> Frank came over and said, "Let's play the game." Jason still wanted to make a song. "How do you make a song?" Frank said, "I'll show you," and he took the mouse and said, "after we play the game."
> Frank went to the rainforest game. Jason still wanted to make a song. They fought for the mouse, and Frank won. He started the game. After a minute, Jason got into the game and didn't complain about wanting to make a song. In the game, you have to answer some questions, more or less related to the rainforest (e.g., unscramble a word like "ecology," answer a multiple-

choice question about where most of the nutrients are in the rainforest, or choose the correct numbered vine that will take you where you want to go–I think this was just a matter of guessing). After one or two questions, Jason was into the game, and Frank gave him the mouse to answer a question. (Fieldnotes, Cindy's classroom, May 11, 1993)

The computer was new to many students, and it was an attractive toy. This was not discouraged because the games (such as EcoExplorer, MathBlaster, Where in the World Is Carmen Sandiego?, InnerBody Works, and The Incredible Machine) were selected for their presumed educational value. However, in the context of students helping students, playing could be a problem when one student was looking for help, and the helper was looking to play with the computer.

The computer also served as a great source of distraction to many students. Marcus was a good example of this.

Marcus came over several times. He tried to help them with several things. Cindy [the teacher] called him away to do spelling, but he stayed by the computer to give them more advice. Cindy called him again, "Marcus, this is the third time." He went with her. But Cindy went back to her desk for a minute, and Marcus went back to the computer. (Fieldnotes, Cindy's classroom, February 28, 1994)

Marcus, in particular, liked to avoid his other classwork by going over to the computer and trying to help other students.

Sharing

Sometimes students offer support by sharing their experiences with the rest of the class as in the following example.

Sarah [the teacher] had all the kids gather in a circle. She said that one of the kids (Ken) had run into some problems, and she wanted to talk about it and show what he did to solve the problem. He had created his stack, but he wasn't able to get a new card or a new stack or a new field. He described the problem; Sarah explained what he was saying. Sally (a volunteer with Sarah's after-school class) showed them how to get around the problem. She had them start HyperCard through the HyperCard application, and then select Open Stack to open Ken's stack. Then they could script. If they just double-clicked on Ken's stack, they could not script. They suspected the problem had something to do with HyperCard Player, but they weren't sure. (Fieldnotes, Sarah's after-school program, October 26, 1993)

One of Sarah's students had run into a problem that she thought others might encounter. After they solved the problem, Sarah had the student share the solution with the class. Whether it was the teacher, the volunteer, or the student who solved the problem was unclear, but the student was actively involved with presenting the solution.

This was part of Sarah's after-school class in which she worked with third-grade students on a HyperCard project. Overall, no one had a lot of experience with HyperCard, so the class spent a lot of time exploring and learning about it. In this exploratory environment, sharing was important–including students sharing with each other and the teacher, and the teacher sharing with the students.

Reading

Many of the computer activities involved a great deal of reading. As third- and/or fourth-grade teachers, Sarah, Cindy, and Jennifer had students at a variety of levels of reading, including some who had a great deal of trouble reading instructions on the computer.

At 10:06 a.m., Sarah started talking to the class about Oregon Trail. She assigned partners to some of the slower readers. (Fieldnotes, Sarah's class at the university computer laboratory, September 23, 1993)

Cindy said they were about ready to get started, and the kids started to head to the computers. She stopped them and was mildly upset. When they settled back into their seats, she reviewed how to get to the tutorial, and she assigned partners to some of the slower readers. (Fieldnotes, Cindy's class at the university computer laboratory, September 30, 1993)

At 9:29 a.m., she reviewed how to get to Microsoft Word. She asked people to work with others if they had trouble reading. She made sure some kids had partners. (Fieldnotes, Cindy's class at the university computer laboratory, October 5, 1993)

In some situations, the teacher or another adult (volunteer, student teacher) helped some of the slower students with the reading, but this can be draining on the adults' time. As in these examples, some teachers have found that pairing slower readers with faster readers allows the adults to spend more time with other problems. These examples are from laboratory situations, but this kind of support can be very effective in the classroom as well. Often the teacher is working with a group of students and cannot spend the time to work with a student on the computer.

Small Help

Small help refers to the small ways that students help other students or the teacher, usually by answering a question or showing how to do something on the computer. Students working on the computer will often get stuck with a problem. Other students are always around, some of whom might know the solution to the problem.

One student didn't know how to change the names in the party [in the game Oregon Trail]. The volunteer did not know either. The parent said, "She made it turn red. How did she do that?" A kid at the next computer showed them how to do it. (Fieldnotes, Nora's class at the university computer laboratory, September 28, 1993)

By 11:07 a.m., about half the kids were in Oregon Trail. Many kids gave other kids pointers in Oregon Trail, but Cindy never showed the game to the class at all. She was too busy checking all the paragraphs [they had just typed] and helping the kids save. (Fieldnotes, Cindy's class at the university computer laboratory, October 5, 1993)

One of the options for erasing [in KidPix] is the firecracker. Jennifer tried to show them this option, but she couldn't get it to work. She clicked on the eraser on the left, and then she clicked on the firecracker on the bottom, but nothing happened. She didn't realize that once she selected the firecracker tool, she had to click on the screen to get it to erase. One of the kids pointed this out to her, and she said "Oh, yeah," and then showed it to the rest of the class. (Fieldnotes, Jennifer's class at the university computer laboratory, October 20, 1993)

Often students become experts or at least knowledgeable helpers and can answer small questions. Although none were observed in these classes, many times students become technical experts, answering questions about configuring software and setting up equipment (matters beyond help with how to play an educational game). Students with expertise at all levels can be very helpful due to their proximity; they are very close to the situation where help is needed and, in some cases, even closer than the teacher.

Small help has its drawbacks as well. Elementary students are often more interested in playing than helping, and they might use offers of small help to get onto the computer. An additional drawback is that children are not trained as helpers or teachers, and when they are given the opportunity, they often give the answer or do the work for someone rather than giving hints or explaining how it should be done.

> Brad came over and said that he had won the game. He asked if they had. They said they were close. They asked him where the antidote was. He wouldn't tell them. He gave them hints. They tried again to find it and couldn't. Finally, Brad agreed to do it for them, and they let him sit down (at first they just wanted him to tell them). (Fieldnotes, Cindy's classroom, May 11, 1993)

> They were having a lot of trouble solving the first puzzle. They went to get help from Tim. Tim came over and did the puzzle for them. (Fieldnotes, Cindy's classroom, February 28, 1994)

Small help can be beneficial when the students answer simple questions and help others to get past roadblocks, but it can be a problem when they do the work for other students.

Becoming Expert

During the 1993-94 school year, Sarah worked with several students in an after-school program to train them how to use HyperCard. The students she trained were third-graders from her class and

Cindy's class. The goal of the program was for these students to become proficient enough in HyperCard so they could train others the following year. The class was limited to third-graders because both Cindy and Sarah's classes were combined third- and fourth-grades. The following year, the graduates of the program would still be in Cindy and Sarah's classes, and they could teach the other fourth-graders and third-graders who would be around the following year.

Sarah made an investment in her students and the use of HyperCard as an integral part of her curriculum. Many of the other types of support that students offered were almost "free" to the teachers, requiring little or no effort on their part beyond creating an environment in which students were free to help others. Having the students become experts required a significant investment in time on Sarah's part. Sarah had been inspired by other projects in her classroom and discussions with others about the effectiveness of HyperCard in her program. She lacked the expertise in HyperCard and a core of experts to help in her class. Sarah got connected with Sally, a university student, to help her for a short time, but she needed a continuing core of experts. She created this core from her students.

Creating the core of experts was a difficult task, especially after Sally did not return to help in the spring, and progress was slow.

> Sarah was talking to Sally about getting the kids to be more independent. Sally seemed optimistic and positive about their progress. Sarah seemed impatient; "I'm anxious to get them independent." Sarah said she was happy with the way Jimmy was able to help the other kids. She thought that soon Ken and some of the others would be up to a level where they could help the other kids. Sally said she was pleased with the progress. Sarah said she was frustrated. (Fieldnotes, discussion with Sarah and Sally after Sarah's after-school program, October 26, 1993)

Sarah knew that next year she would need the help that she could only get from a core of expert students in her class to fully integrate Hyper-Card into her curriculum.

Teaching

After becoming experts, students were enlisted to teach other students. HyperCard is a fairly complex program that requires a great deal of training, but other programs require a smaller amount of training, and students could easily learn the program and be used to train other students. Cindy did this with The Incredible Machine, a game that explores the construction of simple machines.

> I have a child in my room who bought it for home, and two of Sarah's children came in and trained two of mine, and then we went from there, 'cause she did it first. And then we matched up kids who now taught everybody in the class. We had a lot of collaboration and peer work. (Cindy, interview, May 2, 1994)

As with small help, Cindy took advantage of the proximity of other experts: her students. She might not have had the time to teach all her students how to use The Incredible Machine without the help of her students. Having a core of experts, at close proximity, to teach others is difficult without using students for support. This support can be beneficial to the students being taught, to the students doing the teaching, and to the teacher.

Other

The categories of student support listed above were the most prominent ones observed, but students helped in a variety of other less specific ways. Teachers used, as a means of support, the ability of students to learn the technology on their own. While they might have been inclined to teach, they did not always have the time to teach and instead counted on the students to learn by exploring.

> She said that the kids feel real confident with this. She said that the kids are not afraid to "let's just plug it in." (Fieldnotes, discussion with Sarah about Lego Logo, January 26, 1994)

This helped the teachers spend time on other things and not worry about the students learning the technology.

> She said she is not worried about support for Lego Logo. She said the kids are doing well and can mostly learn it themselves. Though she admitted that it might get complicated. (Fieldnotes, discussion with Sarah about Lego Logo, February 15, 1994)

Teachers got support by learning with the students.

At 10:49 a.m., two boys (who I think had played before) started a full game [of SimAnt]. Cindy asked if she could sit with them. "You see, I'm learning along with you guys." (Fieldnotes, Cindy's class at the university computer laboratory, September 30, 1993)

In earlier categories, students gave support by answering questions (small help) and teaching other students. Teachers also got support from knowing that students who could answer questions were around, whether or not they actually did anything.

At 10:20 a.m., she started talking about Oregon Trail. She asked how many had played before. Nine raised their hands. She said that they could ask the kids who had played before or [the student teacher] or herself for help. (Fieldnotes, Virginia's class at the university computer laboratory, October 7, 1993)

All of these other forms of support relied on the proximity of students, mostly to be where the teacher was not or could not be.

DISCUSSION

In terms of support received by the teacher, the most significant categories of support are becoming expert, teaching, and other. These were most significant because the teachers were able to change their curricula in ways that might not have otherwise been possible.

In becoming expert, the teacher was relying on the proximity of a core of experts. The knowledge and support of these experts would be relevant because she was determining what that knowledge and support would be; the support was not added on later but was an integral part of the development of the curriculum.

Teaching was the logical step after becoming expert and part of the process of developing the curriculum. Student support was necessary to implement the teachers' ideas.

The other category was significant because it relied on the students to be helpers. The actual support given was not necessarily anything more than small help, but the reliance of the teacher on that help made it most important.

The reading category can be critical to the students who have trouble reading. Without this kind of support, the teacher or other adults would have to spend more time with the poor readers, or the issue of equity among students could become a major problem for the teacher. Allowing students to help each other with reading allows all students access to the computer.

Small help is the most common form of support. Except in the cases where the teacher relies upon it, this kind of support does not have a major impact on the classroom. It is helpful and, because it is so common, it appears to be the most significant, but the students giving this kind of support are often not credible helpers and not relevant to the needs of the teacher or the student being helped. Playing can be viewed as small help taken to the least relevant extreme, where one student is offering support merely for the opportunity to play.

The instances of sharing observed were not significant in and of themselves, but they helped to create an atmosphere that encouraged helping others.

Proximity is the key to student support in the classroom because students are always present. This is most significant when some students form a core of experts, always available to help, but it is still important in lesser ways, such as small help.

Proximity and a feeling of credibility toward the student allow the teacher more flexibility to create student support (by creating experts and developing a situation where students can teach others) to do what she feels is relevant (such as HyperCard in Sarah's class). The student support is relevant because it is created by the teacher to be relevant. When students have their own agendas (such as playing and wanting to do things for others), their support becomes less relevant and thus less supportive.

As teachers view students as credible supporters/experts, the support and the curriculum can be expanded beyond simple things. Small help is useful, but Cindy's addition of The Incredible Machine was more useful and made possible by her relying on her students. Sarah took it one step further by relying on her students to help her implement a major addition to her curriculum with HyperCard.

REFERENCES

Bruce, B. (1993). Innovation and social change. In B. C. Bruce, J. K. Peyton, & T. Batson (Eds.), *Network-based classrooms: Promises and realities* (pp. 9-32). New York: Cambridge University Press.

Hall, G., & Hord, S. (1987). *Change in schools: Facilitating the process.* New York: State University of New York Press.

Shelley Anne Burgstaller
Dean S. Cristol

HyperStudio
for Grade-One Students:
A Case Study

SUMMARY. *With current advancements in hypermedia, innovative software is being developed with educators in mind. A prime example is HyperStudio, where the user has the ability to manipulate and control the union of sounds, graphics, and automation. In this article, we describe the interactions of a grade-one HyperStudio expert teaching a novice Hyper-Studio classmate how to use the program as a means to publish her story.*

Data were collected through videotaping, QuickTime movies, and observations. The data were analyzed to discover emerging patterns between the two students, the researcher, and the computer. The two students evolved from an unequal power structure of peer tutoring to a more collaborative structure, where the once novice became an equal partner in the publishing process. [Article copies available for a fee from The Haworth Document Delivery Service: 1-800-342-9678. E-mail address: <getinfo@haworthpressinc.com> Website: <http://www.HaworthPress.com>]

KEYWORDS. *Elementary schools, technology, Hyperstudio, peer teaching, cooperative learning, literacy*

SHELLY ANNE BURGSTALLER is English Teacher/Librarian, American International School, Salzburg.
DEAN S. CRISTOL is Assistant Professor, Old Dominion University, Darden College of Education, Department of Education and Curriculum, Education 165-11, Norfolk, VA 23259-0161. E-mail: dristol@odu.edu

[Haworth co-indexing entry note]: "HyperStudio for Grade-One Students: A Case Study." Burgstaller, Shelley Anne, and Dean S. Cristol. Co-published simultaneously in *Computers in the Schools* (The Haworth Press, Inc.) Vol. 16, No. 3/4, 2000, pp. 227-236; and: *Integration of Technology into the Classroom: Case Studies* (ed: D. LaMont Johnson, Cleborne D. Maddux, and Leping Liu) The Haworth Press, Inc., 2000, pp. 227-236. Single or multiple copies of this article are available for a fee from The Haworth Document Delivery Service [1-800-342-9678, 9:00 a.m. - 5:00 p.m. (EST). E-mail address: getinfo@haworthpressinc.com].

227

It was early in the instruction when Ed said to Ella, "Here let me show you," as he gently nudged her aside and began using the mouse and computer. This was a customary action in Ed's early instruction of HyperStudio. At the beginning Ed would take control of the computer when Ella became confused about a procedure. The first time Ed exhibited this behavior was when Ella first attempted to select a font. Instead of explaining to Ella, Ed took control while Ella sat quietly and watched as he showed her the font selection process. She just sat and stared at Ed and the computer, the researcher never knowing whether she was listening or comprehending what Ed was showing her. Ed would ask her a question, and she would respond with a simple yes or no.

As Ella became more skilled with the program, they began to lose the earlier established dominant-passive structure. One day, Ella chose the sound button, but Ed was not ready to show her how it worked. Instead of arguing, she waited until he was ready and let him show her the different sounds and then told him what sounds she wanted and why they were important to the story. This type of verbal interaction was indicative of how each respected one another's decision making.

This vignette is from a study on young children teaching one another to use HyperStudio to publish their personal stories that will be described at some length in this article. The example demonstrates one approach that some teachers are using as they face the challenges of integrating technology into the curriculum. Currently, the implementation of educational technology in the classroom is providing creative teaching and learning opportunities for teachers and students. An example is hypermedia, which allows easy and quick access to greater amounts of information. Hypermedia allows students and teachers to manipulate a combination of text, audio, graphics, and animation in a nonlinear fashion through the use of buttons or "hot spots" (Randall & Higgins, 1991). The user controls the program to best suit his/her own needs. Ultimately, the goal is to process the information for a deeper and more complete understanding of curricular concepts.

A common use of hypermedia in the elementary classroom is the authoring and publishing of student written work (Roblyer, Edwards, & Havriluk, 1997). Students have the ability to go beyond the traditional written text by publishing their works using colored text, sound, and animation. Research has shown that hypermedia provides motivation, flexibility, critical-thinking skills, writing skills, and a positive source for self-expression and active learning (Barron & Or-wig, 1993; Roblyer et al., 1997). Students have many options to explore material in a way that is most appropriate for their own learning (Simonson & Thompson, 1997). While hypermedia allows students the opportunity to explore and create, its use in the classroom is dependent upon the teacher's ability to integrate the program within the curriculum. When used correctly, Simonson and Thompson (1997) predicted that "hypermedia with digitized graphics, visuals, and sounds that are controlled in a flexible authoring system such as Hyper-Studio will be the educational computing system of the future" (p. 43).

Hypermedia has existed since 1987, but until recently hypermedia was not a realistic option for educators of young children (Barron & Orwig, 1993). In 1997, Roger Wagner Publishing (1997) created HyperStudio to get young children involved in the hypermedia experience. Hyper-Studio is a comfortable, low-stress alternative to conventional student publishing, which allows students to create stories that incorporate appropriate multimedia using texture, sound, and animation in an organized and coherent manner (Newby, Stepich, Lehman, & Russell, 1996). There are four elements driving HyperStudio: cards, stacks, buttons, and home pages (Wishnietsky, 1992). These four elements are the tools to create the "pages" of a story. Students explore information in associative, nonlinear ways, allowing them to choose and follow their own paths (Barron & Orwig, 1993). The flexible nature of Hyper-Studio permits teachers to individualize, collaborate, and coordinate instruction in a systematic manner. Along with providing unique publishing possibilities, HyperStudio encourages peer collaboration when working with computers (Forman & Pufall, 1988).

THE FOCUS FOR THIS STUDY

In this article, we describe the processes that grade one students undergo when using HyperStudio to publish personal stories. The case study focuses on the interactions of a grade one HyperStudio "expert" teaching a novice HyperStudio classmate how to use the program as a means to publish her story. The study was guided by the following questions: Can grade one students effectively program HyperStudio without the help of a teacher? Can a grade one HyperStudio expert teach a grade one HyperStudio novice how to publish a personal story using the program?

Our research may be viewed in the context of studies that focus on technology and young children. We maintain that current educational technology provides a wealth of opportunities for students and teachers. However, computers are only as good as the programs used in them, and programs are only useful if the teacher understands how they contribute to a curriculum. The purpose of the study was to understand how the hypermedia program, HyperStudio, can be used as a technological tool by primary elementary students to teach each other to publish personal stories.

METHODOLOGY

The data from this study came from two students, Ed, the HyperStudio expert, who showed a deep interest in the workings of the computer, and Ella, the HyperStudio novice, who had strong writing and drawing skills. The process of publishing Ella's HyperStudio story, "Horses," was analyzed in terms of the verbal and nonverbal interactions of the students. Throughout this study, data were collected using video, QuickTime movies, and observations. A video camera was placed on a tripod directly behind the students to capture them using the monitor, the "Big Keys" (a colored and alphabetized keyboard), and the mouse pad. The students were comfortable being videotaped, often ignoring the video camera as they worked on the computer.

A major concern was that the video camera could only capture the movements of the student's hands and the resulting changes with the HyperStudio stack. In order to capture the facial expressions of the students a QuickTime camera was placed on a small tripod and positioned to the left of the computer screen. The QuickTime camera was explained to the students as an eyeball that was used to make movies of their work. The eyeball was exciting for the students, because they were able to see themselves at work on any given day. The QuickTime camera was connected to a PowerBook 190cs and was used to create QuickTime movies. These movies captured the expressions of the students while they interacted with the HyperStudio program. The hard drive of the PowerBook was a limiting factor for the publishing sessions. Despite the technical restrictions, the PowerBook and the QuickTime videos proved to be key in the data collection.

For consistency, one of the researchers was the participant-observer (Spradley, 1980) during the study. She interacted with the students while observing their interactions with her and each other. The researcher's note-taking followed each session in order to avoid distracting the students by constantly writing about their actions working together. The process of publishing Ella's HyperStudio story, "Horses," was analyzed in terms of the verbal and non-verbal interactions between the students. The videotapes were viewed in 10-minute intervals in order to capture meaningful interactions. The interactions were then grouped and categorized as a way to unitize the data (Lincoln & Guba, 1985).

DISCUSSION

Eleven significant interactions emerged between Ed, Ella, the computer, and the researcher. Each interaction was labeled verbal or non-verbal. These interactions differed depending on whom they were directed to and who they were initiated by. As a result, different combinations of communication could be categorized as both verbal and non-verbal.

Verbal interactions included situations where the students spoke to each other, themselves, or to the researcher (see Table 1). Also, this category included situations when the researcher spoke to the students. The verbal interactions constituted the larger number of incidents in the study. In contrast non-verbal interactions included situations in which the participants made their thoughts known without the use of speech (see Table 2). In this category, the computer played a major role. A silent move toward the mouse conveyed a definite message

TABLE 1
Description of Verbal Interactions

(1)   Ed's verbal interactions with Ella and the Researcher.

(2)   Ed' verbal interactions with Ella.

(3)   Ed's verbal interactions with the Researcher.

(4)   Ella's verbal interactions with Ed.

(5)   Ella's verbal interactions with the Researcher.

that this person wanted, or would not give up, control of the program. Non-verbal interactions also included Ella's pensive "thinking looks" and Ed's wandering gaze.

The QuickTime movies proved to be the most revealing source of data. The movies revealed subtle movements that were not documented by the observations or the video. The most informative aspects included the verbal and non-verbal interactions initiated by Ella toward Ed. Initially, the researcher explained to Ed that he would be teaching a classmate how to publish her book using the computer. Current literature refers to this situation as discovery learning. Discovery learning occurs when the teacher places a learner into an educational situation without telling the student what is already known about the situation (Simonson & Thompson, 1997). According to Webb (1989), "In the process of clarifying and addressing questions, the helper [tutor] may discover gaps in his or her own understanding or discrepancies with others' work or previous work" (p. 29). Peer tutoring is a framework for discovery learning, where the tutor perfects existing skills as he/she teaches the peer. As Ed guided Ella in discovering HyperStudio, he was discovering further nuances of the program.

Verbal Interactions

Initially, Ella was passive and silent. As the sessions continued, she became confident using HyperStudio; and, as a result, she discussed

TABLE 2
Description of Non-Verbal Interactions

---

(1) Ed's non-verbal interactions with Ella.

(2) Ed's non-verbal interactions with the Researcher.

(3) Ed's non-verbal interactions with the Computer.

(4) Ella's non-verbal interactions with Ed.

(5) Ella's non-verbal interactions with the Researcher.

(6) Ella's non-verbal interactions with the Computer.

---

her ideas with Ed, answered Ed's questions with longer responses, and sometimes initiated conversations. The verbal interactions initiated by Ed and directed to Ella increased until Ella reached a level of ability that was similar to Ed's. At this time, the verbal interactions decreased in terms of instructions and increased in terms of suggestions and general communication. As Ella's verbal communication increased, Ed's verbal communication remained consistent with his interactions at the beginning of the sessions.

Ed's teaching style was similar to the way he was taught by adults. This included giving verbal and non-verbal cues, such as pointing at the appropriate areas on the screen. As the study continued, Ed contributed fewer verbal instructions; however, he continued to give more suggestions. In the final sessions of the publishing process, Ella participated in conversations with Ed concerning both the HyperStudio stack and related topics.

Early on, Ed interacted both verbally and non-verbally with the researcher in times of uncertainty. As time passed, verbal interactions initiated by Ed and directed toward the researcher decreased in terms of his need for instruction and increased in terms of general communication. Ed began to engage the researcher in general conversation as Ella was drawing. Her drawing was a timely procedure and Ed appeared to need something to occupy his time.

As the research continued, verbal interactions initiated by Ella and directed toward Ed increased. For the first several days of the research, Ella was relatively quiet. When Ed asked Ella a question, her answer would be a whispered "yes" or "no," or a simple nod. As the publishing continued, Ella became more confident and would answer Ed's questions in her normal speaking voice. In the final days of the study, Ella began to disagree with Ed and demonstrated independence by stating her opinion.

Over time, verbal interactions initiated by Ella to the researcher increased. When Ella was asked a direct question by the researcher, and, if Ed did not jump in with a response, she would initially reply with a quiet "yes" or "no." By the end of the study, Ella would answer questions in full statements.

In the beginning of each session, the researcher would informally ask questions concerning the students' feelings about being videotaped, what they had accomplished the previous session, what they thought they could accomplish in the current session, and how they were feeling in general. Initially, the researchers were concerned by Ella's lack of verbal communication. Due to this concern, the researcher periodically prompted Ed to explain issues to Ella, as opposed to showing her, and negotiated with Ed to be sure that Ella received time making the cards and, therefore, learned the program. As the study progressed, the verbal interactions between the researcher and the students decreased, while the interactions between Ed and Ella increased.

Non-Verbal Interactions

At the beginning of the study, Ed interacted with the researcher mostly by way of verbal questions. As the research continued, non-verbal interactions initiated by Ed to the researcher increased as he appeared to be needed less by Ella. As Ella's ability and confidence increased, Ed became more interested in the QuickTime eyeball, the laptop computer, and the QuickTime movies.

At the onset of the study, Ed was very excited about being a teacher. He mimicked the researcher as he prompted Ella to use HyperStudio. However, as the sessions continued, Ed focused more on creating the cards, and less on teaching Ella. He began to say more frequently, "Here let me show you" and to place his hand on the mouse and gain control of the card. As the study progressed and Ella became more proficient with HyperStudio, she was less willing to let Ed control the mouse, especially when it was not his negotiated turn. The non-verbal interactions initiated by Ed and directed to the computer reached a plateau as Ella's ability increased.

Throughout the study Ella's non-verbal interactions were minimal with the researcher. Ella was content to work on a card quietly and thoughtfully. If she had a question, she would direct it to Ed. As the study continued, non-verbal interactions initiated by Ella and directed to the researcher decreased as she became more confident with the program. As the publishing progressed, non-verbal interactions initiated by Ella and directed to Ed increased and reached a plateau as her ability and desire to contribute equaled Ed's ability. In the final sessions, Ella used one of the non-verbal interactions on Ed, that he had used with her earlier in the sessions. When she wanted to contribute to a card, Ella put her hand over Ed's and waited to see if he would remove it and let her control the mouse. Non-verbal interactions initiated by Ella and directed to the computer increased as her skills and confidence increased. As a result, Ella was able to interact with the computer frequently and successfully.

CONCLUSION

The findings from the study suggest that grade one students can use HyperStudio to publish personal stories, and teach their peers to effectively use the program. While the expertise levels between the two students were evident throughout the study, the peer tutoring relationship evolved from the expert dominating the early interactions to the novice and the expert sharing publishing responsibilities at the conclusion of the study. HyperStudio offers unique publishing possibilities, but it may not be best for all students in all situations.

While Ella was successful in learning and using HyperStudio, it may not have been the best way to publish her work. While she learned to use the program, she stated that drawing with pencil and paper was still preferable. Elementary students should be given the opportunity to experience Hypermedia, specifically HyperStudio, and then judge for themselves if it is a program that they would like to continue to use and explore.

In creating versatile classrooms, teachers should consider providing HyperStudio in writing workshops, but it should not be the only resource for the students. As the study suggested, HyperStudio is an effective hypermedia program, that can help some students become comfortable using technology. While Ed was a good teacher and Ella was a good student, in the end, Ella was more comfortable using traditional means to publish her stories. This outcome is crucial for teachers and administrators to not expect every child to positively embrace the opportunity to use technology. It was not the technology that was difficult or uncomfortable for Ella to learn, but simply not her main choice to publish her stories.

When schools make the commitment to use HyperStudio, the computer specialists and media specialists should be the key resources in integrating hypermedia technology into the language arts, math, science, and social studies curriculum. However, in order to successfully integrate HyperStudio into the curriculum, administrators need to realize the importance of providing a setting in which classroom teachers can take the time to become familiar with hypermedia. Programs like HyperStudio are user friendly and promote exploration and discovery without the need to rely on a manual, but do take time to learn.

REFERENCES

Barron, A. E., & Orwig, G. (1993). *New technologies for education: A beginner's guide*. Englewood, CO: Libraries Unlimited.

Forman, G., & Pufall, P. B. (1988). *Constructivism in the computer age*. Hillsdale, NJ: Lawrence Erlbaum.

HyperStudio. (1997). Home page for HyperStudio by Roger Wagner Publishing [Online]. Available: *http://www.hyperstudio.com*

Lincoln, Y., & Guba, E. (1985). *Naturalistic inquiry*. Beverly Hills, CA: Sage.

Newby, T. J., Stepich, D. A., Lehman, J. D., & Russell, J. D. (1996). *Instructional technology for teaching and learning: Designing instruction, integrating computers, and using media*. Columbus, OH: Prentice-Hall.

Randall, B., & Higgins, K. (1991). *Hypermedia in the classroom: A development handbook for teachers*. Seattle: Washington University Experimental Education Unit.

Roblyer, M. D., Edwards, J., & Havriluk, M. A. (1997). *Integrating educational technology into teaching*. Columbus, OH: Merrill.

Simonson, M. R., & Thompson, A. (1997). *Educational computing foundations*. Columbus, OH: Prentice-Hall.

Spradley, J. P. (1980). *Participant observation*. Fort Worth, TX: Harcourt Jovanich.

Webb, N. M. (1989). Peer interaction, problem-solving, and cognition: Multidisciplinary perspectives. *International Journal of Educational Research, 13*, 21-39.

Wishnietsky, D. H. (1992). *Hypermedia: The integrated learning environment*. Bloomington, IN: Phi Delta Kappa Educational Foundation.

Kathleen Hogan
Damian Gomm

How Can Technology
Enhance Children's Natural Curiosity?

SUMMARY. *We want children to WANT to learn. Since they have a natural curiosity about so many things in their world, it is only right to base our teaching strategies around this curiosity. If we disguise our teaching objectives as child-centered activities, our students will soon realize that learning is fun and not something to dread. People often have a natural bond with animals, especially with cats and dogs. We have used technology to support our students' inquiry as they observed a puppy and kitten throughout several months. By linking technology with our county objectives, the Maryland School Performance Assessment Program science outcomes (MSPAP) and the National Science Education Standards we have provided the students with an exciting, real-world experience. [Article copies available for a fee from The Haworth Document Delivery Service: 1-800-342-9678. E-mail address: <getinfo@haworthpressinc.com> Website: <http://www.HaworthPress.com>]*

KEYWORDS. *Children's natural curiosity, observations, Maryland School Performance Assessment Program (MSPAP), National Science Education Standards*

KATHLEEN HOGAN is Teacher, Hyattsville Elementary School, 5311 43rd Ave., Hyattsville, MD 20781. E-mail: khogan1234@aol.com
DAMIAN GOMM is Teacher, Hyattsville Elementary School 5311 43rd Ave., Hyattsville, MD 20781. E-mail: sirdai@juno.com

Development of this case study was supported in part by NetTech (Northeast Regional Technology in Education Consortium).

[Haworth co-indexing entry note]: "How Can Technology Enhance Children's Natural Curiosity?" Hogan, Kathleen, and Damian Gomm. Co-published simultaneously in *Computers in the Schools* (The Haworth Press, Inc.) Vol. 16, No. 3/4, 2000, pp. 237-246; and: *Integration of Technology into the Classroom: Case Studies* (ed: D. LaMont Johnson, Cleborne D. Maddux, and Leping Liu) The Haworth Press, Inc., 2000, pp. 237-246. Single or multiple copies of this article are available for a fee from The Haworth Document Delivery Service [1-800-342-9678, 9:00 a.m. - 5:00 p.m. (EST). E-mail address: getinfo@haworthpressinc.com].

237

WHY INTEGRATE TECHNOLOGY INTO OUR LESSONS?

When the word *technology* comes to mind, one often immediately thinks of computers. However, the computer is just one aspect of technology. Educators have been using technology in their classrooms for years. Televisions, VCRs, videocassettes, audiocassette recorders, cameras, and copy machines are all examples of technology that have been used for many years without a second thought as to the extreme value they can bring to any lesson. When given new tools for teaching or a new outlook on how to use tools already on hand, many educators are motivated to try them out.

We knew that the newest technology at our school–updated computers, software, and a Smartboard–would motivate us as facilitators of our students' learning, and we were thrilled with the opportunity of presenting lessons to our students using this new technology. We hoped that the existing technology would help as well. Our philosophy is that a motivated educator will promote motivated students. In this article, we will present how an educator can use various technology to enhance children's natural curiosity while still meeting county objectives, state outcomes, and national science education standards. We used puppies and kittens in this case study. This subject can be changed to suit any learning situation. The activities can be modified to suit the subject as well as local and state standards. Paramount is the way in which a motivated educator uses the technology to meet the standards while maintaining student interest.

HOW TO ENHANCE CHILDREN'S NATURAL CURIOSITY

In Maryland a statewide assessment program was developed, the Maryland School Performance Assessment Program (MSPAP), to provide information to help improve instruction in the schools. Tasks involved in the assessment program are related to real-life experiences, require that students write a great deal, and integrate all subject areas. We often used of technology to create MSPAP tasks relevant to our puppy and kitten project. By doing so, we were able to give our students practice for these assessments. Throughout this project we were able to meet MSPAP science outcomes by our students' being able to demonstrate their ability to:

1. *Acquire and integrate major concepts and themes from the life sciences.* (They acquired and integrated major concepts about cats and dogs.)
2. *Employ the language, instruments, methods, and materials of science for collecting, organizing, interpreting and communicating information.* (We emphasized learning the MSPAP vocabulary tasks for science K-3, since understanding these words would greatly increase performance on the assessments. We modified the vocabulary tasks, integrating them into our kitten and puppy project by using specific relevant language.)
3. *Demonstrate ways of thinking and acting inherent in the practice of science.* (Our students had to problem solve when they needed to weigh and measure the animals by writing down their *observations*, not their opinions, as they observed the animals.)

We incorporated the following National Science Education Standards into our project.

1. Standard A: As the *teachers of science*, we *planned an inquiry-based science activity* every visit with the puppy and kitten. The students were able to "play teacher." They led the discussions, asked the questions, and found out the answers together as they observed, weighed, measured, played with, and took care of the puppy and kitten. In follow-up activities, the students continued their discussions and inquiries and eagerly waited for the next visitation day.
2. Standard B: As the *teachers of science*, we *guided and facilitated learning science.* We provided books, computer software, Internet sites, videos, and observation opportunities to help our students learn about puppies and kittens.
3. Standard C: As *teachers of science*, we *engaged in ongoing assessment of our teaching and of student learning.* We used various technology resources to aid us in meeting this standard, including audiocassette and videocassette recorders, cameras, and computers to assess our teaching as well as student learning.
4. Standard D: As *teachers of science*, we *designed and managed learning environments that provide students with the time, space, and resources needed for learning science.* Our puppy and kitten observation days were excellent examples of how this standard was met. Learning about general kitten and puppy behavior and

care was integrated into reading, language arts and math. Various stories and books were read about puppies and kittens. Graphs were made using the computer and then interpreted after learning information about some specific breeds of dogs from the Internet.

5. Standard E: As *teachers of science*, we feel we have *developed a community of science social values conducive to science learning social values conducive to science learning.* Our students continued to make observations, ask questions, and problem solve science issues–not just specifically about puppies and kittens learning. Through our technology and their natural curiosity about puppies and kittens, our students have demonstrated much success in this area.

6. Standard F: As *teachers of science*, we have *actively participated in the ongoing planning and development of the school science program.* We have integrated this project into our county's science program as well as into other discipline areas and are continuing to do so today. We have shared our project with peers, hoping to give them ideas on ways to get their students interested in science learning, and are willing to share with anyone who shows an interest.

SETTING THE SCENE

As educators, we both have similar teaching styles and enjoy creating our own lessons to go along with mandatory local and state outcomes. We decided to work together, not only because of common teaching styles, but because we believe that educators who share their ideas and don't mind the peer mediation will grow professionally. We also realized that teaming up would be mutually beneficial in learning to use the newest technology at our school.

Our first objective was to find someone willing to share his or her new pets with 50 elementary school children. We wanted a very young puppy and kitten–ones that we could observe obvious changes in throughout the weeks. The animals were to visit our classrooms at least once a week. As it turned out, sometimes our first- and third-grade classes would team together, while other times they would remain separate. We shared our work as much as possible.

The following technological resources were available to us: an audio-cassette recorder, computers, camera, digital camera, Smartboard, video camera, videocassette recorder. We also had available to us various software programs, including Microsoft Word, Smart Notebook, KidPix, Graph Club, PrintMaster, and an e-mail program.

Computers and Computer Software

PrintMaster (Mattel Inc., 1998) was used to create transparencies, for borders on letters, to add graphics to journal pages, to create puppy and kitten stories, and for iron-on transfers. Graph Club (Tom Snyder Productions, 1998) was used for graphing practice. KidPix (Broderbund Inc., 1997) was used to create stories and can be used to create slide shows. SmartNotebook (Smart Technologies Inc., 1998) is the necessary software to use with the Smartboard. Microsoft Word (Microsoft Corporation, 1997) was used throughout this project. Teachers used it to create related activities.

Many of the MSPAP vocabulary tasks were modified. We made the MSPAP vocabulary words task-specific to meet the needs of our project. Some students used Word to type their own notes or to type whole-class notes for the students to refer to at a later time. This was a wonderful incentive for those students who lacked the will to write many notes. One first grader was kept motivated by being told that he could type his notes on the computer after he had written some down on his journal page. The students were able to e-mail other students about this project. Students who have home access to the Internet will be able to e-mail the kitten's owner in the summer to find out about his progress. At this time, there has already been an exchange of e-mail about the kitten.

Video Equipment

A video camera was used to record the animal observation times and as a tool to more closely observe our students' thinking and participation. The students' questions and comments were recorded–no need to write as many anecdotal notes. As we watched and listened to the video, it brought back to mind the excitement of our students during the project and it helped keep us motivated as teachers.

For the initial observation, the academically weaker third-graders were paired with academically stronger first-graders as much as possible. This had two advantages. First, it gave the weaker first-graders more support from their partners. Secondly, it gave the weaker third-graders a chance to feel helpful without it being too much of a struggle since their partners were often the more capable first-grade writers. This pairing gave all the third-graders a sense of leadership, and they were eager to "play teacher." The videos clearly showed this.

We were excited to see such wonderful interaction between the two classes. We had a few great surprises as the students worked together. A third-grader was caught on video teaching a first-grader a mini-lesson on subtraction. This resulted when we were trying to figure out the weight of the puppy. One student stepped on the scale and weighed himself. Then he stepped on the scale again while holding the puppy. The students then had to subtract the boy's weight from the combined weight. The third-grader started tearing bits of paper to show the first-grader how to do a subtraction problem with regrouping. Rather than just telling his partner the answer, this student went through the process of getting the answer many times until he felt that his partner understood. Students are able to learn from each other. The adult doesn't always have to be the teacher!

Likewise, we listened to ourselves and to the conversations that were taking place on the tape and made changes in the way these conversations were carried out. We questioned ourselves. Were we dominating the conversations? Were we interacting so much that it hindered the students' chances to take charge or to problem solve on their own? We made mental notes to change the negative things and to continue the positive things.

Another use of the video camera was to record animal observation times for the students who were allergic and unable to participate in observation activities or for students who were absent. One first-grader was highly allergic. She had to leave the room when the animals were visiting. We were unable to have the camera set up for the first kitten visit due to a last-minute change in plans, but this first-grader wanted to record information anyway. She filled in information on her paper as the rest of the class discussed what they had observed. She listened and wrote down what she heard. She was eager to learn as much as possible about the kitten and didn't mind writing. However, her comments about the second day of kitten observations, when the camera was recording, made the teachers very aware that this use of technology would be extremely valuable to help all students feel included. She said, "Cats are my favorite animal. They're so cute–but I'm so allergic. I've never seen one play very long. Wow! Francois (the kitten) likes to run and jump doesn't he? I can see him on TV and it seems like he is here in our class." Her huge grin told the teachers that she had enjoyed her visit with the kitten. A full page of written notes was another sign that showed she was able to make lots of observations from the video. No student felt excluded.

Audiocassette Recorder

An audiocassette recorder was used solely for the teachers to reflect back on the observations and extended lessons. Later we were able to motivate more students by commenting on students' responses heard on the tape. Just as we did with the video camera, we were able to reflect on how the conversations and observations were carried out. Did the children stay on track? Were we as teachers dominating the conversations?

Smartboard

The Smartboard resembles a mobile chalkboard or dry-erase board. It is used with a projector to project the computer screen's image onto it–like an overhead projector. When used with Smart Notebook, software specifically for the Smartboard, it becomes "smart." There is no longer a need to type at the computer's keyboard because the Smartboard is touch-sensitive.

After giving the students the opportunity to observe the animals several times, we introduced our classes to the Smartboard. This piece of state-of-the-art technology is new at Hyattsville Elementary School. Years from now this will probably be a standard piece of technology in all schools. The lesson created for this project was the initial introduction of the Smartboard into the classroom. Using the Smartboard and its software, along with Microsoft Word and the Internet, we prepared a graph lesson on the computer. This lesson was then projected onto the Smartboard. The lesson took the students out onto the Internet to find out information about four breeds of dogs. After reading this information and discussing it, the students voted on their favorite breed for a pet. They took into consideration the size of the dog, where they lived, and how much room the dog would need. We then made a bar graph from this data. The students were able to interact with the Smartboard. They could actually come up to the Smartboard and fill in the labels and color the bars for the graph. While the whole class was involved in creating the graph on the Smartboard, the students shaded in and completed a hard copy of the graph at their seats. This allowed everyone to stay on task while waiting for an opportunity to come up to the Smartboard and "touch." Their individual graph, along with a hard copy of the information found on the Internet, helped them with a homework assignment that night. They were to go home, present the information from the Web site to two people, and have them choose their favorite breed of dog. Then they were to compare these answers with our class graph and write about it. It was easy to keep motivated during this activity. The students were bursting with excitement with the use of new technology, and the teachers were too!

Camera and Digital Camera

We were fortunate to be able to loan a camera to the family who owned the kitten immediately after the kitten was born. Photographs were taken of the mother cat, the father cat, and the other babies. Each week a few photographs were taken. We were able to have a record of the kitten's growth from birth. The students were able to determine who the kitten looked more like–mother or father–and to make more observations about the kitten.

Both cameras were used to record the students and the animals as they interacted. Digital cameras provided instant photos into the computer. Film from regular cameras can be developed and scanned into the computer or can be developed directly onto a disk. Photographs have been used as story starters, to help students create books, and can be used to create slide shows using KidPix.

EVALUATION

Indeed, we want children to *want* to learn. Their natural curiosity toward puppies and kittens has been strengthened through the use of technology. This entire project was evidence that technology can motivate children–especially when paired up with a hands-on, student-centered activity. The technology was the tool to help integrate the science activities with all other academic areas. Our own teaching methods were right in line with the National Science Education Standards–some naturally, while others consciously. The emphasis on the MSPAP vocabulary tasks helped the students understand the necessary terminology used on the test and helped the students learn to think like scientists.

Assessment was ongoing. We were able to determine that most of the students' understanding of what it means to make observations has been strengthened considerably. We were pleasantly surprised and amazed to see that children who didn't like to write and very often gave the teachers little or no writing in the classroom had few or no complaints when taking notes during the observations. One third-grader has written more for these observations than his teacher has seen for any other classroom assignment. We have learned that all of our students can be motivated to write.

Opportune timing for puppy or kitten visitations was sometimes difficult. First-grade and third-grade schedules can be quite different and impossible to change due to annual testing schedules. However, the pet owners were extremely flexible and sometimes the pets only visited one class rather than both classes. The puppy required more immediate attention from the students and only stayed for part of the day. When it visited, the activity was implemented immediately. The kitten stayed at school the entire day. The teachers were able to implement activities around their schedule for that particular day. However, sometimes the kitten decided that it was naptime, and some plans had to be modified or changed for that particular time of day!

Now that the school year is over and the summer days have begun, no doubt these students will keep our puppy and kitten close to heart. Unfortunately, the puppy has moved away. However, in September, since the entire project went so well, we will have a reunion between the kitten and students. We will observe the changes the kitten has gone through during the summer vacation. Then the observations may continue with our new group of students. Perhaps we will invite our former students into our rooms when the kitten visits. They could be a part of the science learning process for our new students. They will be able to report to our new classes what Francois (the kitten) used to do, look like, etc. Our cameras, computers, computer programs, and other technology resources will be valuable tools to help us remember what

Francois was like several months ago. Likewise, these same technology resources will be valuable tools to help us continue to make new observations. No doubt, conversations about this kitten will continue.

Whether discussing past or present observations, kittens or other subjects, the use of technology can indeed enhance students' natural curiosity. Our students showed continuous signs of wanting to learn. The positive attitudes, questioning, comments, and written work have proved this to be a worthwhile project that any educator could modify and use to enhance student learning. We are looking forward to our new school year. We are motivated to continue using technology in a variety of ways. We know that it will enhance our students' curiosity and will help to create a desire to learn.

REFERENCES

Graph Club [Computer Software]. (1998). Watertown, MA: Tom Snyder Productions.

KidPix [Computer Software]. (1997). Novato, California: Broderbund Inc.

Maryland School Performance Assessment Program. (1990). Baltimore: Maryland State Department of Education.

Microsoft Word (Version 97-SR-1) [Computer Software]. (1997). Microsoft Corporation.

National Research Council (1996). *National science education standards.* Washington, DC: National Academy Press.

PrintMaster Platinum 8.0 [Computer Software]. (1998). El Segundo, CA: Mattel.

SmartNotebook [Computer Software]. (1998). Calgary, Alberta, Canada: Smart Technologies, Inc.

Index

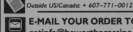